Parents and Children

Parents and Children

The Ethics of the Family

JEFFREY BLUSTEIN

Barnard College

COLUMBIA UNIVERSITY

New York   Oxford

OXFORD UNIVERSITY PRESS

1982

Copyright © 1982 by Oxford University Press, Inc.

Library of Congress Cataloging in Publication Data

Blustein, Jeffrey.
    Parents and children.

    Bibliography: p.
    Includes index.
        1. Family—Moral and religious aspects. 2. Parent
and child—Moral and religious aspects. 3. Family
policy—Moral and religious aspects. I. Title.
HQ518.B634   306.8   81–16921
ISBN 0-19-503072-9   AACR2
ISBN 0-19-503073-7 (pbk.)

Printing (last digit):   9 8 7 6 5 4 3 2 1

Printed in the United States of America

To my children, Lev and Rachel,
for making me think both backward
and forward.

Acknowledgments

This book grew out of my participation in a symposium organized by the Society for Philosophy and Public Affairs in 1976. The paper I wrote, and which Onora O'Neill and Kenneth Henley commented on extensively, forms the basis of much of the argument in part II, chapters two and three. Jane English's views on filial duty, and George Kelling's reflections on the psychology of interpersonal relationships, also helped me to clarify my own ideas in the last few sections of part II, chapter three. Part III, chapter four benefited significantly from the criticisms of Isaac Levi and the other participants in a colloquium held at Columbia University on equal opportunity and the family. The appendix to chapter four is a scaled-down version of a paper read at the New York University School of Law on the ethics of inheritance. Discussions with Edmund Leites, Stephen Darwall, and Amélie Rorty helped orient my thinking on issues relating to marriage and the family. David Hoy was kind enough to read and comment on the portions of part I dealing with Kant and Hegel. Others whom I wish to thank include William Ruddick, Virginia

Held, David Richards, Martin Golding, James Nickel, Michael Bayles, Noël Carroll, and the students in my annual course at Barnard College, "Duty and Feeling: The Ethics of the Family." Finally, I am grateful to Barnard College for awarding me a Mellon grant for 1980–81 to complete the revision of my manuscript.

I am very appreciative of the warm reception my work-in-progress received from many friends and colleagues and of their guidance and supportive criticism.

New York   J.B.
July 1981

Contents

Parents and Children

Some Contemporary Challenges to the Family

By comparison with the average parent today, parents in pre-industrial Europe did not worry much about the moral values implicit in raising children. There was little mobility out of the family; one's life prospects were largely limited by one's family, and one's station in life was likely to be the same as one's father's. The family was a unit of economic production, and the rights and responsibilities of parents were defined in terms of whatever was necessary to maintain its productivity. But with the rise of industrialization, the orderly and predictable transmission of occupation and status from parent to child could no longer be assumed, and the education and training appropriate for children had to equip them for success outside the narrow confines of the family. These broad social and economic changes paved the way for some serious rethinking of parenthood. Reflecting on the instability of social life brought about by the industrial revolution, Rousseau asked the following rhetorical question:

> When we consider the fleeting nature of human affairs,
> the restless and uneasy spirit of our times, when every

generation overturns the work of its predecessor, can we conceive a more senseless plan than to educate a child as if he would never leave his room, as if he would always have his servants about him?

Modern conditions, in Rousseau's view, demand new ways of educating the young and a new conception among parents of their parental responsibilities. Education for a predetermined social role may have made sense in a world without cultural change, but when social roles are themselves in flux, it is unreasonable for parents to aim for a particular outcome of their children's choices. They should rather seek to develop their children's capacity to make choices in a certain way, namely, autonomously.

Today it is a widely, though not universally, held belief in our society that parents should see to it that their children have the opportunity to adopt a variety of social roles and life styles. Yet children can only become autonomous agents if they are given the freedom to make certain kinds of choices, do certain kinds of things, and accept certain kinds of responsibilities, and many of us are uncertain where to draw the line between freedom for children and encroachment on the legitimate prerogatives of parents. Autonomy for children is not the only kind of autonomy that enters into our thinking about family relationships. Equally important to citizens in a democratic society is the idea of parental autonomy, that is, the right of parents to raise their children as they think best, in accordance with their own notions of childrearing. Some of us, perhaps, do not feel comfortable with the mode of childrearing practiced in, for example, the Amish and Hassidic communities, because of the extreme isolation from the larger community it encourages, though we are willing to concede that it is quite arbitrary to limit the scope of parental autonomy to childrearing that is based on secular values alone. Closer to home, many parents today are uneasy about their right to exercise authority over their own children. We believe that, as parents, we are entitled to command our children's obedience, but we worry that our use of authority may actually be inhibiting our children's growth to autonomy. As a result of this insecurity, parents are frequently inconsistent in their use of authority, alternately failing to set limits for their children when they need to have demands imposed on them and then reacting to their children's perceived rebelliousness with excessive discipline and other authoritarian measures.

I mention these doubts here not so much to resolve them as to suggest that much of our current perplexity about the family stems from the fact that we are committed to both kinds of autonomy, parents' and children's, and yet do not have any clear sense of how to reconcile them to one another. The advocates of children's rights press their case, and we are becoming increasingly aware of the heavy reliance on power and authority by which adults impose excessive and arbitrary controls on children. At the same time, we don't want the recognition of children's rights to significantly alter the traditional balance of power in the family. This tension between parental autonomy and autonomy for children can also be looked at as a tension within the notion of parental autonomy itself. On the one hand, parents' right to raise their children as they think best is thought of as a particular instance of the right to privacy that belongs to every mature citizen in a free society. Like the right to be free of annoyance in one's house, or the right to enjoy the use of a piece of property without interference from others, the right to autonomy in childrearing recognizes the individual's legitimate interest in having a well-defined zone within which one need not be on the alert against possible observations and intrusions. The interest protected by parental autonomy is here the *parent's* interest, just as the interest protected by the right of private property is the property owner's interest. On the other hand, the right of parents to raise their children in accordance with their own notions of childrearing is regarded as being necessary for the healthy growth and development of their children. Children, it will be said, need to feel safe within the confines of the home, need to believe that their parents are omniscient and all-powerful, and these needs are thwarted if parents are not free from outside control or coercive intervention. Here the interest protected by parental autonomy is the *child's* interest in having a permanent and secure place in a family of his own.

The contrast between these two justifications of parental autonomy, the one in terms of the legitimate interests of parents, the other in terms of the legitimate interests of children, may strike some readers as being too artificial. For, it may be asked, is it not in the interest of parents to see to it that their children's interests are served, and don't children likewise have a second-order interest in the interests of their parents being served? The family is not merely a collection of separate individuals, but a community in which the satisfaction of one kind of interest entails the satisfaction of the other.

To illustrate the difficulty, and perhaps inadvisability, of trying to separate the lives of children from those of their parents, consider the case of religious training. Our Constitution guarantees citizens the right to the free exercise of religion, and this right is not lost when a citizen decides to become a parent. On the contrary, it might be said, the right to the free exercise of religion simply expands to include the right to bring up one's children in the religion of one's choice. Their instruction in that religion is just one way in which parents may exercise a right they would have had even if they had had no children. But this is only part of the story, for it considers only the interests of parents. The welfare of the child, so the argument continues, is also promoted when parents have autonomy in matters of religious instruction. If parents practice a religion and are not at the same time free to educate their child in that religion, this will weaken the familial bonds critical to every child's healthy growth and development. Parental values, explicit and implicit, normally become the child's own, and where they cannot, an essential ingredient of family integrity is lacking. From the point of view of the welfare of the child, therefore, as well as from that of the parents, parents should be allowed to bring up their child in the religion of their choice.

This argument is plausible as far as it goes, but it doesn't go far enough. It is true that there is no way to avoid the influence of parents' religious beliefs on their child. It is also true that the child's training must conform to the intricate developmental processes of childhood. But what is missing from this argument is any explicit recognition of the fact that children have distinguishable interests in need of protection and that these interests do not necessarily coincide with the interests of their parents. Parents quite understandably want their children to share their most important values, to participate with them in forms of life that rest on and develop around common values. This is not, however, the primary end of childrearing, for the maintenance of family life, satisfying as it may be to parents, should not take precedence over the rights and interests of the children who take part in it. Children must be helped to attain a separate identity from that of their parents, which is to say only that parents must prepare children to make conscientious and autonomous decisions about such matters as religion, not that they must prepare them to reject their religious values. (This would be asking too much of parents.) Exposing children at a young age to a variety of religious and nonreligious ways of life is probably not the best way to prepare them to make such decisions. It is more likely, in fact, to confuse them and to convince them that religion is not something worth taking seriously. Parents, therefore, should be allowed to bring up children in the religion of their choice, but only *as long as* they do not at the same time make it too difficult for the children to choose to abandon that religion as they mature.

For the advocates of children's rights, or the more radical

among them, even this argument does not go far enough. Some contend instead that autonomy for children demands a fundamental revision in our traditional notions of parental autonomy and familial integrity. Let us look at what one writer, John Holt, has to say on this subject, in his book *Escape from Childhood*. "Instead of trying to make sure that all children get only those experiences we think are good for them," Holt says, "I would rather make available to children, as to everyone else, the widest possible range of experiences (except those that hurt others) and let them choose those they like best." To accomplish this, Holt proposes that the law grant to children, of all ages, the same freedoms it now grants to adults alone. In granting children such rights, the law does not say that children must or shall exercise them. "It simply says that it will not allow other people to prevent" children from exercising them if they so choose. The kind of right Holt is talking about here is what some philosophers have termed an "option-right" and is to be distinguished from what is sometimes called a "welfare-right." Option-rights are rights to noninterference by others, spheres of autonomy to which are annexed legal and nonlegal demands upon the behavior of other members of society. Welfare-rights, in contrast, are rights to services from particular others, to the goods necessary for a happy or satisfactory life as defined by the ideals of the community. Simply put, an option-right is a right to be left alone in some area of life; a welfare-right is a right to receive assistance, goods, and benefits, so that a fulfilling human life is possible.

Holt is aware of some of the objections that might be raised to his proposal. He notes that young children are not likely to want to exercise the rights granted them by law. He notes also that even if they do want to exercise their rights, they will probably be influenced by the opinions and values of those adults whose approval they seek. But these problems, Holt argues, do not constitute a sufficient reason to deny children these rights altogether. "The possibility of exercising responsibility draws people toward it," and in the long run, Holt believes, children will become more responsible individuals because the law gives them the opportunity to accept responsibility. Merely knowing that they could do what adults can do "would be like an open door and a beckoning hand to the larger adult world."

Having defined what he means by "rights" and set out the rationale for legal reform, Holt proceeds to discuss a number of particular rights that he wants the law to grant children. These include the right to vote, the right to work for money and to use it as they see fit, the right to travel and live away from home without the permission of parents, and the right to control their own learning. All of these rights, to varying degrees, conflict with our traditional norms of parental autonomy, but one in particular seems to do so more than the others. This is the right of a child to choose his or her own guardians. Holt distinguishes between two types of guardians: primary guardians—the child's natural or adoptive parents, who have a preexisting obligation to take care of the child and must do so if no one else wants to; and secondary guardians, who have no such obligation, but who may volunteer to take care of the child if some mutually agreeable arrangement can be worked out between them. The right to choose one's guardian amounts to this: the right of the child to seek out and choose secondary guardians, to live under the control and supervision of his or her primary guardians, or to have no guardian at all. The choice is the child's, and parental autonomy, which consists of the right of parents to raise their children as they think best, and by implication the right of parents to raise their children as well, is severely curtailed. Parents, in Holt's view, have a right to raise their children only if their children choose to be raised by them or at least do not choose to be raised by other, secondary, guardians.

Is such a fundamental abridgment of parental autonomy

warranted? I think not. The child is not born with autonomy, nor is the ideal of autonomy promoted by giving children of all ages the right to be free of all adult control. Autonomy develops gradually, within the context of a stable, continuous, and authoritative (not authoritarian) parent-child relationship. Most of us believe that it is best for children if the ultimate authorities in charge of them are their natural parents, joined in a stable marital union. We may be mistaken about this. But questions having to do with the permissible variety of family structures need to be distinguished from those having to do with the psychological prerequisites for attaining physical, emotional, and moral self-reliance. The family as we normally conceive of it may not in fact promote such self-reliance in children, but then some other more adequate childrearing arrangement must be found. In any case, Holt's proposal is not the answer.

Another way of making the same point is to say that any proposal that aims at self-determination for children must adjust itself to the fact that the achievement of autonomy is a developmental process and that this development advances through stages, beginning with a stage when issues of autonomy are of secondary concern, and only gradually passing to the stage when children attain their separate identities. It is only when children's welfare-rights have been secured and respected that their option-rights can be meaningfully asserted and exercised. Moreover, parental autonomy is necessary if parents are to take pride in their work and willingly embrace their responsibilities, and this is a considerable benefit to children.

Let us recall here the two justifications for parental autonomy. In the one, parental autonomy is the right of parents, part of a more general right to privacy that individuals possess as citizens of a free society. In the other, parental autonomy is the right of children, grounded on their interest in a form of upbringing that furthers their growth to autonomy. I would like to suggest now that to give equal moral weight to both justifications of parental autonomy is to misconstrue the moral basis of parenthood. Parents, as individuals, do have the right to a certain degree of autonomy within the family, and their children ought to honor this right. To deny parents the right to take their own interests into account in rearing their children and to transmit their own ideals and values to them is also to undermine the integrity of the family. But such autonomy is justified only insofar as it is not inconsistent with the performance of parental responsibilities; indeed some autonomy seems to be required, for it keeps childrearing from becoming an intolerable burden for parents and is thus beneficial for children. To express this another way, individuals do not forfeit all of their individuality by founding families and becoming parents, but then, as parents, they also have a responsibility to serve their children and so must adjust their individual needs and personal goals to the needs and legitimate demands of their children. As Locke put it so well, the rights that parents have over their children are, at bottom, "rather the Priviledge of Children, and Duty of Parents, than any Prerogative of Paternal Power."

I now want to shift the discussion to another area in which our traditional notions of parental autonomy are seriously challenged. I have spoken so far about children's rights and about how an undue emphasis on parental autonomy leads to a profound misunderstanding of the grounds of parenthood. The state ought to protect these rights and has a responsibility to the individual child to set relatively precise limits on parental judgment so as to prevent parents from exploiting the inherent inequality between themselves and their children. But society should not only be concerned about the individual child; it should also be concerned about children generally and about how A's opportunities for autonomous action measure up against B's, where A and B are children from different families. The issue here is one of ensuring justice for all children, and equality is a basic requirement of justice.

What does parental autonomy have to do with the rights of children to equal opportunity? To answer this, let us first see what it means to say that A and B have an equal opportunity to receive some good. Take admission to college as an example. Suppose college admissions committees tell a high school graduate that they will not admit him because he is black. He is fully qualified, and known to be so, and since he is being turned down solely because of his race, he is being denied an equal opportunity to attend college. Now suppose instead that he is not fully qualified and that the college admissions committees tell him he is not being admitted because he lacks the credentials, skills, motivations, or competences necessary for college work. Has the candidate in this case also been denied an equal opportunity to attend college? If the absence of these motivations, competences, etc., is itself the result of prior inequalities of opportunity, then the claim that he has not is unconvincing. We do not give children an equal opportunity to go to college merely by applying the same criteria for college admission to them at the point when they become candidates. For what we may actually be doing is applying the same criteria to one individual, as affected by earlier favorable conditions, and to another, as affected by earlier unfavorable conditions. A better secondary school education for the latter might have reduced somewhat the disparity between the candidates, but as many social scientists have maintained, socially induced inequalities in opportunities cannot be corrected in school alone. Children fortunate enough to have been born of middle- or upper-class parents usually begin life with advantages that the children of poor parents can never hope to enjoy. Some of these advantages are of a directly economic kind, but probably more important for children, though harder to measure, are the effects of parental interest in education, attitudes toward achievement, and the like, which are correlated with class membership. Even within the same so-cial-class group, families differ widely in the kinds of home environments they provide their children. These differences in family background, economic as well at attitudinal, affect children's abilities and motivations to grasp educational opportunities quite unequally. The elimination of these differences to create genuine equality of opportunity for children requires actual equality of conditions during childhood as the basis for the future distribution of goods according to merit. More precisely, it requires actual equality of conditions that are causally effective for the attainment of these goods.

We can only bring about actual equality of conditions in childhood, however, if we take control of children's lives to an extent not envisaged by schools today and if we are willing to restrict parental autonomy to an extremely narrow compass. Governmental regulation, now confined to such matters as child labor, compulsory education, and immunization, would have to concern itself with the intimate details of day-to-day parent-child interactions. Short of such measures, equal opportunity for children will lack a secure foundation in the early childrearing years. To be sure, economic, social, and educational support services can be made available and readily accessible to all parents. They can be made aware of the importance of children's early experience and of what constitutes a good environment and adequate care. But as long as these services are voluntary, as long as children benefit from them only if and as their parents choose to utilize them, children will continue to have unequal abilities, motivations, and life chances. We cannot suppose otherwise unless we assume not only that all parents want what is best for their children, but also that they all want this to the *same* extent and will, with the proper education, all want the *same* things for their children.

I want to stress that the points I have been making in the last few paragraphs concern the family as a childrearing institution, not the individual family; that is, I have been speaking about the distribution of treatment under the family system, not about relationships within families. In the best of families, the children feel wanted and valued, their inborn capacities are stimulated, and they acquire the ability to think for themselves and to pursue their own conception of their good. But as an institution for rearing the young, into which the state intrudes only in unusual and extreme circumstances, the family as we know it is an obstacle to the complete realization of a basic principle of social justice.

Should we, then, abolish the family? There is no simple answer to this question. If we want equality for children, the price must be paid in parental liberty. Some form of common upbringing, in which the physical, emotional, and intellectual development of all children is continually monitored and uniform standards of adequate care are imposed, seems to be the best way to accomplish this. If we want somewhat greater equality for children and only some sacrifice of liberty, we can try to affect the opportunities of children by, for example, requiring that prospective parents be licensed before they are allowed to start a family. If we want to retain liberty and yet do something to reduce inequality of opportunity among children, we can offer loans to children in the form of tax credits to their families, create new and support existing child-care services, disseminate information about child care, or provide educational opportunities for parents. In order to decide whether the family should be abolished, we have to balance liberty against equality, and there are several ways of doing this.

The first alternative, that of a common upbringing, has frequently been criticized on the ground that it would not give infants and young children the individualized attention they need for healthy psychological development. Like all bureaucracies, communal childrearing institutions would tend to treat people and situations alike in order to achieve precision and efficiency and would have little regard for a person's individual tasks and requirements. Parental autonomy may be a barrier to equal chances between individuals, but such an extreme curtailment of parental autonomy, it might be argued, would also tend to homogenize society, to promote conformity rather than diversity, and to suppress the development of genuine autonomy in children. I agree with these objections to this extent: common upbringings can offer constant care, but they are unlikely to offer children the deeply personal care that good parents can provide. The fundamental philosophical issue, however, has to do with the human ideals that underlie our commitment to such deeply personal care. To say that individualized attention is necessary for healthy psychological development or that children need to feel that they are the center of the universe if they are to attain self-reliance is implicitly to adopt a certain normative conception of the self. Advocates of common upbringings, on the other hand, will either not subscribe to these ideals or will maintain that other values outweigh them. (We should not be too quick to suppose that in a communal arrangement, self-determination is necessarily precluded. It may just take on a different meaning and hence call for different processes of identity formation.)

I conclude these introductory remarks much as I began, by drawing attention to the normative assumptions and preconceptions that shape some of our thinking about the contemporary family. My unifying theme has been the notion of parental autonomy, and I have tried to explore its relation both to children's rights and to social justice. In so doing, I hope I have given a long-neglected area of social philosophy a certain amount of philosophical respectability and shown how important it is, particularly now, to critically reflect on our strong commitment to family institutions and values.

This book is divided into three parts. Part I surveys a number of important contributions to philosophy of the family from Plato to Russell and provides some historical background and perspective for the discussion that follows. Their views on the nature of parenthood, the rights and responsibilities of parents, and the duties and virtues of children are taken up at several points in part II and, by way of amplification and criticism, are used to help develop my own arguments.

Part II offers a moral theory of parenthood, focusing on the interests rather than the rights of children and on parental responsibility to promote children's interests and long-term good. I adopt this orientation not because I believe that moral rights language cannot be correctly applied to children, but because it makes it possible for us to discuss a wider range of issues pertaining to family life. Part II then separates the question of what duties parents have from that of who has these duties, and proposes broad guidelines for the assignment of duties by childrearing practices. The last chapter of part II deals with children's duties—a topic that may have lost much of its traditional appeal but one that we must nevertheless think more about if we are to understand why the family is more than just a temporary arrangement for the purpose of childrearing.

Part III examines some of the factors to be considered in making policy decisions with respect to justice for children and marriage. Here I show how our commitment to the family is put to the test by our commitment to equal opportunity and how this challenge can be met. Next I draw a distinction between the institutions of family and marriage and stress that the growing incidence of marital breakup forces us to reevaluate the traditional practice of linking family rearing to marriage. Part III concludes with a comparison of marital and nonmarital family policies.

PART I

The Family in Western Philosophical Thought: From Plato to Russell

Philosophy of the Family and Its History

Philosophers have been criticized for writing very little about families. It would be more accurate to claim, however, that it is historians of philosophy, rather than philosophers in general, who have been guilty of this. Contemporary histories of political theory and ethics abound, but philosophical writing on the family also has a history of its own, and so far there has been no attempt to reconstruct this history in a systematic and comprehensive fashion. To be sure, some histories of political theory contain brief discussions of, say, Aristotle's vindication of the family or Locke's refutation of patriarchalism. But we cannot hope to piece together a history of the family in philosophical literature from these accounts alone, because it is a history that only occasionally converges with that of political theory. Modern histories of ethics devote even less attention to the family, because they tend to conceive of ethics as the study of those principles that determine how *any* two individuals are required to regard, and behave toward, one another. We might then get the erroneous impression that moral philosophers seldom took the organization of private affairs very seriously.

The history of philosophy of the family is complex for a number of reasons. First is the problem of conceptual analysis. It would be a great mistake to think that, in the history of philosophical reflection on the family, the concept of a family has a univocal meaning. Apparent agreement on the defining features of the family—marriage and the marriage contract, socially recognized rights and duties of parenthood, reciprocal obligations between husband and wife—may belie fundamental theoretical differences. The concept of duty, for example, as in "duties of parenthood," has undergone change as different forms of social life have provided different roles for the concept to play. Unlike the modern, post-Kantian, understanding of duty, the Greeks did not conceive of duty in contrast to inclination, or as distinct from the requirement to fulfill a specific social role. The theological ethics of, say, Aquinas, also attaches importance to the concept of duty, but here again what is meant is different from the modern and Greek senses. Nevertheless, notions of the family in different philosophical traditions are not totally irrelevant to one another. There may be breaks in the history of this concept, owing to breaks in the history of concepts like rights and duties which are embedded in the definition of a family, but there are continuities as well.

The history of philosophical writing on the family is complex for another, related, reason. Changes in social life are associated not only with changes in the concept of a family, but also with different perceptions of the family's emotional and psychological significance, and the amount of attention philosophers devote to the family is partially a function of the degree to which ordinary men and women put their emotional hopes for fulfillment into their family life. In this context, we might note that many critics of Plato's proposal to abolish the family make the unwarranted assumption that present-day convictions about the importance of the family were also shared by Plato's contemporaries. Further, the family consists of different kinds of relationships—parent-child, husband-wife (the master-servant relationship is also included in Aristotle's "household")—and even when the family remains at the center of emotional life, the relative prominence of its constituent relationships continues to vary with changes in social life, leading to a redirection of philosophical inquiry. The modern, child-centered conception of the family, as Phillipe Ariès tells us in *Centuries of Childhood*, is of comparatively recent origin, dating back only to the sixteenth century.

The history of philosophy of the family is further complicated by the fact that philosophers have traditionally been concerned with two different sets of norms pertaining to the family: those that regulate the family's relation to the state, and those that regulate the relationships among family members. This is not to suggest that these sets of norms have no bearing upon one another. On the contrary, not only the emotional tone of family life, but also the specific virtues, responsibilities, claims, and obligations of family members, are affected by different forms of social regulation of the family. Nevertheless, as Plato clearly saw, the moral issues raised by family-state relations are basically issues having to do with the distinction between private and public spheres of life, and the private/public distinction only establishes a framework within which individuals must still decide how to conduct themselves in their families. Even if it is true, for example, that the state has no right to dictate to parents how they shall educate their children, it does not follow that parents may educate them in any way they choose.

Bearing these preliminary remarks in mind, I shall present first a broad picture, then a more detailed examination, of some of what has been thought about familial institutions and family life. The purpose of this survey is three-fold: to show that the sorts of concerns expressed in the following chapters have numerous philosophical precedents, to demonstrate how my own arguments build upon or diverge from those of previous philosophers, and to provide a historical context for many of the assumptions I make about the emotional and psychological importance of family life, the nature of childhood, the place of children in families, and the relations between familial and other social institutions. In many respects, this book is not so much about the ethics of the family as it is about the ethics of the contemporary family, but this distinction cannot be fully appreciated without some sense of how concepts and values have changed in the traditions of philosophical commentary on the family.

This history is divided into four periods: the Greek and Roman, the Christian, the modern (dating approximately from the sixteenth to the early nineteenth century), and the contemporary. Only Western views on the family are included, and even then the account is not intended to be exhaustive. Further, the discussion concentrates on one (for us, the central) familial relationship, the relationship between children and those who bring them up.

An Overview of the Literature
from Plato to Russell

The family as we understand it, as a sphere of intimacy to which we retreat in order to find ourselves, does not exist in Greek writing. Plato regarded the family as a nest of individualism and wanted to eliminate it altogether from the ruling class of his ideal city. (In the second-best city of the *Laws*, he allowed the family to remain, but regulated marriage, education, etc., so as to reduce its exclusive and antisocial tendencies to a minimum.) It was the family as a social institution that Plato disapproved of, not the sentiments of family life, which he believed could be transferred to the entire community of guardians. Even when the family was distinguished from political government and its retention vindicated, as in the first two books of Aristotle's *Politics*, family life was regarded as existing for the good life in the polis. In the polis, men could distinguish themselves through unique deeds and achievements, and in an atmosphere of freedom, attain human excellence (*aretē*); it was the role of the family to master the necessities of life and free men for the nobler pursuits that were possible only in public life.[1] When Aristotle discussed the affective side of family life in the *Nicomachean Ethics*, his purpose was to illuminate the nature of *philia* as a phenomenon of personal and private life, not to suggest that among relationships based on personal affection, family friendships are especially valuable. Under these conditions, "the full development of the life of hearth and family into an inner and private space" (Arendt, p. 59) could not occur, and the Greek philosophers could not give the family the kind of consideration that we believe it deserves.

The decline of the polis and the rise of the large-scale state transformed the milieu of moral life and was partially responsible for the family's new prominence in philosophical writing. Under the Roman Empire, with its sharp antithesis between the individual and the state, individuals could no longer think of themselves in terms of the life of the larger community, and they retreated into the privacy of the family to escape the burdens of civic life and the sense of powerlessness engendered by the new political arrangements. The rise of Christianity reinforced the withdrawal from public affairs, and issues of family life became colored by theories of man's relationship to God and the future of his soul. Early Christian thinkers, who were interested in the licitness or illicitness of forms of sexual behavior at least as much as in parenting, linked the having and raising of children to mo-

1. See Hannah Arendt, *The Human Condition* (Chicago: University of Chicago Press, 1958), pp. 28–37.

nogamous marriage. Monogamous marriage represented a partial concession to lust for the sake of procreation, and the family was assigned the dual function of providing for the parenting of children and providing for and protecting an exclusive sexual relationship between a man and a woman. Much later in the Christian tradition, writing out of very different historical and cultural circumstances, Thomas Aquinas divided domestic society into its component parts and focused considerable attention on the parental society of parents and children. The sexual aspect of the marital union was less problematic for Aquinas than it had been for Augustine, and Aquinas turned at some length to the issues of parent-child friendship and love, parental authority and its limitations, and parental and filial obligations. His analysis of filial obligation in particular is unsurpassed for its subtlety and the richness of its moral vocabulary.

In the early modern period, extending from Bodin through Hobbes and Filmer to Locke, the family became a focal point of debates on the nature and justification of political authority. With the breakup of the medieval Church, the framework of the older forms of political thinking had collapsed, and it was no longer possible to conceive of a realizable order in Christendom in terms of obligation to the Church or to justify political authority in terms of the authority of a universally recognized Church. Some other focus of political obligation had to be found before order could be restored, and political authority had to be justified on different grounds. The relationship between parental and political authority was not, of course, a totally new concern in this period; it had been a recurring theme of social and political philosophy since antiquity. But the period's emphasis on parental authority definitely reoriented thinking about the family and gave new prominence to issues of obedience and discipline in family life. In contrast to the Greeks, parental authority was not regarded merely as something to be reflected on or understood or as one element of a larger problem of family-state relations, but as something on which to focus moral judgment. Plato's *Republic* does not question the authority that parents exercise in raising their children so much as the privacy of the family, of which parental authority is only one aspect. And in contrast to Aquinas, for whom parental authority was a moral issue, the interest in drawing analogies or disanalogies between parental and political authority tended to concentrate discussions of familial relations on a relatively narrow range of issues. In Locke, for instance, the core of family life is not its emotional togetherness, but the child's need for submission to the parents' rational judgment and control.

Discussions concerning the connection or similarity between familial and political institutions are found with considerably less frequency in eighteenth-century political literature, in no small measure due to the influence of Locke's *Two Treatises.* Rousseau, in the *Social Contract,* was merely going over familiar terrain when he argued that civil society could not be derived from the natural authority of parents. Moreover, with the demise of patriarchal theories of political obligation, the family largely disappeared from the domain of political theory, at least until Marx. But while philosophers became less preoccupied with the political inferences that could or could not be drawn from familial life, this did not mean that they left the domestic sphere untouched. Locke's treatise on education, though colored by the political debates of the seventeenth century, laid the groundwork for Enlightenment educational theory, and his emphasis on the parental duty of education recurs in the writings of Rousseau, Kant, Fichte, and Hegel. To be sure, the eighteenth and early nineteenth centuries' interest in education, like the seventeenth century's interest in parental authority, was not without precedent. As far back as the first century A.D., Plutarch had claimed that "to receive a proper education is the source and root of all goodness,"[2] and Aquinas too had argued that the primary end of marriage is both procreation and education of offspring. But it is with Locke that modern educational theory really begins, as a response to the demands of an increasing rationalization of the world, and as an expression of a new conception of the child. According to this conception, never fully developed in the Middle Ages or before, children have their own rights, their own rhythm of development, and their own pedagogical requirements. Moreover, Locke advanced a view shared by many in the modern period when he argued that education, rather than generation, gives rise to filial obligation.

The grounds of parental and political authority having been defined and demarcated, philosophers turned their attention to the ends which that authority ought to promote. The family soon found itself in a somewhat precarious position. Rousseau set extremely demanding standards for parents, in particular fathers, and reluctantly conceded that some of them will have to delegate their educational responsibilities to tutors. Kant placed less arduous demands on parents, but he too had serious reservations about their capacities as dispensers of education. "Parents," he observed,

> exercise forethought for the home, princes for the state. Neither have for their ultimate aim the good of the world and the perfection for which man is intended, and for which he also has the capacity.[3]

It seemed that the parental duty of education could best be discharged by delegating tasks to persons and agencies outside the family. Children needed more than their families could provide.

The family's shortcomings with regard to education were

2. "The Education of Children," in *Moralia*, trans. F. C. Babbitt (Cambridge: Harvard University Press, 1949), vol. 1, p. 19.
3. *Lecture-Notes on Pedagogy*, trans. E. F. Buchner (Philadelphia: J. B. Lippincott Co., 1904), sec. 16.

brought out even more forcefully by Hegel. Education, he asserted, "operates in a negative way on the family,"[4] but his point was only partly that the family should prepare children to lead lives of their own choosing, free of parental authority. More fundamentally, his point was that education must operate in this way because its rationalistic aims clash with the sentimental ethos of family life. Family members are bound together by love and do not relate to one another according to rational and impartial principles of justice. Education, in contrast, concerns what is universal, the community. It is to prepare the child for membership in the larger society, not for civil society, which is only a collection of family units, but for a social order in which the individual is subject to demands that are more rational, because more universal, than the claims of the family.

Though Hegel believed that the family is ultimately inadequate as a means of education and that there are persistent tensions between family society and the polity that cannot be resolved, it was not his intention to present a case for the abolition of the family. On the contrary, Hegel viewed the family as an intrinsically valuable form of social life, a sphere of intimacy in which the claims of individual members are restricted by the common task of looking after the welfare of the family generally. Moreover, because the family was for Hegel a distinctive form of social life, characterized by particular connections between particular persons, he could not follow Plato in advocating the absorption of familial arrangements into the political sphere.

In Hegel, a number of currents in the history of philosophical writing on the family converge. Hegel returned to the ideals of Greek social life, blended them with views of marriage and family life that entered Western thought through the Christian tradition, and advanced a theory that at once

4. *The Phenomenology of Mind,* trans. J. B. Baillie (New York: Harper, 1967), p. 469.

provided the family with a secure position in ethical life and
emphasized the radically different concerns of the family
member and the citizen. Education of children, which Locke
had maintained should be conducted at home under the
direction and supervision of parents, was eventually seen to
require a less restricted form of relationship than the family.
At the same time, by sharpening Locke's distinction between
familial and political arrangements, Hegel enriches our understanding of the nature of familial relations. He conceived
of the family not as a locus of individual rights and duties,
nor as an institution whose primary value consists in guiding
the child to adulthood, but as preeminently a community of
love.

  Through the rest of the nineteenth, and into the twentieth,
century, writing on the family took two new directions: the
Marxist and the feminist. Marx and Engels stressed the family's integration into the economic and political structures of
each era and revealed the economic and political functions of
the division of labor between the sexes, the nature of women's
employment, and the management of childrearing. But traditional moral concepts do not play an important role in their
assessment of social institutions, and moreover, they were
more interested in what the family could become in socialist
and communist society than in exploring the options available to family members in capitalist society. Feminist writing, which embraced both Marxist and non-Marxist perspectives, reflected the political climate of the mid and late parts
of the nineteenth century, when campaigns for women's
rights were conducted in England, France, and elsewhere.
Liberal feminists like John Stuart Mill argued for legal and
political equality of women as the means of achieving egalitarian marriage and parted company with the Marxists who
believed that egalitarian marriage could only be realized by
transferring the care and education of children from the family to society at large. The kind of egalitarian marriage Mill

envisaged, however, was not one in which childrearing and domestic duties were shared equally between husband and wife. The woman was to have an equal share in the legal rights and responsibilities of the relationship, but she was still expected to take primary responsibility for the management of the household and the bringing up of a family.

One exception to the general neglect of the moral aspects of parent-child relations among philosophers of this period is Henry Sidgwick. Like his predecessors, the eighteenth-century British moralists, Sidgwick thought seriously about the content of plain men's moral judgments and regarded the deliverances of the normal moral consciousness as data for moral theory. Shaftesbury, Hutcheson, Butler, Smith, and others, in their revolt against the cynicism of Hobbes, had concentrated on the ordinary person's experience of benevolent affections, on the operations of sympathy and gratitude. The phenomenon of parental affection was singled out to support the view that there are elements in human nature not derivable from the individual's desire for private pleasure. Sidgwick did not share the British moralists' uncritical acceptance of common sense or their preoccupation with the theory of selfishness, but like them he was interested in the psychology of the ordinary man, and in the close, affectionate relations that play such an important role in everyday human life. Wanting to better understand the family and not merely to use it in order to resolve an abstract problem in ethical theory, Sidgwick expressed the position of common sense on such issues as the grounds' of parental and filial duty and the relationship between familial and other moral responsibilities. Common sense, he claimed, distinguishes the duties arising out of family relations from the duties of friendship, gratitude, and special need. It is clear, for example, that parental duties are not thought to rest solely on special need, for we would normally criticize parents for handing their children over to other caretakers, even when those caretakers could fully provide for them. Yet "in attempting to formulate the different domestic duties as recognized by Common Sense," Sidgwick found "a large vague margin with respect to which general agreement could not be affirmed, and which, in fact, forms an arena for continual disputes." It was just this margin which, in his view, clearly revealed "the latent Utilitarianism of common moral opinion"[5] and the standard (utility) to which all moral problems arising out of family life should ultimately be referred.

Twentieth-century philosophy of the family opens with Bertrand Russell. Though a proponent of feminism and libertinism, he did not take them to the point of advocating the abolition of the family. On the contrary, he had a deep conviction that family relationships can be fulfilling and liberating. Cooperation in the serious business of rearing children, he argued, can "produce so deep a tie between a man and woman that they will feel something infinitely precious in their companionship"[6] even if they can no longer fulfill each other sexually. Moreover, in contrast to Mill, who did not believe that parenting should be shared equally between mothers and fathers, Russell was bothered by the increasingly marginal role fathers were playing in the actual day-to-day rearing of their children. He perceived the family losing ground to the state, and warned that this trend would eventually leave fathers without any outlet for their parental impulses and children without the parental affection and individualized attention so vital to their development.

Russell's philosophy of the family, concerned as it is with the rapid decay of the family in modern industrialized countries, foreshadows contemporary worries about the survival of the family as an institution. Radical transformation of the family was no longer the utopian fantasy of the philosopher but, as Russell saw it, the direction in which powerful social

---

5. *The Methods of Ethics* (Chicago: University of Chicago Press, 1962), pp. 435–436.
6. *Marriage and Morals* (New York: Bantam, 1968), p. 96.

and economic forces were working. The family was at a cross-roads, and a reappraisal of the value of family life was never more urgently needed. Russell may not have said the last word about the psychological benefits of parental as opposed to institutionalized upbringing, but he was not only interested in how elimination of the family would affect the development of children. He was also interested in how it would affect the well-being of parents. Parents derive important satisfactions and pleasures from a relationship with their child, satisfactions and pleasures, Russell believed, as central to human emotional life as the love of man and woman. The substitution of state for parental rearing, he speculated, would probably have an enormous effect on married life and on the quality of relations between the sexes and personal relations generally, quite apart from benefits or losses to the child.

The Greek and Roman Period: Plato, Aristotle, and the Stoics

The Family in Plato's Republic and Laws

For Plato, the ideal state cannot coexist with private property or the private family. Private property, as an institution, encourages acquisitiveness and tends toward the unrestricted pursuit of private fortunes at the expense of other citizens and the community. One of the principal motives for the accumulation of private wealth and possessions is the desire to protect and improve the condition of one's private family. Among the poor, men are engaged in a continual struggle for money to secure "the necessities of life for their households,"[7] and among the rich, their homes are "literal private love nests in which they can lavish their wealth on their women and any others they please with great expenditure" (548b). Eliminating the private family, therefore, would also eliminate one of

7. *The Republic,* in *Plato: The Collected Dialogues,* ed. E. Hamilton and H. Cairns (New York: Bollingen Foundation, 1961), 465c.

the main supports for the institution of private property. However, Plato appears to think that a modified type of private family might remain even after the institution of private property is annulled. Men might continue to devote themselves to the interests of their individual families, even though the nature of their involvement with their families would change. For this reason, Plato's aim is only half achieved with the abolition of private property. He regards communal ownership of property as a necessary, not a sufficient, condition of the ideal state and maintains that abolition of the private family would "tend to make them [the rulers] still more truly guardians and prevent them from distracting the city by referring *mine* not to the same but to different things" (464c).

Plato does not merely believe that the private family is one focal point of loyalty alongside the state or that, in deciding to retain the private family, we merely tolerate the possibility of occasional conflict between private and public interests. Rather, he is convinced that when familial claims are recognized and admitted into social life, they draw off energies and affections from the common purpose of the larger community and detract from the patriotism demanded of the true citizen. "Excessive love of self," considered by Plato to be inborn in most people, would, if given the opportunity, express itself through an excessive devotion to the interests of one's family and a corresponding disregard of public interests. Rivalries between families would disrupt society, and in time, as family members withdraw more and more from the active pursuit of civic well-being, the community would cease to exist as a community at all.

Much later, Cicero would call the family "the seedbed of the state,"[8] but for Plato, the habits and attitudes necessary for the maintenance of the ideal political state cannot be acquired within the family circle. The state first has to control

8. *On Moral Obligation,* trans. J. Higginbotham (London: Faber and Faber Ltd., 1967), bk. 1, ch. 17.

and mandate procreation in order to ensure a constant supply of genetically superior offspring. Children of guardians and soldiers then have to be removed from their mothers at birth and placed in public nurseries, where their care and early education would be supervised by guardians not directly involved in affairs of state. Freed from the demands of home and childrearing, both men and women would be able to pursue public functions unstintingly and would also be able to relate to children without possessiveness and anxiety. Women in particular would have the opportunity to join the ranks of the guardians and soldiers, though it is not in order to liberate women that Plato wants to dismantle the system of private upbringings. Rather, his argument is premised on the belief that children have to be reared communally if they are to be trained to live communally as adults, and that communal living among the guardians and soldiers of the ideal state promotes solidarity and identity of interests among those responsible for the welfare of the entire society and hence the unity of the state.

Plato's recommendations regarding the private family are closely bound up with his theory of the tripartite division of the human soul and the psychological basis of class division in the ideal republic. Despite the socially disruptive tendencies of private property and private family, Plato does not advocate their elimination from the economic class. He does not do so because the economic class represents for him the element of appetite, and appetite is satisfied only if it is allowed to express itself through devotion to family and the accumulation of private possessions. The members of the guardian class, in contrast, represent for Plato the element of reason, and their reason would either be dormant or distracted by desire if the private family were to remain among them. The prominence of reason in their souls means that their innate love of self can be controlled through proper education and living arrangements that do not include the private family, and the public good demands that we provide them with such.

In the *Laws,* Plato offers practical proposals for legislation to govern the imaginary, about-to-be-founded, Cretan city of Magnesia. This is not the "first-best society" of the *Republic,* with its "community in womenfolk, in children, in all possessions whatsoever,"[9] but a second-best society in which private property and the private family are retained. At the same time, extensive legal regulation of the private family is required, according to Plato, for "while the right regulation of the private households within a society is neglected, it is idle to expect the foundations of public law to be secure" (790b). Female curators in charge of wedlock are to supervise many areas of family life: the early upbringing of children, conditions of marriage, divorce, and filial responsibility. Yet Plato also understands that in certain respects the family must remain unregulated if it is to continue to exist, that childrearing in the private family will to some extent reflect the idiosyncracies of parents, and that therefore the fit between private upbringings and the requirements of the polity will be a loose one at best:

> The privacy of home life screens from the general observation many little incidents, too readily occasioned by a child's pains, pleasures, and passions, which are not in keeping with a legislator's recommendations, and tend to bring a medley of incongruities into the characters of our citizens. Now this is an evil for the public as a whole. . . . [T]hey are a real danger to such law as we do impose, since the habit of transgression is learned from repetition of these petty misdeeds. (788a–b)

While it would be "both improper and undignified" (788b) for the law to intrude on the intimacies of family life, the legislator must help parents become aware of the importance of children's early experience and of what constitutes appro-

9. *Laws,* in *Plato: The Collected Dialogues,* 739b–c.

priate physical and mental training of the young. He must hope that the citizen will come to regard these instructions "as so many laws for his own conduct, and, so regarding them . . . be happy in the administration alike of his own household and of his city" (790b).

Plato reintroduces private property and the family into the second-best city for primarily practical, not moral, reasons: he recognizes that the citizens of this city, not being gods or sons of gods, are incapable of holding their property, wives, and children in common. At the same time, the reintroduction of these institutions goes hand in hand with a new way of thinking about the relationship between reason and appetite in the human soul, and this new conception may have lessened Plato's anxiety about those institutions. In the *Republic*, the relation between reason and appetite is characterized solely in negative terms: reason has to harness, goad, and curb our feelings. In the *Laws*, this restraint is replaced by the positive development of desirable habits and traits. Now our feelings can be educated and cultivated; we can be taught to feel things that we would not otherwise have felt. On this view, though the family is still a temptation to self-seeking, reason does not require the repression of particular familial attachments. Family feeling can be enlightened by precepts of virtue, and therefore a communistic life, in the sense of a life divested of the appetitive element, is no longer necessarily connected to the supremacy of reason in the state. The result of Plato's new conception of the human soul is that the private family does not pose as great a danger to social unity as he had thought it did in the *Republic*.

Aristotle's Critique of Plato in the Politics

One of Plato's strongest critics is Aristotle. Aristotle opens the *Politics* by sharply criticizing the identification of "political science" and "the science of household management," a view he ascribes to Plato in the *Statesman*. The essential difference, according to Aristotle, between the statesman and the manager of a household does not involve the numbers of people over whom they rule. It is rather that the former handles the affairs of a political association where all are equals, whereas the latter exercises authority in a form of association where the strictest inequality prevails. And since equality is the essence of freedom, "the authority of the statesman is exercised over men who are naturally free . . . [while] the authority generally exercised over a household by its head is that of a monarch."[10] Though the family satisfies the material wants of daily life and assures the survival of the species and can also provide a context within which the father can exercise moral influence over his children, it is only within the state that an individual's moral needs can be completely satisfied and that full human development is possible. In the *Nicomachean Ethics,* another distinction is drawn between the state and family, viz., that the same kind of justice cannot obtain in both. A young child is, as it were, an extension or part of his or her parents. Since no one is voluntarily treated unjustly, and "the just and the unjust always involve more than one person,"[11] parents cannot act justly or unjustly toward their young children.

Aristotle admits that his theory of the household, as presented in book 1 of the *Politics,* is incomplete in a number of respects:

> There remain for discussion a number of questions—the relation of husband and wife, and that of parent and child; the nature of the goodness proper to each partner in these relations; the character of the mutual association of the partners, with its qualities and defects and

10. *Politics,* trans. E. Barker (New York: Oxford University Press, 1962), 1255b.
11. *Ethica Nicomachea,* trans. W. D. Ross (Oxford: Clarendon Press, 1966), 1138a19.

the methods of attaining those qualities and escaping those defects. (*Politics,* 1260b)

The subjects of marriage and parenthood are reserved for further treatment as part of his theory of education in book 7. As it turns out, however, these chapters do not really address themselves either to the nature of the goodness proper to parents and children as family members, or to the character of the mutual association of parents and children. In book 2, Aristotle proceeds to a criticism of Plato's proposed abolition of the family in the *Republic.* The problem is not that Plato sought to promote civic friendship and social solidarity, but that the methods he recommended for achieving them are self-defeating. The community of wives and children is not merely a larger family, different from the private family only in respect of the number of people with whom one enjoys fraternal relations. Rather, the attitudes of mind and forms of conduct characteristic of family life cannot be transposed to the wider circle of guardians. To believe otherwise is to deny the following true psychological principle:

> There are two things which particularly move men to care for an object and to feel affection for that object. One of them is that the object should belong to yourself; the other is that you should like it. (1262b)

Love for children cannot exist as something general but only in particular forms through which individual parents relate to individual children. It is only when individual parents relate to individual children that parents can think of their children as their own, and most people are incapable of devoting themselves to children unless they can think of them in this way. A civic education that teaches citizens to "like" all children will not produce the same effects as ownership. Plato's community of wives and children results in a "watery sort of fraternity" (ibid) not merely because the guardians are forced to spread their affections too thinly, but because they are expected to

show concern for those in whom they have no personal stake
or investment.

Recent critics like Ernest Barker have credited Aristotle
with the following insight into the importance of family life:

> Some there are indeed, but they are few, to whom a
> great cause is more than a group of persons, and who
> can give wife and child and much that men care for to
> identify themselves with this wider and fuller being.
> Ordinary humanity seeks its fulfillment in a narrower
> sphere; and of the vast majority it is true, that the love
> of their family (along with an interest in their profession
> and its circle) is, and is quite rightly, the sum of their
> life.[12]

However, this interpretation of Aristotle reads more into his
remarks about parent-child relationships than is warranted.
Aristotle does not argue that family and profession are the
center of the ordinary man's emotional life. (Of course, neither does he deny that there are pleasures, "arising from the
satisfaction of a natural feeling of self-love" (*Politics*, 1263b),
associated with being a parent and viewing your child's life
as a continuation of your own.) Rather, as I have said, his
argument is that parents and children will not feel especially
wanted, valued, and cared for by one another unless those who
do the childrearing feel personally and primarily responsible
for the well-being of specific children. Communal rearing,
such as Plato proposes, does not extend the warmth of family
feeling over the whole state, but alienates parents, so that the
quality of child care and the attachment between parents and
children suffer. If there is to be a strong sentiment of common
interest between parents and children, childrearing cannot be
left to the community in general, for then nobody in particular is likely to do it:

12. *The Political Thought of Plato and Aristotle* (New York: Dover, 1959),
pp. 399–400.

What is common to the greatest number gets the least amount of care. Men pay most attention to what is their own: they care less for what is common; or, at any rate, they care for it only to the extent to which each is individually concerned. Even where there is no other cause for inattention, men are more prone to neglect their duty when they think that another is attending to it: this is exactly what happens in domestic service, where many attendants are sometimes of less assistance than a few. (1261b)

References to Aristotle's arguments against Plato in contemporary debates on the merits of communalism versus the nuclear family sometimes reveal a misunderstanding of Aristotle's intentions. Aristotle's main concern is to show that one cannot destroy the exclusivity of family life without also seriously weakening the sentiment of common interest that exists between children and those who bring them up. Contemporary critics of communal upbringing share Aristotle's insistence on the importance of preserving affective ties between individual parents and individual children, but they are usually concerned less with communalism's effects on social unity than with its effects on the personal growth and self-actualization of children. Further, Aristotle claims that children who are raised communally are likely to be neglected, since each of their caretakers is inclined to shirk his or her responsibility and pass the buck to someone else. Contemporary theorists also call attention to a very different problem, viz., that caretakers in a communal setting will have a strong tendency to treat children "by the book," without much regard for their individual tasks and requirements.

Aristotle on Familial Friendship in the Ethics

While the *Politics* says little about the character of the mutual association of parents and children, books 8 and 9 of the

Nicomachean Ethics characterize the family as the sphere of a peculiar friendship. Aristotle distinguishes among three basic types of friendship: those based on shared pleasure, mutual usefulness, and common virtue. The most perfect form of friendship for Aristotle is virtue-friendship, because virtue-friendship normally lasts longer than either pleasure- or utility-friendship, and because virtue-friends are both pleasant and beneficial to one another, while pleasure-friends are not necessarily beneficial to one another and utility-friends are not necessarily pleasant to one another. It has also recently been suggested by John Cooper that there is another reason why Aristotle groups these three sorts of relationships under a common name:

> If . . . Aristotle means to adopt in *Nicomachean Ethics,* VIII, 2 the *Rhetoric*'s definition of friendship as always involving well-wishing to one's friend for his own sake, then the types will have much in common: in every friendship, of whichever of the three types, the friend will wish his friend whatever is good, for his own sake, and it will be mutually known to them that this well-wishing is reciprocal.[13]

According to Cooper, Aristotle holds the view that even in friendships based on pleasure or utility, one eventually comes to wish one's companion or associate well for his own sake, in recognition of the pleasure or utility he has brought one.

Cutting across the distinction between three types of friendship is Aristotle's other distinction between equal and unequal friendships. Friendship is possible even between persons who are not equally morally good or who bring each other unequal amounts and kinds of pleasure and utility. Family friendships are examples of unequal friendships:

> But there is another kind of friendship—that which involves an inequality between the parties, e.g. that of

13. "Aristotle on the Forms of Friendship," *Review of Metaphysics,* 30 (June 1977), pp. 630–631.

father to son and in general of the elder to the younger, that of man to wife and in general that of ruler to subject. (*Ethica Nicomachea*, 1158b12)

Aristotle probably believes that sons are morally inferior to their fathers for the same reason that he believes wives are morally inferior to their husbands. Like women, children may be perfect of their kind, but their kind is naturally and inherently lower than that of men. However, sons, unlike women, do outgrow their natural condition of dependency, and so we have to ask whether they can then become their fathers' equals in virtue. Aristotle does claim that children owe their parents honor and deference, but he argues that this is because of the benefits children received from them when young, not because of a continuing moral inequality between fathers and sons. Moreover, even if sons owe their fathers honor in part for the same reason that younger people generally ought to be deferential toward older ones, this still does not show that equal virtue-friendships between fathers and their grown sons are impossible. Friendships between the elder and the younger might be unequal in respect of pleasure or utility, rather than virtue.

For a number of reasons, it would seem, Aristotle thinks that parents normally derive more pleasure from their children than children from their parents. Some of these reasons are specific to parents; others are true of benefactors in general. With respect to the former, Aristotle begins by asserting that "parents love their children as being a part of themselves, and children their parents as being something originating from them" (1161b17). Parents love their children because their children are not completely individuated from them, because they see their children as reproducing some aspect of themselves or their lives. Parents identify with their children much the same way that painters identify with their paintings, and their love for their children closely approaches the love with which they love themselves. Children,

in contrast, come to love their parents not because they value
themselves as continuations of their parents' lives, or because
they see themselves reflected in their parents, but insofar as
they realize that their parents are responsible for conferring
on them the benefits of life, nourishment, and upbringing.

Parental and filial love are not, however, merely different:

> Parents know their offspring better than their children
> know that they are their children, and the originator
> feels his offspring to be his own more than the offspring
> do their begetter; for the product belongs to the pro-
> ducer . . . but the producer does not belong to the
> product, or belongs in a less degree. And the length of
> time produces the same result; parents love their chil-
> dren as soon as these are born, but children love their
> parents only after time has elapsed and they have ac-
> quired understanding or the power of discrimination by
> the senses. (1161b19)

As children grow older, they concentrate more and more of
their time and energy on achieving an identity separate from
that of their parents. Even as adults, the fact that they are who
they are—indeed, that they are at all—because of their parents
does not occupy as central a place in their lives as in the lives
of their parents. Parents identify with their children more
consistently and more deeply than their children identify
with them. Parents also love their children from birth, and
consequently love them over a greater length of time than
children love their parents. The very young child does not
really love his parents, because he is not yet capable of distinguishing them from others and understanding their special
relationship to him. For these reasons, Aristotle concludes
that parents love their children *more* than their children love
them. And if they do, then parents will derive more pleasure
from associating with their children because they are their
children, than children will derive from associating with their
parents because they are their parents. As between parents,

mothers usually get more pleasure than fathers, since the mother's affection for her child is rooted in early biological attachment and strengthened by the division of labor in the home.

Parents are their children's benefactors, bestowing on them the benefits of life, nourishment, and upbringing, and of benefactors in general Aristotle states, "benefactors are thought to love those they have benefited, more than those who have been well treated love those that have treated them well" (1167b17). The good of benefactors consists in their acts of beneficence, and they delight in their beneficiaries as in that in which they find their good. Moreover, "most pleasant is that which depends on activity" (1168a14) and "all men love more what they have won by labour" (1168a22), and since it is not an act of virtue to receive benefits from another, and since beneficiaries receive benefits without any labor on their parts, beneficiaries delight less in their benefactors than the benefactors delight in them. Even when the act of beneficence is past, the benefactor continues to delight in it, because moral good does not pass out of existence, but is enduring. The beneficiary, on the other hand, is left only with the memory of useful goods which were once received from the benefactor, and the memory of useful goods is less delightful than the memory of moral good when at some point their utility comes to an end. With respect to parents and children, parents will always delight in the memory of having bestowed upon their children numerous benefits while they were growing up, but when the children reach adulthood, they no longer need the care and guidance of their parents, and they tend to forget or underestimate their parents' earlier usefulness to them.

To the extent, therefore, that friendship between parents and children is based on pleasure, Aristotle's view seems to be that these friendships cannot be, or are not normally, equal. Under alternative descriptions of the parties involved in the friendship, equal pleasure-friendships may be possible, for example, between parents and children as travelling companions or sexual partners. But when the friendship is between parents and children *as* parents and children, the situation is different. As to the utility for parents and children of their association with one another, Aristotle points to yet a further disparity. Parents bestow upon their children the *greatest* of benefits—life, nourishment, and upbringing—but from their children "they can get no honour which will balance their services" (1164b5). Even if, as Aristotle discusses in one of his examples (1165a1), the child should ransom his father from robbers and thereby possibly save his life, the child has still not returned to his father the equivalent of what was received from him. To be sure, grown children can be of great utility to their aged parents, of greater utility than the parents can then be to them (1165a22). But the parent-child relationship does not commence with the maturity of the child. It has a long history, and when we consider the whole span of this relationship, we see that no matter what we do for our parents, we can never benefit them to the same extent as they have benefited us.

Parents, then, get more pleasure from their children than they give them; children derive greater benefits from their parents than their parents do from them; and at least as between parents and young children, parents are morally superior. But if in respect of utility parents are superior to their grown children, and if "the better man think[s] he ought to get more, since more should be assigned to a good man," and "the more useful similarly expects this" (1163a27), how are parent-child friendships possible? Aristotle's answer rests on the view that "in all friendships between dissimilars it is . . . proportion that equalizes the parties and preserves the friendship" (1163b32). One can never return to one's parents, as authors of one's being, the equivalent of what one received from them, but friendship is in any case more a matter of mutuality than reciprocity of benefits. Friends offer what they can give, and help one another when in need, without regard for the total amounts of benefits exchanged:

> Loving seems to be the characteristic virtue of friends, so that it is only those in whom this is found in due measure that are lasting friends, and only their friendship that endures. It is in this way more than any other that even unequals can be friends. (1159a34)

How do we decide whether children are loving their parents "in due measure?" "Who is to fix the worth of the service; he who makes the sacrifice or he who has got the advantage?" (1164a22). In general, where a service is rendered with a view to a return, the return should be one that seems fair to both parties or, if there is no such agreement on the appropriateness and fairness of the return, the receiver of the service should fix the reward according to the advantage received. Where there is no formal agreement on service and remuneration between the one who provides a benefit and the one who receives it, Aristotle argues, everything depends on their mutual intention. As long as we do the best we can for our parents, nourish and care for them when they are in need and we are able to help, and in general give our parents the honor that is due them when we can do no more, we compensate for the inequality between ourselves and our parents, and friendship between us develops and persists. What counts is that children should make an effort to befriend their parents, and it is intention rather than success that establishes when they are doing the best they can, "for it is purpose that is the characteristic thing in a friend and in virtue" (1164b2). In such friendships, the children, throughout their lives, display in their actions a respectful and deferential attitude toward those who are both older than themselves and responsible for the blessings of life that they enjoy.

It is not Aristotle's intention to argue that a child's debt to his parents is based on, or results from, the friendship that exists between them. Children would still be deeply indebted to parents with whom they have no friendship. Nor is it Aristotle's intention to argue that children ought to honor their parents, because in this way friendship with parents would develop and endure. Rather, Aristotle is interested in friendship as a phenomenon of family life because he believes that friendships of a close and intimate kind are a necessary constituent of the good or eudaemonistic life. Familial friendship is thus not a ground of filial obligation for Aristotle, but the desirable outcome of "children render[ing] to parents what they ought to render to those who brought them into the world, and parents render[ing] what they should to their children" (1158b22).

Aristotle's conception of familial friendship, situated within a general theory of friendship, his discussion of the basis of parental love, of the role that filial honor plays in equalizing parents and children, and of the grounds and stringency of children's indebtedness to their parents constitute a major contribution to philosophical writing on the family. Plato was too impatient with the family as a social institution to offer a serious philosophical treatment of infrafamily relationships, and though subsequent philosophical discussions of parent-child relations did emphasize the child's duties of honor and respect, the connection between honor and friendship was for the most part neglected. Only in Aquinas's philosophy of the family do we find a range of moral, political, and emotional concerns comparable to Aristotle's, and of course Aquinas chose Aristotle's views on family relations as his point of departure.

Generosity and Gratitude in the Stoics: Cicero and Seneca

Like Aristotle, Cicero holds that human society is necessary, or natural, because individuals are not sufficient to meet all

their wants by themselves: "It is natural for man to live together in communities, for only in this way have they learned
the advantages of mutual help and interdependence" (On
Moral Obligation, bk. 1, ch. 4). Again like Aristotle, Cicero
traces "from the fountain-head the natural principles on
which human society rests" (bk. 1, ch. 16). Society begins with
the nuclear family, with man and wife, parents and children.
The nuclear family then becomes part of a broader kinship
system, interlocked with other kin groups in a vast web of
kinship. This web of kinship is based on genealogical ties,
both consanguineal and affinal:

> Next comes the relationship of brother to brother,
> then that of cousins and second cousins, who some-
> times become too numerous to inhabit the same house.
> . . . Marital relationships come next, resulting in the
> extension of the family. (Bk 1, ch. 17)

Finally, in the complex series of social relationships formed
on the basis of these genealogical bonds, the state takes root:
"It is from the offspring of these unions that states are formed.
Blood relationship then is the prime factor in uniting men in
bonds of love and goodwill" (ibid.). The fellowship enjoyed
by family members is generalized through the kinship system,
which provides a simple foundation, easily recognizable and
usually unchallengeable, upon which a stable and unified
state can be erected.

While the "greatest bonds" are to be found between members of the same family, the state represents the most comprehensive of human societies, and according to Cicero, its claims
on our loyalty and devotion outweigh the claims of "parents,
children, relatives, and friends." As between the latter, our
obligations to our parents outweigh those to children, relatives, and friends, for we are bound to our parents "by great
debts of gratitude" (ibid.). Gratitude is an obligation in the
sense that, like all obligations for Cicero, it is "right and

fitting" (bk. 2, ch. 3). Our supreme obligation is to live "in accordance with nature" (bk. 3, ch. 5), that is, in accordance with the requirements of continued and fruitful mutual co-operation. From this point of view, ingratitude is wrong because it is "antisocial," "it discourages generosity" (bk. 2, ch. 18). In the particular case of ingratitude toward parents, the natural society of the family would be undermined if parents were not rewarded for their generosity by the gratitude and general good will of their children.

Before repaying any benefits, Cicero argues, we must discriminate between the quality of the benefits we have received. Two criteria should be employed: the value of the benefit to the recipient, and the state of mind of the benefactor in conferring the benefit. Benefits can be conferred "deliberately, eagerly and generously," or "rashly and injudiciously as though spurred on to indiscriminate benefactions by some infectious urge or by a sudden blast of good will" (bk. 1, ch. 15). Gratitude, Cicero suggests, is due only in the former case, and so children owe a duty of gratitude to their parents only for those benefits bestowed upon them in that spirit. Beyond this, however, Cicero does not tell us here what it is that children should be grateful to their parents for, nor does he tell us whether and how the child's debt of gratitude can ever be completely discharged. For a discussion of these and related issues, Seneca's treatise *On Benefits* is well worth our attention.

Benefits, says Seneca, are of three types: "things necessary, then profitable, thirdly agreeable, and permanent."[14] Among the "things necessary,"

> we rank those things, which alliance and parentage, familiar conversations, and long use, hath made us always repute and accopt most dear and precious: as

14. *On Benefits*, trans. T. Lodge (London: J. M. Dent and Co., 1899), bk. 1, ch. 11.

> our children, our wives and houses, and all these things
> whereunto we have so much addicted and dedicated our
> hearts and desires, that we had rather die than divide
> ourselves from their company. (Ibid.)

It would be wrong to conclude, however, that because children are such an important part of personal happiness for many people, parents always raise their children in order to derive pleasure or receive services from them in return. On the contrary, the things that parents do for their children are often bestowed as gifts in order to benefit them, and as Seneca asserts, there is a crucial difference between bestowing a benefit and expecting recompense:

> An honourable benefactor never thinketh of the good
> turn he doeth, except he that hath received the same,
> refresh the memory thereof by repaying him: because
> otherwise it ceaseth to be a benefit, and becometh a
> debt. (Bk. 1, ch. 2)

For an "honourable benefactor," the principal motive is benevolence, the desire to promote another's welfare not in order to create a debt but for that other's own sake, and the benefactor is requited when the object of his benevolence is in fact benefited and receives the benefit gratefully and in a spirit of good will. Though the beneficiary may not be able to do as much for his benefactor as his benefactor did for him, he can still "be thankful even with his will and heart" (bk. 2, ch. 31), and this is sufficient. The services the benefactor receives from a grateful person are, in one of Seneca's more memorable phrases, "not the remnant of an imperfect duty, but an income and accession to a perfect one" (bk. 2, ch. 33).

In the context of human reproduction, life is not a gift in the usual sense. Unlike saving a life, creating a life is not conferring a benefit upon someone, for it is only through the creation of life that there *is* anyone at all upon whom to confer benefits. Seneca does not discuss this conceptual difficulty, but argues instead that the mere granting of life by parents is not a benefit, or is the least of benefits, "except other things accompany it" (bk. 3, ch. 31):

> Can there be a greater care, and more circumspect diligence in this world, than that which the parents have over their children? and yet their pains should be lost, if so be they should abandon them in their infancy: if their devoir and paternal piety should not nourish them long, and tenderly protect that unto the end which nature hath recommended unto them. All other benefits are of the self-same condition; except though helpest them, thou losest them. (Bk. 2, ch. 11)

Life is only a precondition of the true end of parenting, virtuous living, and parents fail to fulfill their obligations if they do not continue to nourish and educate their children after they are born. The parents who abandon their child in infancy have merely given the child that which he has in common "with brute beasts, yea, with the least, the most despised, and the most loathsome" (bk. 3, ch. 30).

Even if parents do sustain and care for their children past infancy, Seneca observes, parents cannot adequately rear their children alone. Parents' efforts on behalf of their children are "assisted and seconded by the favours of diverse other persons" (bk. 3, ch. 35), for example, physicians, nurses, and educators. The life itself that parents confer on their children could not have been conferred unless parents had themselves received life from their parents, and so on through past generations: "But if I owe wholly to my beginning, whatsoever I more can do, think you that neither my father is my true beginning, nor my grandfather indeed" (bk. 3, ch. 30).

The father's motives in having children must also be considered. According to Seneca, he may have children out of respect for the law of his country, or in order to garner praise and reward from his parents, or to perpetuate his house and family, and not primarily out of a desire to bring another human being into the world to enjoy the blessings of life. Moreover, children are often the unplanned result of sexual acts undertaken purely for the sake of pleasure or at least the result of acts not clearly motivated principally by generosity toward prospective offspring. For these reasons, we should be somewhat skeptical of the claim that parents, in bestowing life, are acting as true benefactors of their children and that children (assuming Cicero is right) owe their parents a duty of gratitude for life itself.

It is in light of the above points about the benefit of life itself that Seneca addresses the question, "whether children at any time can give greater benefits to their parents, than they have received" (bk. 3, ch. 29). He considers the Aristotelian argument that "whatsoever I have done for my father, how great soever it be, it is nothing to be esteemed in respect of the benefit he hath done me, for I had not bin, had he not begotten me" (bk. 3, ch. 30), and rejects it on a number of grounds. Suppose a grown son saves his father from the peril of death. In this case, the son has not only conferred on his father a benefit *equal* to that conferred on him, by saving a life in return for being born, but in Seneca's view has actually surpassed his father. For first, in terms of quality of life, the infant, being "deprived of reason and judgment" (bk. 3, ch. 31), is not his father's equal. Second, the son's benefit is conferred by someone who knows what he gives upon someone who knows what he receives, whereas the father's act of begetting was both unintentional (in many instances) and as yet only potentially beneficial to the child. The father participates in procreation, and then must work toward the day when his child will have reason to be thankful to him for being alive. But the son gives something to his father that he (the son) knows the father will esteem as a benefit when he receives it. Third, "he that hath received a good turn, the more he needeth that which he hath received, he hath received the greater goodness" (bk. 3, ch. 35). The father has a greater need to stay alive than the son has to be born, if indeed the latter makes any sense at all. Even if the son never saves his father's life, the son can still outdo him in beneficence. For "there is something better than life" (ibid.), and the child bestows this on his father when he raises him from "a base degree . . . to high estate," and "from the meanest and ignoblest race of men" gives him "eternal and indefinite honours" (bk. 3, ch. 37).

For Aristotle, as we have seen, the child must honor and revere his father in acknowledgement of the father's superiority, and honor and reverence transform an unequal friendship into something resembling a friendship of equals. Seneca likewise believes that children must revere their fathers throughout their lives, but since he maintains that fathers are not in every case superior to their sons in terms of beneficence, his rationale for filial duty could not be the same as Aristotle's. In Seneca's view, the function of reverence is not to equalize unequals, and though the child's debt to the father *can* be completely discharged (if we want to speak about the child being "in debt" to the father at all), this does not render filial reverence obsolete. For reverence is not a sign of inferiority, but an attitude that expresses itself through the child's continuing desire to make his parents proud of him, to bring them the happiness that can only come from witnessing his eagerness to bestow kindnesses and favors on them. "Whence so great happiness to parents," Seneca asks rhetorically, "as to confess that they cannot equal their children's benefits?" (bk. 3, ch. 36). That parent is happiest whose child can truthfully say, "thou gavest me unto my self both rude and ignorant, and I gave my self to thee such a son, as thou mayest rejoice that ever thou begottest me" (bk. 3, ch. 31). In contrast, Aristotle's conception of filial reverence, the idea that children can never benefit their fathers as much as they have been benefited by them, gives children "means to excuse themselves" and, if repeatedly brought to their attention, tends to make them "more slow and retchless in acknowledging their father's benefits" (bk. 3, ch. 36).

The Christian Period: Saint Augustine and Saint Thomas Aquinas

Augustine and the Sinfulness of Children

Seneca places much more emphasis upon parental responsibility than Aristotle. Parents' obligations, Seneca holds, only *begin* with the birth of their child, and those who decide to have a child also necessarily take upon themselves the further task of teaching or enabling that child to lead the right kind of life. Parental responsibility is also an important theme of Saint Augustine's writing on the family, but due to his conception of the child as essentially sinful and his view of the relationship between original sin and human sexuality, Augustine pays particular attention to the child's need for parental discipline.

The term *original sin*, as Augustine uses it, refers to a theological, not an ethical, fault or deficiency. It is an interpretation of human existence since the Fall, a way of referring to man's alienation from God, rooted in prideful self-centeredness. Original sin is thus not to be confused with sexual desire, lust, or concupiscence, which Augustine holds to be particular sins. These particular sins are signs and symptoms of the corruption of human nature since the Fall, in the sense that sexual excitation and desire are incompatible with rational self-control and represent a kind of disobedience of the sexual organs parallel to the original human revolt against God's commands.

Further, all children, with the sole exception of Christ, are conceived in original sin, because no child can be conceived without the operations of lust and concupiscence, and these would either be entirely absent or under the strict control of the rational will if man had not originally disobeyed God's commands. Not only are children conceived *in* original sin: they are also born *with* it. The sin of Adam is passed down to his descendants, so that, like Adam himself, children are domineering, willful, egoistic, and self-centered. (Again, it is not Augustine's intention to claim that children are born sinful in the sense that they are born unjust or immoral. These are not terms that can appropriately be applied to agents who have no conception of right and wrong, who are incapable of understanding the connection between their actions and the consequences of those actions, and who do not yet have the ability to empathize with other human beings.) Original sin generates certain needs during childhood. Children must not have their every whim and impulse gratified, for otherwise they will never develop that sense of humility without which human happiness is impossible. The secret of human happiness, for Augustine, lies in accurately assessing one's real needs, specifically one's need for God, and children who are permitted to tyrannize over their parents and teachers will grow into adults who cannot escape from the hazards and temptations of mundane life to find their true resting place in the understanding of eternal truth.

Parents must attend not so much to the wishes as to the welfare of their children, for children are willful and passionate and need the firm tutelage of a stern master. In the rightly ordered family, the young children accept their beliefs on trust from their parents, and act confidently on such beliefs accepted on authority. As in the understanding of ultimate reality, faith must precede reason. But parents themselves, Augustine admits, typically treat their children as means to their own self-satisfaction and thus teach them, by example, to become even more self-centered. The child, says Augustine,

> when learneth he to love ought, save what his parents
> have whispered into his ears? They teach him and train
> him in avarice, robbery, daily lying, the worship of
> divers idols and devils, the unlawful remedies of en-
> chantments and amulets. What shall one yet an infant
> do, a tender soul, observing what its elders do, save
> follow that which it seeth them doing.[15]

Parents may even command their child to do something "contrary to the Lord his God" (p. 315). The good parent, then, is
a rare phenomenon.

The obvious question to ask at this point is why, given this
fact, Augustine never seriously questions the advisability of
allowing parents to rear their children. Part of the answer is
contained in the following passage from his treatise *The
Good of Marriage*:

> Marriage has also this good, that carnal or youthful in-
> continence, even if it is bad, is turned to the honorable
> task of begetting children, so that marital intercourse
> makes something good out of the evil of lust. Finally,
> the concupiscence of the flesh, which parental affection
> tempers, is repressed and becomes inflamed more mod-
> estly. For a kind of dignity prevails when, as husband
> and wife they unite in the marriage act, they think of
> themselves as mother and father.[16]

Though the chief end of marriage, for Augustine, is procreation, marriage also has a secondary, nonprocreative, relational
purpose. Parents should raise their children, and children
obey their parents, because parenting benefits both husband
and wife by affording them a means of salvation from sex.
Marriage provides an honorable and regulated outlet for concupiscence by confining it to the production of children; and

15. P. Schaff, ed., *A Select Library of the Nicene and Post-Nicene Fathers,*
(New York: Christian Literature Co., 1888), Vol. 8, p. 632.
16. *The Good of Marriage,* trans. C. T. Wilcox, M.M. (New York: Fathers
of the Church, Inc., 1955), p. 13.

while parents may often treat their children as a means to their own self-gratification, and parental affection may often be no more than a disguised form of self-love, cooperation in the serious business of bringing up children represses the sexual desires of husband and wife after procreation.

Aquinas and the Virtue of Piety

Saint Thomas Aquinas does not reject Augustine's claims about the sinfulness of children or the doctrine of original sin on which they are based. But by returning to Aristotle rather than Augustine in order to develop his own conception of the family, Aquinas could attend to aspects of family life that Augustine had neglected or whose importance he had underestimated. Essentially, the difference between Augustine and Aquinas is that Augustine does not think of the family as a domestic society so much as a form of association made necessary by God's command to be fruitful and multiply. This is evident, for example, in Augustine's repeated, almost exaggerated insistence upon procreation as the primary end of marriage and his tendency to deemphasize mutual aid between spouses as one of the legitimating purposes of marriage. It is also evident in the prominence he gives to notions of discipline and obedience in characterizing parent-child relationships, at the expense of notions like mutual friendship and love.

Aquinas's debt to Aristotle was immense, but Aquinas was quite selective in what he took over from him, and whenever he used Aristotelian notions, fitted them into a theological view of virtue and the moral life that Aristotle did not share. He agrees with Aristotle, for example, that children can never discharge the debt they owe their parents and that since "parents are in the position of superiors . . . their love tends to express itself by giving, whereas children's love shows itself by honouring."[17] On the other hand, Aquinas does not share

17. *Summa Theologiae*, vol. 34, trans. R. J. Batten O.P. (New York: Blackfriars, 1975), 2a2ae, question 31, article 3.

Aristotle's views on the limits of parental authority. He faults Aristotle for failing to distinguish between the child qua child and the child qua individual human being. The child qua child is part of his or her father, and since, as Aristotle had said, justice "presupposes the distinction of one individual from another,"[18] there can be no justice in the usual sense between a father and his children. But what Aristotle did not acknowledge was that the child is also an individual human being who "subsists in himself and distinct from others" and, as such, is "an object of justice in some manner" (ibid.). Fathers, therefore, do not have absolute authority over their children, and children do have rights in regard to their fathers.

Parents, of course, have rights over their children, but for Aquinas these rights are constrained by parents' obligations to provide their children with physical, mental, moral, and religious education, as well as by the needs of domestic life. Like Seneca, Aquinas holds that it is incumbent on those who bring a child into the world to follow up this beginning with many further benefits. Similarly, children have duties as well as rights, and these duties are of two types: those of a temporary nature, lasting until the child reaches maturity—duties of obedience; and those of a permanent nature—summed up in what Aquinas calls duties of piety.

> Obedience in general, says Aquinas, necessarily includes the will being prompt with respect to the objective of virtue, not with regard to what runs counter to the will. But what is peculiar about the objective of obedience is that it is a precept issuing from the will of someone else, so that obedience makes a person's will ready to carry out the will of another, i.e., a superior.[19]

Obedience is, however, only one of the duties inferiors owe their superiors. First, obedience must be distinguished from

18. *Summa Theologiae*, vol. 37, trans. Thomas Gilby, O.P. (New York: Blackfriars, 1975), 2a2ae, question 57, article 4.
19. *Summa Theologiae*, vol. 41, trans. T. C. O'Brien (New York: Blackfriars, 1972), 2a2ae, question 104, article 2.

reverence, in that obedience "has to do with the precept of
the person of rank," while reverence "has to do directly with
the person who has some sort of eminence" (ibid.). We do not
obey superiors, we obey their commands; we revere superiors
because of their superior personal qualities, we do not revere
their commands. Second, obedience must be distinguished
from respect, for the former presupposes the latter. A person
owes a duty of obedience only to someone who exercises rightful authority over him, and those who have rightful authority
over others, even if they occasionally abuse that authority, are
at least entitled to respect in virtue of their superior rank, if
not reverence as well:

> In the instance of one holding authority we should
> take into consideration, first, his superior status with
> power over subjects, and secondly, the actual duty of
> governing them. On grounds of superiority, he has a
> right to honour, which means in fact the acknowledge-
> ment of another's eminence. On grounds of the task of
> governing he has a right to homage, which consists in a
> definite service, namely that his commands be obeyed
> and his good offices be recompensed in due measure.
> (Question 102, article 2)

In short, obedience has to do with commands, respect with
positions of authority, and reverence with character or personal attainments. As regards the relationship between children and parents, children owe their parents all three, obedience, respect, and reverence, but obedience to parental
commands and respect for parental authority are the duties
only of young children.

Parents have eminence, and ought to be revered (not just
respected) by their children, because of the kind of benefits
that children receive from them. Next to God, parents are
the "closest sources of our existence and development" (question 101, article 1), surpassing even country, for it is only be-

cause parents give their children existence, food, the support
needed for life, and education, that they are able to share in
the benefits of homeland. Since the benefits parents bestow
touch the whole of our existence, our entire personality and
not just one relatively minor aspect of it, the degree of our
indebtedness to them is particularly great, and it is incumbent
on us to revere them in a special way, to acknowledge and pay
back our debt to them by the virtue of piety. Whenever we
are dependent on another for a whole side of our life, piety
comes into play, and filial piety shows itself, first, through
honor or appreciation, which involves a certain attitude of
mind toward one's parents as well as the outward manifestation of this attitude when occasion requires; and second,
through actual service, which entails assisting parents when
in need, visiting them when sick, caring for them in their old
age—in general, doing "whatever plain decency shows to be
suited to their situation" (question 101, article 2). Even when
parents do not *need* the services of their children, there are
still many ways in which the children can demonstrate appreciation to their parents for all that they have done for them.

The virtue of piety can perhaps be further clarified in the
following way. According to Aquinas, filial obligation is a
matter of "making a return for benefits received,"[20] and "return for a good received can be the concern of any one of
three virtues, justice, gratitude, or friendship."[21] The term
justice here refers to what Aristotle calls "particular" as opposed to "general" justice, that is, to a particular virtue rather
than to the sum of all virtues. More specifically, it refers to
the kind of particular justice Aristotle calls justice in exchange, or commercial justice. When return for benefits received falls under the heading of justice in this sense, the
beneficiary has a legal or quasi-legal debt and must return to
his benefactor goods or services whose value is commensurate

20. *Summa,* vol. 34, 2a2ae, question 31, article 3.
21. *Summa,* vol. 41, 2a2ae, question 106, article 5.

with that of the benefactor's goods or services: "the amount given is the measure of the recompense." Gratitude, in contrast, is not a legal, but a moral, debt, and "repayment made out of gratitude regards the sentiment of the giver more than what he has given." The person who has a duty of gratitude is not expected, and may not be able, to give back the equivalent of what he has received. Likewise, friendship gives rise to moral, not legal, debts, and "in reciprocation out of friendship, that on which the friendship is based should serve as the norm" (ibid.). What friends should or should not do for one another depends on the nature of their friendship, on whether their friendship is based on utility, pleasure, or virtue.

It is clear that for Aquinas, filial obligation is not a matter of justice, as above defined. Our relationship to our parents is not analogous to a business transaction in which we receive certain benefits or services from them, as it were, on loan. Rather, our indebtedness to our parents should involve elements of imprecision, latitude, even friendliness. Moreover, children cannot exactly acquit the debt they owe their parents, because, as Aristotle also believed, "we can make no equal return to our parents for the great benefits they have given us."[22] (The point here is not merely that we can't literally do for our parents what they did for us, but more importantly, that no matter what benefits we confer on our parents, they will not be as valuable to them as their benefits are to us.) Though Aquinas borrows heavily from Seneca's discussion of gratitude in *On Benefits,* his position on the issue of equal return does not seem to have been affected in any significant way by his reading of Seneca. He agrees with Seneca only to the extent of saying that "from the standpoint of willingness to give and repay, it is possible for a child even to surpass parents."[23] Filial obligation is also not a result of

22. Mary Clark, ed., *An Aquinas Reader* (New York: Image Books, 1972), p. 495.
23. *Summa,* vol. 41, 2a2ae, question 106, article 6.

friendship, in Aquinas's view. Friendship between parents and children promotes the fulfillment of filial duties by fostering reverence and service;[24] it does not create these duties. And though friendship between parents and children "is safeguarded by the acknowledgement of favour received"[25] from parents, this act itself is not directly the concern of the virtue of friendship.

The one remaining virtue is that of gratitude, and while Aquinas is perhaps not completely consistent in his explanation of its relationship to piety, there are at least a few occasions on which he strongly suggests that piety is a form of gratitude. The gratitude we owe our parents is, of course, distinct from the gratitude we owe just "any benefactor from whom we have received some special, personal kindness":

> We do not . . . offer what we owe to God, parents or civil authority to everyone who does us a personal favor. This is why gratitude, which returns thanks for kindness, ranks after religion, by which we offer worship due to God; after piety, by which we honour parents; and after respect, by which we honour public officials. Gratitude is distinct from these others in the way that anything secondary is distinct from something primary, namely as something less. (Ibid.)

But just as "religion is a preeminent form of piety" as well as "a higher form of gratitude" (ibid.), so too piety can be thought of as a higher form of gratitude. Gratitude does not obligate us to respond to all our benefactors in the same manner, with the same degree of devotion. On the contrary, "the nature of the case requires that a recipient respond to his benefactor in a way that reflects their relationship" (question 106, article 3), and since our relationship with our parents is

24. See *Summa*, vol. 23, trans. W. D. Hughes, O.P. (New York: Blackfriars, 1969), 1a2ae, question 65, article 3.
25. *Summa*, vol. 41, 2a2ae, question 106, article 1.

so closely bound up with who and what we are, more is required to demonstrate our gratitude and appreciation to them than to any other benefactor, with the exception of God. Just what is required of children cannot be determined with the precision that would be possible if filial obligation were a matter of justice, for gratitude looks to the nature of the particular family and of the particular relationships within it, and not, as in the case of justice, to an "equality . . . of external objects" (question 106, article 6).

Piety, gratitude, and justice all concern themselves with a beneficiary's indebtedness to a benefactor, but according to Aquinas, the indebtedness to which justice responds is quite different from the indebtedness to which either piety or gratitude respond. In the case of justice, the thing that is owed is not "reckoned as part of the debtor's belongings, but as part of the true owner's."[26] It is an obligation of justice to make a return for a benefit received only when the benefit in some way still belongs to the benefactor, as when the benefactor confers upon the beneficiary only a right to use the benefit in question. When the benefactor freely confers a right of ownership, and not merely a right of use, upon the beneficiary, the indebtedness to the benefactor cannot be based on justice. With piety and gratitude, on the other hand, "the thing that is owing is reckoned as part of the debtor's, not the creditor's, goods" (ibid.). Here a good or favor possessed as one's own becomes the basis of a debt toward the source, and as beneficiary, one does not attempt to rectify a moral imbalance by restoring something that rightfully belongs to another, but rather tries to show one's appreciation for what rightfully belongs to oneself. On this view, parents who demand that their children repay them for all that they have done on their behalf operate on the assumption that justice, not piety or gratitude, is the basis of filial obligation.

26. *Summa,* vol. 34, 2a2ae, question 31, article 3.

The Modern Period:
Bodin Through Hegel

Bodin and Absolute Parental Authority

Jean Bodin's *Six Books of the Commonwealth* (1576) marked the transition from specifically medieval to specifically modern ways of political thinking. The disorder and violence of the times in which he lived seemed to validate the traditional Augustinian teaching that the state is necessary to curb man's natural rebelliousness and formed the background against which Bodin defined the state in terms of its government, "a rightly ordered government," and citizenship in terms of subjection to absolute sovereign power. Writers in the next century continued to define the central problems of political philosophy as Bodin had done, and repeated all or part of what he had to say about the nature of the state and citizenship. Filmer and Hobbes, for example, took over Bodin's absolutism; Locke shared his belief that the essence of sovereignty is the authority to make law. As far as the family was concerned, Bodin was only interested in the relationship between political authority and domestic power, and this too had a significant impact on the way in which family life was discussed through Locke. The family, whatever other purposes it might have, was for Bodin a nursery of the state, and a training ground for citizenship. Therefore, the habits proper in a subject of the commonwealth had to be learned within the family. This much was uncontroversial. The debate in the next century revolved instead around the characterization of these habits, and the view, put forward by Bodin, that the family is not merely the "principal constituent" of the commonwealth, but its "true image" and "the model of right order in the commonwealth."[27]

27. Jean Bodin, *Six Books of the Commonwealth,* trans. M. J. Tooley (New York: Macmillan, 1955), bk. 1, chs. 2–5, p. 6.

Actually, it would be more accurate to say that Bodin does not offer a familial model for the political order so much as a political model for the familial order. Domestic government, which Aquinas had regarded as only one of the elements of the family, becomes for Bodin its defining feature:

> A family may be defined as the right ordering of a group of persons owing obedience to a head of a household, and of those interests which are his proper concern. . . . I understand by domestic government the right ordering of family matters, together with the authority which the head of the family has over his dependents, and the obedience due from them to him. (P. 6)

Further, because Bodin believes that "children who stand in little awe of their parents, and have even less fear of the wrath of God, readily set at defiance the authority of magistrates" (p. 13), he proceeds to develop a conception of parental authority that dovetails with his conception of political authority. As regards the sovereign in the political sphere, he is absolute in relation to his subjects, though not so in his relation to God. The sovereign must respect and guarantee certain rights pertaining to the individual prior to the state, but if he fails to do so, he has wronged God, not his subjects. The father, too, must have absolute authority over his children, even to the extent of having the power of life and death over them. As in the case of the political sovereign, absolute parental authority is not the same as arbitrary parental authority, for the father has genuine obligations toward his children. But again it is to God, not to his children, that the father is answerable for failure to carry out these obligations.

Once the young are trained by their fathers in the habits appropriate to a citizen, that is, in the habits of obedience and submission, a rightly ordered commonwealth can be achieved. But obedience and submission do not exhaust the virtues of the citizen, for Bodin. The end of the state, as well as the "sovereign good of the individual," consists "in the constant contemplation of things human, natural, and divine," and it is only within a rightly ordered commonwealth that the individual can achieve "true felicity" (bk. 1, ch. 1). The ultimate purpose of parenting is to help children develop those qualities of mind whereby men distinguish good and evil, true and false, pious and impious, and absolute parental authority is a necessary means to this end.

If the granting of absolute authority to parents was something Bodin believed he had to defend, he appears to have taken it as a given that consent plays no role whatsoever in the obligation to obey parents. This belief about the relationship between consent and legitimate parental authority provides Bodin with yet another point of similarity between parental and political authority, for in his view legitimate political authority likewise does not rest on the consent of the governed. The political sovereign is subject to divine and natural law, and the ultimate sanction of the individual's liberty, the guarantee that the restrictions placed on it in political society shall be reasonable, is the imprescriptibility of divine and natural law. Bodin further bolsters the analogy between parental and political authority with his voluntarist conception of law. He makes no sharp distinction between loyalty to the person of the sovereign and loyalty to the laws governing the commonwealth, for he holds that law is simply the command of the sovereign. The citizen's loyalty to the sovereign is not contingent on the conformity of civil to divine and natural law. Rather, the citizen is expected to obey the law solely out of loyalty to the sovereign. Similarly, in the family the young child experiences the authority of the parents and the authority of their commands as one, and the child's ultimate allegiance is given to the persons of the parents. Bodin wants parents to keep their children in this position of unquestioning obedience throughout childhood, for only then will they be prepared to transfer their ultimate allegiance from the persons of their parents to the person of the sovereign.

Bodin realizes that there will be objections to his recommendation that "princes and legislators should revive the ancient laws touching the power of fathers over their children" (pp. 13–14). If the laws are to give fathers the right to exercise absolute authority over their children, then what is there, other than their consciences, to prevent fathers from abusing the power they have over the life and property of their children? Bodin admits that sometimes it will be necessary for the law to step in to protect children from their fathers, when they demonstrate gross unfitness to raise their children. Normally, however, "the affection of parents for their children is so strong . . . that they will only do those things which are of benefit and honour to their children," and the law ought to presume that children are sufficiently protected against "cruelty and abuse of power" by the "natural affection" (p. 14) their parents feel for them.

By using the term *natural affection* Bodin does not mean to suggest that parental affection is completely independent of institutional forms of familial arrangement. He argues, in fact, that there are certain modes of childrearing, the Platonic, for example, which are not conducive to the development of strong parental affection, and hints that in them parental affection might not be intense enough to deter fathers from abusing their absolute authority. Following Aristotle, Bodin maintains that Plato's abolition of the family would not eliminate quarrels and animosities between the guardians, but would only destroy

> affection between husband and wife, and the love of parents for their children, the reverence of children for their parents, and the goodwill of parents towards one another. Such are the consequences of ignoring the tie of blood, the strongest bond there is. It is common knowledge that no one feels any very strong affection for that which is common to all. (pp. 8–9)

If parents are to have absolute authority over their children, and if, as Bodin suggests, children should be provided with a type of familial arrangement that minimizes the opportunities for abuse of that authority by parents, then it follows that Plato's system of common upbringings should not be adopted. It is not clear whether Bodin meant to use Aristotle's vindication of the family in order to quiet the fears of those who objected to absolute parental authority. Even if he did, it should not be supposed that Bodin's vindication of the family was addressed solely to the problem of parental abuse, or that he used Aristotle's remarks about the family only for the rather un-Aristotelian purpose of shoring up his own defense of absolute parental authority. For Bodin also shared Aristotle's view that "those things which are public property are habitually neglected" (p. 91), and seems to have been concerned about protecting children from parental neglect as well as from parental abuse.

Hobbes, Paternal Dominion, and the Consent of Children

There are, Hobbes claims, only three ways in which one person comes to have "right and dominion over another"[28] in the absence of civil society: "voluntary offer, captivity, and birth" (part 2, ch. 4, sec. 1). The only difference between the kind of dominion that is instituted by voluntary offer ("sovereignty by institution") and the kind that is acquired by captivity or birth ("sovereignty by acquisition") is that in the former case, the "men who choose their Sovereign, do it for fear of one another, and not of him whom they Institute," while in the latter, "they subject themselves to him they are afraid of."[29]

28. De Corpore Politico, in Body, Man, and Citizen, ed. R. S. Peters (New York: Collier, 1967), part 2, ch. 3, sec. 2.
29. Leviathan, ed. C. B. Macpherson (Baltimore: Penguin, 1968), part 2, ch. 20.

Both the child and the citizen submit themselves to another—
the child to his or her parents and the citizen to the political
sovereign—out of fear, and in Hobbes's view there is no more
of a loss of liberty in obeying the commands of parents, out of
fear of them, than in obeying the commands of a political
sovereign, out of fear of others. If I perform some action because I am afraid that I shall suffer some unpleasant experience if I do not do so, then I act of my own volition. And if
my voluntary action is not hindered by external impediments,
that is, by impediments outside my body, then I act freely:

> A Freeman, is he, that in those things, which by his
> strength and wit he is able to do, is not hindered [by
> external impediments] to do what he has a will to do.
> (Part 2, ch. 21)

Further, it is because children freely agree to submit to the
authority of parents, not because of the fact of birth itself,
that parents acquire their right of dominion over their children. Sovereignty by acquisition derives from "Covenants of
the Vanquished to the Victor, or Child to the Parent," and
there is "no Obligation on any man," including the child,
"which ariseth not from some Act of his own; for all men
equally, are by Nature Free" (ibid.). The obligations of children are not natural, but as artificial and consensual as the
obligations of citizens or of subjects. In this way, Hobbes de-
parts both from Bodin, who maintains that neither parental
nor political authority derives its legitimacy from consent,
and from Locke, who argues only that consent is the foundation of legitimate political, not parental, authority.

The child's consent may either be "expresse, or by other
sufficient arguments declared" (part 2, ch. 20): express when
children enter into a covenant with parents similar to that by
which servants subject themselves to lords, and "by other
sufficient arguments declared" when children act in ways that
imply they have consented. About express consent, Hobbes

says little. Regarding the propriety of applying the notion of tacit covenant to the child-parent relationship, he offers two arguments. First,

> And though the child thus preserved, do in time acquire strength whereby he might pretend equality with him or her that hath preserved him, yet shall that pretence be thought unreasonable, both because his strength was the gift of him, against whom he pretendeth; and also because it is to be presumed, that he which giveth sustenance to another, whereby to strengthen him, hath received a promise of obedience in consideration thereof.[30]

In other words, when children are within the power of parents to preserve or destroy (as they are in a state of nature), and the parents choose to preserve rather than destroy them, it is to be presumed that the parents do so only on condition that the children shall not grow up to be their enemies, that they shall obey them, for no one is so unreasonable as to sustain or breed his own enemy. This is a presumption of reason regarding parents in general, not a presumption that particular children make about their parents. Children tacitly agree to obey parents because they instinctively want to remain alive and because they are given to understand that the parents may kill or abandon them if they do not obey. Such a consent is free, although forced; terror of the alternative only makes it more prudent to consent. When a child lacks the capacity to understand the connection between his actions and risks of harm to himself, this argument obviously does not apply.

If parental power derives from an implied contract between children and parents, do children consent to obey parents only for as long as they remain within their power to preserve or destroy, or do they also consent to obey their par-

---

30. *De Corpore Politico*, part 2, ch. 4, sec. 3.

ents even after they have ceased to be dependent on them for protection? When, if ever, do children cease to have an obligation to obey their parents? Hobbes's answer seems to be that we consent to obey them into adulthood and must obey indefinitely. Our "pretence" of equality with our parents "shall . . . be thought unreasonable," because "we intend always our own safety and preservation" (part 1, ch. 1, section 13), and a child who becomes his parents' equal can also become their enemy. In preserving their child, parents do not intend that he shall become equal, and the child must accept the parents' protection on these terms. It doesn't matter that it may not be prudent for the children to obey their parents once they are free of parental power. For Hobbes's point is that children must be presumed to consent *now* to obey their parents *later on,* and must actually do so later on even if it is not prudent to do so, because they would never be in a position to disobey their parents at all if the parents had known, or had good reason to believe, that the children would grow up to be disobedient. Our adult obligation to obey our parents is thus essentially a moral, not a prudential, obligation. We do not have the right to disobey our parents, because we have an obligation to keep the promise we (tacitly) made to our parents when we were dependent on them for protection.

The question *For how long do children consent to obey?* should be distinguished from this other: *When do children consent to obey?* Hobbes seems to regard the tacit consent of children as the consent given by each child under the threat of present or future probable death, that is, as the consent each child gives while still a child and subject to the power of his or her parents. His argument that "Feare and Liberty are consistent" (*Leviathan,* part 2, ch. 21) can thus be read as an attempt to show that the tacit consent of children can be free, and hence the means of transforming mere "Naturall force" into sovereignty. But this interpretation of tacit consent seems to clash with the following remark:

Over naturall fooles, children, or mad-men there is no
Law, no more than over brute beasts; nor are they capable of the title of just, or unjust; because they had never
power to make any covenant, or to understand the consequences thereof; and consequently never took upon
them to authorize the actions of any Sovereign. (Part 2,
ch. 26)

On this view, the claim that "Feare and Liberty are consistent" seems irrelevant to the issue of legitimate parental authority over children, for now submission to parental power,
motivated by fear of parents, is not also consensual, and hence
not free. Fear and liberty might be consistent, but in the case
of children, there is only fear, not liberty, in submission.

Hobbes does not appear to have recognized any problem
in his account of tacit consent. He does not seem to have
noticed that sometimes he speaks of tacit consent in a way
that suggests it can be given even by a child, and other times
maintains that a child lacks the rational capacities required
for meaningful consent. It may be, however, that this discrepancy is more apparent than real. For first as Gordon
Schochet has argued, Hobbes might have meant to equate
tacit consent of children with the consent given by each child
as he comes of age and becomes master of his own reason,
in other words, with what could be called future-oriented
consent.[31] Though children, as children, do not actually consent, eventually they will come to see that obedience was a
small price to pay for protection and that in obeying they
only did what they would have wanted to do if they were
fully rational. This future-oriented consent obligates even
the very young to obey their parents. A second way of removing the discrepancy in Hobbes's derivation of parental authority would be to argue that he uses the concept of *child* in two
different senses. When he suggests that children can consent,

31. *Patriarchalism in Political Thought* (New York: Basic Books, 1975),
p. 232.

he might have been thinking of children as those who are dependent on their parents for protection; when he asserts that children cannot consent, he might have been thinking of children as those who lack emotional and cognitive capacities required in order to make rational decisions. Since children may still need the protection of their parents even though they are rational enough to "understand the consequences" of covenanting, these two definitions are not coextensive. The contrast here is between the immature and the mature child and not, as before, between the child and the adult. As for immature children, they do not consent at all, either actually or prospectively, and so their obedience is merely a fact, not an obligation.

In a state of nature, parents and children are potential adversaries. Parents preserve and sustain their children only on condition that they will not grow up to become their enemies, and children promise to obey in return for the protection they receive from their parents. But Hobbes does not seem to rest his entire case for the consensual nature of children's obligations on these grounds alone, and he could have offered another argument to those who are unwilling to accept his adversarial conception of parent-child relationships. According to this argument, while children's obligations are not contractual, they are nevertheless consensual, because by accepting the benefits offered by the preserver, children sufficiently declare, by their own acts, their consent. (This formulation, of course, raises the same problems about tacit consent discussed earlier.) Children oblige themselves according to the fourth law of nature, the law of gratitude, which requires

> that a man which receiveth Benefit from another of meer Grace, Endeavor that he which giveth it, have no reasonable cause to repent him of his good will. (*Leviathan,* part 1, ch. 15)

Thus, even if obedience to parents cannot be thought of as something each child consents to render in consideration of some return, and thus as a matter of justice, it can still be thought of as something each child consents to render in recognition of "Antecedent Grace," that is, as a matter of gratitude. The obligation of gratitude includes the obligation to obey parents and the more general obligation to honor them as well.[32]

We should note, however, that Hobbes's argument from gratitude does not replace an adversarial conception of the family with a conception that emphasizes unselfish love and selfless sacrifice. For in Hobbes, there is no such thing as genuine benevolence, even between parents and children:

> No man giveth, but with intention of Good to himselfe; because Gift is Voluntary; and of all Voluntary Acts, the Object is to every man his own Good. (*Leviathan*, part 1, ch. 15)

In a state of nature, there is no known authorized sovereign competent to make and enforce rules upon all heads of households. With the establishment of civil society and the coercive power of the state, the Hobbesian sovereign ensures that heads of households will not be placing themselves at a disadvantage or exposing themselves to danger by keeping their covenants with one another. The sovereign only underwrites covenants between heads of households or competent adults generally, not between parents and children, because parents and children are not in a state of nature with respect to one another. Though there is no common power over every child, each child is subordinated to the power of his particular parents; and though there is no common power over every family, each family is in itself a small society. Nevertheless, there are important changes in the moral basis of parent-child relationships once we pass from a Hobbesian state of nature to political society. In political society, unlike the state of nature, people do not have the right to judge for

32. See *De Cive*, in *Man and Citizen*, ed. B. Gert (Garden City, N.Y.: Anchor, 1972), 9, 8.

themselves between right and wrong, and children are within the power of their parents to preserve or destroy only insofar as the state grants them this power or does not proscribe its use. The state may instead impose unconditional obligations of care and support upon parents, and if parents fail to meet these obligations, may intervene to protect children. In addition, since the political sovereign significantly reduces the danger of death at the hands of others, parents do not have to fear that their children will grow up to become their enemies. The consent of children, therefore, can no longer be based on the presumption that people never sustain or breed their own enemies. The state does not secure a covenant between parents and children whereby parents now preserve their children in exchange for a promise to obey them in the future. Rather, the state removes the adversarial element from parent-child relationships, and eliminates both the parents' and the child's need to enter into such a covenant in the first place. Of the two arguments that Hobbes offers for the implicitly consensual nature of children's obligations, the argument from gratitude is the only one that can be consistently applied to families within political society.

Locke on Parental Right Versus Parental Duty

Locke's *First Treatise* is a sustained, often exasperatingly tedious, critique of Sir Robert Filmer's theory of divine-right patriarchalism. For the sake of argument, Locke accepts Filmer's contention that procreation, individuals creating other individuals by begetting them, gives parents a right of superiority over their children, and then proceeds to show that Filmer's political doctrines receive no support from this account of parental authority. The moral relevance of procreation is not seriously challenged until chapter 6 of the *Second Treatise,* where Locke offers his own justification of parental authority, a justification that does not appeal either to children's consent or to procreation.

Filmer holds that the foundation of legitimate parental power cannot be the consent of children, for far from being born free, all people are born into families, and consequently into subordination to the heads of families. The right of parental domination arises naturally, and as Locke expresses Filmer's view, "the Act of begetting being that which makes a Man a Father, his Right of Father over his Children can naturally arise from nothing else."[33] Filmer further ascribes three properties to parental authority, each of which plays an important role in his political argument that paternity imposes on individuals indefeasible obligations of absolute obedience to the existing ruler of a political society. Parental authority is (1) absolute, "Unlimited, and Unlimitable" (Treatise 1, sec. 6), extending even to the right of life and death over children, (2) it can only be possessed by the father, and (3) it can be transferred or inherited. Locke's criticisms of these claims, consisting in large measure of Biblical exegesis, contain much of philosophical interest as well.

Locke's refutation of (1) partly rests on the belief that people do not make themselves and hence do not own themselves, because they are the workmanship and property of God:

> Those who desire and design Children, are but the occasions of their being, and when they design and wish to beget them, do little more towards their making, than *Ducalion* and his Wife in the Fable did towards the making of Mankind, by throwing Pebbles over their Heads. (Treatise 1, sec. 54)

To Locke, all this was merely common sense, and it did not seem worthwhile to question it seriously. The more interesting part of Locke's critique consists of two *reductio ad absurdum* arguments. According to the first, if A has absolute authority over B, and therefore the right to intervene in B's relationship with B's issue, C, then A can relieve C of any

33. *Two Treatises of Government*, ed. P. Laslett (New York: New American Library, 1965), Treatise 1, sec. 50.

obligations to B. But there is one obligation, Locke claims, that A cannot relieve C of, the obligation to "Honour thy Father and Mother," because this commandment is "an Eternal Law annex'd purely to the relation of Parents and Children" (Treatise 1, sec. 64). Does this mean, then, that procreation is the origin of filial obligation, even if not of parental authority? Unfortunately, Locke is somewhat indecisive on this subject. At one point, he seems to agree with Filmer that "the Title to this *Honour* is vested in the Parents by Nature, and is a right which accrews to them, by their having begotten their Children" (Treatise 1, sec. 63). The mother in particular can be said to have a right to honor in virtue of her having nourished her child "a long time in her own Body out of her own Substance" (Treatise 1, sec. 55). But on the whole, Locke, like Seneca, is more interested in the nature and extent of parental commitment after procreation. Parents, Locke holds, can forfeit their right to honor by actions of their own, but once they have earned it, then no third party, whether individual or state, can cancel a child's duty to show it. Locke's second *reductio* is as follows: If the fact of procreation entitles parents to absolute authority, this should hold both for a child's parents and for the child as well, when he becomes a parent. But if the parents of the first generation have absolute authority over their children, then the former have the right to determine how their grandchildren shall be raised, to take over the raising of their grandchildren themselves, or even to give their grandchildren to strangers. None of this is compatible with the absolute authority the second generation parents are supposed to have over their own children:

> *Adam,* by a Natural Right of Father, had an Absolute, Unlimited Power over all his Posterity, and at the same time his children had by the same Right Absolute Unlimited Power over theirs. Here then are two Absolute Unlimited Powers existing together, which I would have

anybody reconcile to one another, or to common Sense.
Treatise 1, Sec. 69)

As regards (2), Locke argues that since the mother and the
father both play a role in procreation, procreation can give
the father "but a joynt Dominion with the Mother" (Treatise
1, sec. 55) over their children. Indeed, the woman "hath an
equal, if not the greater" (ibid.) share of parental authority,
not only because, as Locke points out, she lends her body to
the growth of the fetus, but also because she must actively
maintain her body during pregnancy in order to protect her
developing fetus. Childbirth is not the only kind of labor in
which the mother engages; pregnancy itself is work. Whether
or not husband and wife are equal in marriage—and Locke
believes they are not—they *are* equal in the family, for power
in the family, which consists in the exercise of parental authority over children, is equally shared between them.

Finally, in response to (3), Locke asserts: "A Father cannot
alien the Power he has over his Child, he may perhaps to
some degree forfeit it, but cannot transfer it" (Treatise 1,
sec. 100). If paternal power must derive from procreation,
then a father cannot transfer paternal power to his heirs, for
no heir can be transformed into a natural parent by decree
alone:

> *Fatherly Power* I easily grant our A_____ if it will do
> him any good, can never be lost, because it will be as
> long in the World as there are Fathers: but none of
> them will have *Adam's* Paternal Power, or derive theirs
> from him, but every one will have his own, by the same
> Title *Adam* had his, viz. by *Begetting*, but not by In-
> heritance or Succession, no more than Husbands have
> their conjugal Power by Inheritance from *Adam*. (Trea-
> tise 1, Sec. 103)

Indeed, even if Filmer's account of parental authority is
wrong, Locke suggests in the *Second Treatise*, paternal power

is still not transferable. Paternal (or more properly, parental) power, we learn here, consists of two different sets of moral requirements: one encompassed by the parents' duty to educate their child, the other by the child's duty to honor the parents. The first of these "terminates at a certain season; when the business of Education is over it ceases of itself, and is also alienable before" (Treatise 2, sec. 69). Parents may delegate their educational responsibilities to a tutor, though they should realize that in doing so they waive most of their claim to the child's obedience. But the duty of honor, the other part of parental power, "remains never the less entire to them" (ibid.), for parents can fulfill their duty of education not only by educating their children themselves, but also by making provision for them to be educated by competent and willing others. Either way, parents are entitled to honor, and in the latter case, the tutor has to earn the child's honor and respect: it cannot be handed over in the same way that educational tasks can.

According to Locke, parental power does not primarily procede from simple paternity, but from the acceptance of responsibility for the child's growth and development:

> This *power* so little belongs to the *Father* by any peculiar right of Nature, but only as he is Guardian of his Children, that when he quits his Care of them, he loses his power over them, which goes along with their Nourishment and Education, to which it is inseparably annexed. (Treatise 2, sec. 65)

The perpetual "Title to Duty or Honour from the Child" can only be acquired by one who performs "the Office and Care of a Father" (Treatise 1, sec. 100), and it is clear that in Locke the temporary right of parents to restrict their child's freedom in various ways during the childrearing years is not a right in the usual (discretionary) sense. Ordinarily, when we say that we are at liberty to do x, we mean that we are free of a duty not to do x as well as of a duty to do x. Lockean parents, however, have only what Joel Feinberg calls a "half-liberty to do x."[34] They are not at liberty to interfere or not to interfere with their child's freedom of action as they choose, for God has laid on them "an obligation to nourish, preserve, and bring up their Off-spring" (Treatise 2, sec. 66), and this obligation can only be discharged if parents "govern the Actions" (Treatise 2, sec. 58) of their children so as to create in them an unswerving habit of submission to reason. Moreover, as if to drive home the point that parenthood is primarily a matter of duty, Locke uses the language of parents' *rights* in only two cases: when honor is called for, and when parents impose conditions on the acceptance of bequests by their children.

> Though the Obligation on the Parents to *bring up* their children, and the Obligation on Children to *honour* their Parents, contain all the Power on the one hand, and Submission on the other, which are proper to this Relation; yet there is *another Power* ordinarily *in the Father,* whereby he has a tie on the Obedience of his Children. (Treatise 2, sec. 72)

It is not the power, or right, to disinherit children who are still in need of parental support and maintenance, for "men being by a like Obligation bound to preserve what they have begotten, as to preserve themselves, their issue come to have a Right in the Goods they are possessed of" (Treatise 1, sec. 88), both during and after their lifetimes. Rather, it is the power or right of a father to bequeath more than what is obligatory, "according as the Behaviour of this or that Child hath comported with his Will and Humour (Treatise 2, sec. 72). This right is a consequence of the father's right of private

34. "A Postscript to the Nature and Value of Rights," in *Bioethics and Human Rights,* ed. E. Bandman and B. Bandman (Boston: Little, Brown, 1978), p. 33.

property, and while the child is free to reject the bequest, acceptance may entail an obligation of continuing obedience beyond the years of nonage. If the bequest is accepted on these terms, then parents may claim obedience as their due, just as they may claim honor as their due if they have carried out the duties of parenthood. The "right" to educate, in contrast, is more properly thought of as "the Priviledge of Children, and the Duty of Parents" (Treatise 2, sec. 67), than as something that belongs to parents for their own sake or benefit.

The only time Locke invokes the notion of children's consent to justify parental authority is in the case of continued parental power resulting from inheritance. Otherwise, consent plays no more of a role in his account of parental authority than procreation. Locke's departure here from Hobbes can be explained to some extent in terms of their differing conceptions of the state of nature. Unlike Hobbes, Locke draws a distinction between the state of nature and the state of war. "The State of Nature, and the State of War," he says, "are as far distant, as a State of Peace, Good Will, Mutual Assistance, and Preservation, and a State of Enmity, Malice, Violence, and Mutual Destruction are from one another (Treatise 2, sec. 19). People are by nature sociable, favorably disposed toward one another; they have what Peter Laslett calls "natural political virtue."[35] Under these conditions, people can trust each other. Parents in particular can be trusted to protect and promote the welfare of their children (hence the notion of parenthood as a trust) (Treatise 2, sec. 59), and actual or prospective consent need not be invoked in order to explain how fear for one's own survival can be consistent with legitimate parental authority. Trust, not consent, is the key to understanding Locke's theory of parental authority, and since people trust each other even

35. "Introduction," in Locke, *Two Treatises,* pp. 122ff.

before entering political society, there should be no radical change in the moral basis of parent-child relationships as a result of so doing.

Rousseau and Kant on Autonomy for Children

It is Filmer, not Locke himself, who sets the terms of the discussion on paternal power in the *Second Treatise,* and this explains why Locke places such importance on the distinction between parental duty and parental right. Here Locke offers a theory of parenthood in order to draw the following conclusions from it: since parents do have duties to their children, their authority over them cannot be absolute; and further, given the particular responsibilities that parents have, parental authority cannot serve as a model for political authority. Locke's stress on the parental duty of education provides the bridge between his theory of parenthood and his educational theory in *Thoughts Concerning Education,* and after Locke, some of the most important contributions to philosophy of the family were made in the area of educational, rather than political, theory.

According to Rousseau, the next major philosopher of the family, there are two clearly differentiated parental roles, one naturally appropriate for the female parent, the other for the male: "The real nurse is the mother and the real teacher is the father."[36] Good parents do not exchange their responsibilities with one another, nor do they delegate them to outsiders:

> A man . . . has no right to be a father if he cannot fulfill a father's duties. Poverty, pressure of business, mistaken social prejudices, none of these can excuse a man from his duty, which is to support and educate his own children. (P. 17)

36. *Émile,* trans. B. Foxley (London: J. M. Dent and Sons, Ltd., 1974), p. 16.

A father may be able to find a tutor who excels him in knowledge of theories of child development, and of techniques and methods of childrearing, but what the father lacks in expertise, he can more than make up for in commitment and involvement:

> He [the child] will be better educated by a sensible though ignorant father than by the cleverest master in the world. For zeal will atone for lack of knowledge, rather than knowledge for lack of zeal. (P. 16)

Moreover, even if we could find a tutor who combined both zeal and knowledge, there would still be reason to prefer the natural father. For in Rousseau's view, handing children over to professional educators involves more than the delegation of educational tasks; it also jeopardizes the integrity and intimacy of family life:

> The charms of home are the best antidote to vice. . . . There is no more charming picture than that of family life; but when one feature is wanting the whole is marred. If the mother is too delicate to nurse her child, the father will be too busy to teach him. Their children, scattered about in schools, convents, and colleges, will find the home of their affections elsewhere, or rather they will form the habit of caring for nothing. Brothers and sisters will scarcely know each other; when they are together in company they will behave as strangers. (Pp. 13, 16)

Children gain valuable social, moral, and emotional experience in the home, just by being part of a family society, and when the father transfers his educational responsibilities to a private tutor or a public agency, the cohesiveness of family life is undermined. It is unlikely, Rousseau suggests, that any tutor could fully compensate for the loss of this experience.

Apparently, therefore, it is only a necessary, not a sufficient, condition of the ideal education for children that their teachers conscientiously attend to their duties; the teacher should also be the child's natural father. Yet in Rousseau's view, society corrupts the education of the young in two mutually supportive ways: it prescribes a mode of education in which individuals are taught to conform their judgments and actions to the opinions of their fellow citizens, and it imposes demands upon fathers, "the duties of public and private business" (p. 16), that conflict with and are allowed to take priority over their duties to their own children. The mode of education facilitates the neglect of parental duty, and the weakening of family ties makes the child more amenable to social prejudices and opinions. To deal with this situation, Rousseau advocates a new kind of education in which nature, the nature of both children and parents, "would regain her rights" (p. 14). Children would be emancipated from social prejudice so that the true direction of their natural dispositions could be determined; and natural parents would be emancipated from those social incentives and pressures that induce them to delegate the duties of parenthood. In the short run, perhaps, only a tutor can achieve the first objective, because undesirable parental attitudes toward childrearing are deeply entrenched, and because parents, themselves the products of a conventional education, will try to transmit false traditions and habits to their children. But in the long run, Rousseau believes, the tutor would be replaced by the natural father, for children who are always treated according to their natural capacities will themselves become parents who do not think it fitting to delegate their educational responsibilities to anyone.

Yet even the ideal father, the end product of Rousseau's system of natural education, cannot give his children the constant and undivided attention that Rousseau demands of the perfect tutor. The ideal father will also be a husband and thus will have duties to his spouse; he may also have more than one child and thus have to apportion his time between them. But if the ideal father cannot be the perfect tutor in this sense, and if children need constant and single-minded attention from their teachers if they are to become good and happy men, then Rousseau's ideal of the virtuous family man, devoted to raising his children, conflicts with his ideal of education. In other words, if the family is inherently, and not just accidentally, inadequate as a way of educating the young, then the regeneration of the family is not so much the culmination of, as an obstacle to, a truly liberating education for children. This unresolved problem in Rousseau's philosophy suggests a deep-seated ambivalence on his part toward the value of family life.

The aim of education, according to Rousseau, is to make self-sufficient adults who live at peace with themselves, and it is one's duty to bring up one's own children in this way (or the tutor's duty to bring up another's child in this way, if the natural father, to his dishonor, delegates parental authority to him). If the child is made to feel dependent on the will of others, whether they deal with him generously, overgenerously, or whether they deny him, his personality structure will be adversely affected. Since he is taught that others hold the key to his own satisfaction, he will come to think of them as "tools to be used," and in his attempts to gain his will through those on whom he is forced to depend, he will become "tiresome, masterful, imperious, naughty, and unmanageable" (p. 34). But children do not enjoy acting in these ways; on the contrary, they do so out of frustration. They can be happy only if they are autonomous, and they are not autonomous when they are motivated by desires that they cannot satisfy through their own natural powers and capacities. As long as they need others, the possibility remains that the satisfaction of their needs will be withdrawn. And since it is not within their power to secure the continued service of others, children find themselves in a position of weakness, of impotence. The task of the educator, then, is

to give children more real liberty and less power, to let
them do more for themselves and demand less of others;
so that by teaching them from the first to confine their
wishes within the limits of their powers they will
scarcely feel the want of whatever is not in their power.
(P. 36)

Rousseau's strong position on the pernicious character of
dependency relations does not sit comfortably with his ideal-
ization of family life. An autonomous man, in Rousseau's
sense, is not likely to suffer any personal attachments. Moreover, in the family, dependency is, if anything, more difficult
to overcome than in the one-on-one tutor-pupil relationship.
We are well-advised by Rousseau's warning that parental
overprotectiveness and indifference foster unhealthy forms of
dependency in children and inhibit the growth of autonomy.
But family life is also very appealing to us, and probably to
Rousseau as well, because we see the family as a cooperative
institution supporting fruitful and healthy interdependence.
In the family, dependency need not, and often does not, have
the fearful aspect of inviting almost certain exposure and
failure. If there is any kind of interaction that would seem
to be a counterexample to Rousseau's account of social relations, it is precisely that which Rousseau himself occasionally
praises, the interaction of family members.

Kant, too, emphasizes autonomy as the end of education,
both intellectual and moral, but he disagrees with Rousseau's
conception of the preconditions of autonomy and with the
educational methods he proposes for achieving it. In Kant's
view, the best education for autonomy is not one that avoids
instructing and informing the child. Autonomy is not
achieved by indoctrinating children in the values and opinions of society, but then neither is it achieved by keeping children in an intellectual and social vacuum. Moreover, Kant
does not share Rousseau's fear of dependency relations or his
belief in the natural goodness of children, so he does not insist

that early exposure to social relations necessarily contaminates a child's moral development. Rousseau is wrong when he argues that only children who "experience resistance in things and never in the will of man" (p. 33) can become adults who are not subject to the will of another. Autonomy, as Kant understands it, is self-rule, of which self-sufficiency is only one form, and to achieve self-rule the child does not have to be educated *against* society.

The autonomous agent, for Kant, is one whose will is

> not only subject to the law but subject in such a way that it must be regarded also as self-legislative and only for this reason as being subject to the law (of which it can regard itself as the author).[37]

Self-rule is threatened not only by external forces (in the sense of other agents), but also by the internal forces of one's own phenomenal self, in particular one's empirical inclinations. The principles of action one ought to adopt cannot be accounted for by any contingent facts about one or one's social and biological circumstances: their selection can only be explained by reference to one's nature as a rational being. Further, if we have reason to believe that other human beings are like ourselves in respect to the possession of autonomy, then we have an obligation not to treat them in ways that are inappropriate for autonomous beings:

> The subject of ends, i.e., the rational being itself, must be made the basis of all maxims of action and must thus be treated never as a mere means but as the supreme limiting condition in the use of all means, i.e., as an end at the same time. (P. 56)

Children, however, do not yet possess autonomy, as Kant himself acknowledges in his educational writings; at most

---

37. *Foundations of the Metaphysics of Morals,* trans. L. W. Beck (Indianapolis: Bobbs-Merrill Co., 1976), p. 49.

they have the capacity to develop it. Indeed, the process of moral education, according to Kant,

> is that by which man is to be so formed that he can live as a freely acting being. . . . It is the education towards personality, the education of a free being who can maintain himself and become a member of society, but who can also have an inner worth peculiar to himself.[38]

What obligations do we have toward children, whose moral education has not yet been completed and who have not yet developed autonomous characters? Do we merely have an obligation not to treat them unkindly or callously, or is there also an obligation to develop their capacities for autonomous choice and action? Kant's answer is clear. While "rational beings are designated 'persons' because their nature indicates that they are ends in themselves" (*Foundations*, p. 46), children too are persons, even though they are less than rational and autonomous. As persons, they should not be treated as if they were already rational and autonomous, but rather in a manner that respects their "original, innate (not inherited) right" to *become* rational and autonomous beings.[39]

In addition to invoking the notion of rights, Kant offers another, utilitarian, reason for promoting the autonomy of children. The full development of the species' intellectual and moral capacities is the destiny of humanity, he argues, and it can be fulfilled only within the history of the species as a whole. Without education, however, we could never move from barbarism to culture, or transform "a *pathologically* enforced social union . . . into a *moral* whole."[40] Education, therefore, is not a social luxury, but a basic racial need; it is

---

38. *Lecture-Notes on Pedagogy*, sec. 31.
39. *Metaphysik der Sitten* (Hamburg: Felix Meiner, 1959), part II, ch. 2, sec. 28 (author's translation).
40. "Idea for a Universal History with a Cosmopolitan Purpose," in *Kant's Political Writings*, ed. H. Reiss (Cambridge: Cambridge University Press, 1970), p. 45.

not optional, but compulsory. On this view, the obligation to foster autonomy in children is owed to the human race rather than to the individual child:

> One *principle in the art of education,* which those men who devise educational plans should especially have in mind, is this: children should be educated, *not* with reference to their present condition, but rather with regard to a possibly improved future state of the human race,—that is, according to the *idea of humanity* and its entire destiny. (Lecture-Notes, sec. 15)

The duty to educate children falls, in the first instance, upon their parents:

> Through the act of procreation we arbitrarily bring a person into the world without his consent; for which act parents have an obligation, as far as they are able, to make him satisfied with his conditions. . . . From this duty there also necessarily springs the right of parents to the management and education of their children . . . until the time of their emancipation.[41]

But while natural parents do have a natural duty to educate their children, there are also reasons for thinking that parents do not do the best job preparing their children to make good use of their freedom and hence for thinking that educational responsibilities should be discharged by others. Parents, whether for selfish or benevolent reasons, "are usually anxious only that their children should prosper in the world" (*Lecture-Notes,* sec. 16) and hence that they should be able to adapt themselves to change so as to compete successfully with others. Since parents know that they cannot possibly foresee every situation their children will have to face in their lives, they

> seek to let their children learn a great many things and provide for skill in the use of means to all sorts of arbi-

41. *Metaphysik,* part 1, ch. 2, secs. 28–29 (author's translation).

trary ends among which they cannot determine whether any one of them may later become an actual purpose of their pupil, though it is possible that he may some day have it as his actual purpose. (*Foundations*, pp. 32–33)

But in concentrating their attention on skills, on the means for achieving a variety of ends, parents neglect the ends:

> And this anxiety is so great that they commonly neglect to form and correct their judgment on the worth of things which they may make their ends. (Ibid.)

From their parents, children typically learn only how to pursue arbitrary ends efficiently; they do not learn how to evaluate these ends according to relatively settled ideals and convictions, nor to subject the inclinations and desires that set these ends to the test of reason. Capricious, not autonomous, adults are the products of such an education, and parents delude themselves if they think that merely by expanding their children's range of possible life choices they also increase their autonomy.

Can we not educate parents to take a broader view of their educational responsibilities so that they will then be able to raise their children to full autonomy? In Kant's view, this can only be done to a limited extent. For if parents are anxious that their children should prosper in the world, perhaps too anxious, it is because they have a predilection, a preference, for their own children. Parents make no pretense of treating strangers the same as their children. Yet it is an important part, perhaps the most important part, of all moral training that children learn to subject their impulses to *universal* laws, and parents can give them only an incomplete training in universalizability. How can children learn impartiality, we might ask, from those who treat them as if they were the center of the universe? How can parents teach their children to do unto others as others do unto them, when parents feel that they ought to do much more for their

own children than for outsiders? It is because Kant perceives
a tension between the requirements of moral education and
family loyalty that he advocates public rather than private
or domestic education:

> In general, it appears that public education is more ad-
> vantageous than domestic, not only from the view-point
> of skillfulness, but also as regards the character of a citi-
> zen. Domestic education not only brings out family
> faults, but also fosters them. . . . Here public education
> has the most evident advantage, since in it one learns to
> measure his powers and the limitations which the rights
> of others impose upon him. In this form of education
> no one has prerogatives, since opposition is felt every-
> where, and merit becomes the only standard of prefer-
> ment. (*Lecture-Notes,* secs. 25, 30)

Hegel and the End of the Modern Period

The principle of choice for the Kantian autonomous individual is the categorical imperative: Act only on that maxim
which one can at the same time will to be a universal law.
Hegel, in response to this notion of freedom, objects that the
test of the categorical imperative is logically empty in at
least two respects. First, when some "particular content for
acting comes under consideration," the principle provides us
with no criterion "for deciding whether it is or is not a
duty."[42] Kant's criterion of right and wrong does not actually
rule out many—indeed, according to Hegel, any—immoral
actions. Second, even if the doctrine of the categorical imperative could provide us with a useful test for evaluating
proposed maxims, it does not tell us whence we are to derive
the maxims that first create the need for a test. The Kantian
doctrine is parasitic upon already existing, socially established
values:

42. *The Philosophy of Right,* trans. T. M. Knox (New York: Oxford University Press, 1967), par. 135.

With regard to property, for instance, the law of my actions is this: Property ought to be respected, for the opposite of this cannot be universal law. That is correct, but it is quite a formal determination: If property is, then it is. Property is here presupposed, but this determination may also in the same way be omitted, and then there is no contradiction involved in theft.[43]

We are never in the *Kantian* position of being able to make up our minds for ourselves, or of setting ourselves our goals, for moral choices are not made in a vacuum, but always against the background of, and under the influence of, social norms and expectations. The moral life of the individual (*Moralität*) is embedded in the ethical life of his community (*Sittlichkeit*), political as well familial, and different forms of ethical life can be organized according to the way in which the individuals within them characteristically conceive of their relationship to the larger community of which they are members.

Hegel takes the family to be a clear example of a community, rather than merely an aggregate of independent persons. Family capital is the material, children the spiritual, embodiment of family unity. But the family is not an ethical community, if this is taken to mean that family members normally do things for one another out of a sense of duty or moral propriety. "The family," says Hegel, "is specifically characterized by love," which "means in general terms the consciousness of my unity with another."[44] It is only in fairly exceptional circumstances that family members become conscious of their duties to one another as moral duties, and act accordingly. One such circumstance is described by Hegel in the section on Antigone in the *Phenomenology of Mind*.

As Hegel describes it, Antigone's conflict with Creon is

---

43. *Lectures on the History of Philosophy*, trans. E. S. Haldane and F. Simson (London: Routledge and Kegan Paul, 1963), part. 3, sec. 3.
44. *Philosophy of Right*, para. 158 and addition.

symbolic of a fundamental conflict between two markedly different conceptions of individuality. In political society, represented by Creon, individuals lose their determinate individuality and become citizens; in the family, represented by Antigone, determinate individuality is preserved, for family members do not usually regard one another merely as instances of the general category of spouse or child, but as this particular spouse and this particular child. The family is based on consanguinity and love and involves an emotive rather than an abstract, legalistic, principle of individuation. Hegel does not maintain, however, that family ties are always sentimental and that they never have an overtly ethical dimension. On the contrary, he views Antigone's defiance of the king's edict against burying her brother as a dramatic expression of the family's distinctive ethical function. By claiming an exclusive right to take possession of her brother's body, Antigone reaffirms his determinate individuality; and by burying him in accordance with divine law, she invests his death with spiritual meaning and performs a positive ethical act toward him. Her act,

> which embraces the entire existence of the blood relation[,] does not concern the citizen, for he does not belong to the family, nor does it deal with one who is going to be a citizen and so will cease to have the significance of a mere particular individual: it has as its object and content this specific individual belonging to the family, takes him as a universal being, divested of his sensuous, or particular reality. (*Phenomenology*, p. 470)

Though Hegel's discussion of the family in the *Phenomenology* is closely tied to his interpretation of a particular work of dramatic art, and Antigone's predicament seems remote and of little contemporary relevance, his analysis actually does raise a problem of quite general and enduring significance. Individuals typically belong to a number of distinct groups simultaneously. In particular, they belong to a family, where membership begins with birth or adoption, and to the state, which is for most people the most inclusive organized society of which they are members. These two groups have their own ideals, conditions of membership, and characteristic forms of interaction, and each generates its own peculiar obligations. Moreover, while the purposes and ideals of the family may not usually bring it into conflict with the larger society, the possibility always remains that some situation will arise in which the family will have to demand that the state recognize its primacy in some particular area of social life, and so limit its own. At these times, the family transcends the purely sentimental, and family members assert the rights and duties they have qua members of a family. In Antigone's case, the family claimed a preemptive right to its dead members and challenged the state on religious grounds. In a society whose basic structure is not divided along Sophoclean lines, the family may have to take its stand elsewhere. It is only the form, not the root, of the conflict that changes: the individual can belong to such distinct groups as the family and the state, but one can't belong to them in the same way.

Hegel's typological distinction between the family and the state, as well as the priority he gives to the community over the individual, bring Plato to mind. But Hegel does not advocate the abolition of the family, and we must try to understand why if we are to appreciate what is most original in his philosophy of the family. Hegel does not argue, as Aristotle does, that Plato's proposal regarding the family rests on a misunderstanding of human motivation. He argues rather that Plato's proposal represents a basic defect in the Hellenic social ethos:

> In this *Republic,* Plato displays the substance of ethical life in its ideal beauty and truth; but he could only cope with the principle of self-subsistent particularity, which in his day had forced its way into Greek ethical life, by

setting up in opposition to it his purely substantial state. He absolutely excluded it from his state, even in its very beginnings in private property and the family, as well as in its more mature form as the subjective will, the choice of a social position, and so forth. (*Philosophy of Right,* par. 185)

Plato posits an immediate link between the will of the community and the will of the individual, but the modern world, in Hegel's view, has come to accept a new normative picture of human life and in so doing has brought about a genuine advance in self-consciousness for the human spirit. We now believe in the principle of moral individualism, in other words, that one must be free in the sense that one's reason must approve as valid the principles upon which one acts. Further, it is in terms of this principle that Hegel explains the family's crucial contribution to modern ethical life. Though the family imposes demands on the individual that may conflict with the demands of citizenship, it also fosters and reinforces in children a sense of their own particularity, prevents them from being totally absorbed in the public life of the wider society, and thereby lays the foundation for that "subjective freedom" and interiority characteristic of a moral agent.

At the same time that the family arouses in children a sense of their own particular worth, Hegel believes, it also weans them away from particularity by teaching them to become aware of and take into account the desires and needs of others. In an atmosphere of "love, trust, and obedience," ethical principles are "implanted in the child in the form of feeling" (*Philosophy of Right,* par. 175 and addition), and attitudes and dispositions are developed that in due course will lead the child to comply with ethical principles for their own sake. But if the process of moral development typically begins in the home, where the child's feelings of love and trust are especially intense, it cannot end there, Hegel would argue, for the family is inadequate as a means of socialization. Children must internalize the discrimination between their particularistic role as family members and their universalistic role as members of the community, and must eventually acquire an attachment to ethical norms that does not largely spring from ties of affection for particular individuals. A social order that takes its character from the family is, however, only a "civil society," a system within which men are forced into complex patterns of interdependence in order to satisfy their particular interests as heads of households. Here the institutions of communal life are not valued for their own sake, and social responsibility and consideration for others are no more than means to the successful pursuit of private aims.

Unlike other philosophies I have discussed in this chapter, Hegel's philosophy of the family is intended primarily as *meta*-philosophy. Even in the *Philosophy of Right*, he is not especially interested in formulating a moral theory of parenthood, nor does he have much to say about the obligations that grown children may owe to their parents. Indeed, he is more interested in making the point that the education of children culminates in the dissolution of the family than in considering whether there are any moral bonds that unite family members over the life course. Moreover, though Hegel does stress the affective side of family life, it is the affection between husband and wife or between sister and brother rather than between parents and children to which he devotes most of his attention. After Hegel, philosophers did not stop talking about the normative aspects of parent-child relations altogether. What happened was that they no longer attempted to systematically apply their most dearly held moral and social values to the study of parenthood. The resolution of problems relating to the upbringing of children and to our expectations of them became a sideline, and the most profound issues affecting the lives of human beings in society were seen to lie elsewhere.

Directions for Further Exploration

With the exception of Plato (in the *Republic*) and socialist theorists writing after Hegel, all the thinkers referred to or surveyed in this chapter regarded the family as a necessary and fixed human institution. Aristotle, Cicero, Augustine, Aquinas, Bodin, Locke, Rousseau, Kant, and Hegel—each opposed the idea of transferring children from the charge of families to the charge of state agencies. Their commitment to the family was based to a large extent on the simple consideration that virtually all parents love their children, as well as on the belief that parental affection is a sufficient safeguard against the abuse of parental authority. For Hume, the love parents naturally feel for their children was the very foundation of parental duties:

> We blame a father for neglecting his child. Why? because it shows a want of natural affection, which is the duty of every parent. Were not natural affection a duty, the care of children cou'd not be a duty; and 'twere impossible we cou'd have the duty in our eye in the attention we give to our offspring.[45]

Throughout this study of philosophers' ideas on the nature of intrafamilial and family-state relations, the aims and imperatives of parenthood, and the responsibilities of children, I have deliberately chosen not to discuss one shortcoming from which most of their analyses suffer: their reliance on certain assumptions about the family and its relation to society that effectively deny women equality with men. Women's interests were not regarded as distinct, but were subsumed within those of the private, male-dominated family; it was a woman's natural condition to be in the family, to serve as

45. *A Treatise of Human Nature*, ed. L. A. Selby-Bigge (Oxford: Clarendon Press, 1975), bk. 3, part 2, sec. 1.

companion for her husband and to bear and rear children. Criticism of these philosophers' conceptions of and arguments about women must therefore be directed at basic assumptions "having to do with the family and woman's traditionally dependent and subordinate role within it."[46] Yet there may also be a great deal in their writings that can stand independently of these assumptions and that we can build on in developing a nonsexist philosophy of the family. What we have to do is to disentangle those claims about parents and children that presuppose the patriarchal family from those that can be transposed to a more egalitarian family structure.

Since there are good reasons for thinking that abolition of the family is not a prerequisite for sexual equality, the issues we have explored in this chapter will not simply disappear once the traditional attitudes toward women and women's work have been rejected. Plato's criticism of the family and Aristotle's response to it raise the problem of the relationship between social justice and the family and lead us to ask whether the family is compatible with justice in a more modern sense, one that includes a commitment to equality (see pp. 199–216). Aristotle's discussion of familial friendship reminds us that there is more to the moral life of the family than the rights and obligations of individual family members (see pp. 101–4 and 186–93). The frequent emphasis on the child's duty of gratitude, beginning with Cicero and extending through Aquinas and Sidgwick, provokes commentary on the nature of gratitude and its plausibility as a basis of filial obligation (see pp. 175–86). Seneca's remarks on reverence for parents help us to articulate a conception of child-parent relations in which filial obligation is a matter of spontaneous generosity rather than debt repayment (see pp. 172–75 and 193–95). Beliefs about marriage and family life that stem from the tradition of Augustine and Aquinas are still prevalent and re-

46. Susan Moller Okin, *Women in Western Political Thought* (Princeton: Princeton University Press, 1979), p. 10.

quire rethinking in light of changing attitudes toward child-bearing and childrearing outside conventional marriage (see pp. 228–36). The distinction in Aquinas between three bases of reciprocity—justice, gratitude, and friendship—helps us to organize our thoughts on the question of whether children owe their parents anything beyond obedience (see pp. 175–93). The discussion of Hobbes brings out some of the problems that consent arguments pose for the family (see pp. 104–14 and 167–72). Locke's views on the legitimacy of parental authority cannot be overlooked by any philosopher in the democratic tradition who wants to argue that children, like adults, have natural rights that need to be protected (see pp. 104–20, and 162–67). Continuing in this tradition, a theory of parental duties can be developed out of the Kantian notion of respect for the autonomy of persons (see pp. 130–36). And finally, Hegel's work draws our attention to an enduring feature of personal and public life, the potential conflict between the demands of the family and those of the greater society (see pp. 147–56 and 217–23). These are just some of the issues from the philosophical literature that are still very much with us, and some of the areas in which an analysis of key historical writings on the family can contribute to an understanding of the moral decisions and dilemmas of contemporary family life.

The Duties of Parents and Children

CHAPTER ONE

A Moral Theory
of Parenthood

Parenthood and the Family

A moral theory of family relations should start with parents rather than children. Parental decisions and choices affecting the welfare of children begin before parenthood itself. In addition, children develop distinct interests and desires only gradually, and their capacities for self-determination have to be nourished over many years of parental guidance and supervision. The young need to be cared for more than they need to be left alone, and good parents are those who do what they must to meet their children's basic needs, and more besides. Though the pleasures and rewards of raising children may often disguise the fact, parenting is a job involving nonreciprocal obligations, immense self-discipline, and personal sacrifice. The duties that go with being a parent are the tasks and assignments for which a person becomes responsible as a result of having taken on this job.

The notion of parental duty figures prominently in a moral theory of parenthood, as well as in definitions of the family offered by anthropologists and sociologists. Anthropologist William Stephens defines the family as a social arrangement based on marriage and the marriage contract, including recognition of the rights and duties of parenthood, common residence for husband, wife, and children, and reciprocal obligations between husband and wife.[1]

In all societies, parents have legal or quasi-legal obligations to care for and bring up their children, though as Stephens shows, care and upbringing may take very different forms in different cultures. The family, so understood, essentially involves relations having to do with parenthood and is to be distinguished from marriage, which is a complex of customs centering on the relationship between sexually associating adults within the family. Like all definitions, of course, a definition of the family is acceptable only relative to the purposes which that definition is designed to serve. A definition of the family may be adequate in that it makes explicit the meaning that the word is felt to have in everyday discourse, and yet it may be unsatisfactory because it cannot be used in rigorous scientific discourse or because, when incorporated into social policy, it fails to promote the public good. Stephens's definition satisfies the second criterion and, at least until recently, in our society, the first as well. With respect to the third, however, it might be argued that it would be better to adopt a definition of the family that includes persons who are not connected by the relation of potential or actual parenthood, or that excludes marriage and the marriage contract. Perhaps the family should not be defined in terms of marriage at all, because the moral bases of marriage and parenthood are distinct, and because it is, after all, an empirical matter whether the welfare of children is best served when child-rearing primarily occurs in the context of marriage (see chapter five for a discussion of this issue). In order to properly evaluate this suggestion, we need to have a theory of parent-

1. William N. Stephens, *The Family in Cross-Cultural Perspective* (New York: Holt, Rinehart, and Winston, 1963), p. 8.

hood: a theory that explains the nature of the parent-child relationship, that shows what good or adequate parents must do for their children, and that describes the conditions under which children are most likely to receive this care.

Before saying more about the duties of parents, I want to anticipate a possible objection to my whole project in these next two chapters. The objection, in brief, is that my approach subsumes family life under abstract moral principles and thereby obscures what is most valuable in parent-child relationships, viz., their intimate and affectionate character. Family relationships, like all close interpersonal relationships, are not constituted by duties, but by bonds of sympathetic identification, caring, and love. Duties introduce an element of formality, or if you will, puritanism, into the spontaneous emotional life of the family. One might even go further to claim that my project in these chapters is symptomatic of a common misunderstanding among moral philosophers of the proper limits of moral reflection. Morality represents only one sphere of value, and it does not necessarily have supremacy over the other spheres. The attempt to understand parenthood in terms of duties is a clear case of moral imperialism, of excessive moralizing.

It is important to respond to this objection in order to clarify the relatively modest assumptions I am making about what a discussion of parental duties can contribute to an understanding of family life. It is not my intention to argue that being a good parent merely involves doing what one ought to do, or that the existence of duties toward children constitutes a demonstration of the value of parenthood itself. In fact, rigid adherence to moral duty might actually weaken family attachments and threaten enjoyment of the other goods of family life. I wish to claim only that the natural relationship between parents and children typically carries with it duties to children, and that a conventional relationship between parents and children (e.g. adoption), no less than the conventional relationship between husbands and wives, always gives rise to duties. (The precise content of parental duties will depend on the nature of the particular society.) Moreover, I would concede that the notion of duty might not be very prominent in the way people normally deliberate about the options available to them in their family lives or the way family members normally think about parenting. Parents do not always, or even usually, need to be reminded of their duties in order to be good parents, and children (at least young ones) do not usually measure their parents' actions according to some standard of parental duty. Nevertheless, the natural affection that parents feel for their children, though prompting them in the right direction, is not always so strong that all the actions required of them come easily to them, and a general concern for the well-being of one's children does not imply that parents wish their children well at all times and in all respects, or that parents know what they should do for their children in particular circumstances. In these circumstances, it makes perfectly good sense to speak of, and there is a point in speaking of, parental duties.

The Priority Thesis

Even if we confine our attention to the moral aspects of parenthood, the issue of duties is not the only one to be considered. Parents also have rights over their children, grounded, perhaps, on the right of parents to paternalistically intervene in their children's lives, or on the right of parents to bring up their children in any way they choose, or on the right of parents to have their integrity as independent individuals respected, or on the right of parents to reciprocal services from their children. All or some of these might be legitimate grounds of parental rights. I do not believe, however, that we can say much more than this, or that we can give specific content to parental rights, until we first try to clarify the

structure of the moral dimension of parenthood, that is to
say, the relationship between parental duties and parental
rights in general. To help do this, I shall juxtapose two
theories of parenthood discussed separately in part I: those of
Hobbes and Locke.

In a passage from *De Cive,* Hobbes writes:

> If . . . she [the mother] breed him, because the state of
> nature is the state of war, she is supposed to bring him
> up on this condition; that being grown to full age he
> become not her enemy; which is that he obey her. For
> since by natural necessity we all desire that which ap-
> pears good unto us, it cannot be understood that any
> man hath on such terms afforded life to another, that
> he might both get strength by years, and at once become
> an enemy. But each man is an enemy to that other,
> whom he neither obeys nor commands.[2]

The fundamental human motives, according to Hobbes, are
the desire to dominate and the desire to avoid death, and in a
state of nature, where everyone is a potential enemy of everyone else, parents will take measures to protect themselves
against the aggression of their children. They are entitled,
by virtue of the right of self-preservation, to keep their children in a permanently weakened condition, or, as an extreme
measure, to take their lives. If parents decide not to do the
latter, it is with the understanding that their children shall
not become their enemies when they gain "strength by years."
Children, in turn, have a duty to submit to the will of their
parents.

Do *parents* have any duties toward their children in a
Hobbesian state of nature? In particular, do parents have a
duty to preserve the lives of their children? The correct answer seems to be that for Hobbes preservation of children
could *sometimes* be a duty of parents. He maintains only that

2. In *Man and Citizen,* ed. B. Gert (Garden City, N.Y.: Anchor, 1972), 9, 3.

the actions that tend to one's own preservation must be left to the bona fide estimate of each one, and that there is no way in which any specific action, such as the action of destroying one's children, could be ruled out in general. Parents are obliged to preserve their children when they have sufficient security against them, but when preserving a child's life puts the parents in mortal danger, the duty may not stand. It would seem to follow, therefore, that parents have a duty to preserve their child at least until the child gains "strength by years," for it is only then that children are able to pose a real threat to parents. In fact, however, this conclusion is contradicted by Hobbes's remark that a mother "may rightly, and at her own will, either breed him [her child] up or adventure him to fortune" (ibid.); if she thinks it fit "to abandon, or expose her child to death,"[3] she is within her rights to do so. This right to destroy one's child, even when the child is in a weakened condition, is still presumably grounded on the right of self-preservation, and in order for this derivation to succeed, Hobbes has to argue either that children can pose a clear and present danger to their parents' security and survival even before they have gained "strength by years," or that the right of self-preservation is not limited to defense against clear and present danger. The latter is suggested by the following:

> A man . . . that hath another man in his power to rule or govern, to do good to, or harm, hath right, by the advantage of this his present power, to take caution at his pleasure, for his security against that other in time to come. (*De Corpore,* part 1, ch. 1, sec. 13)

Thus, even though the young child does not pose any imminent threat to the parents, the child's destruction might still be reasonable in light of the parents' fears for their future

---

3. *De Corpore Politico,* in *Body, Man, and Citizen,* ed. R. S. Peters (New York: Collier, 1967) part 2, ch. 4, sec. 3.

safety and estimate of their future position. If, for example, parents are naturally weak and so have reason to believe that they will not be able to keep their children in a permanently subordinate position, they may have the right to destroy them before the children surpass them in physical strength.

On the above interpretation of Hobbes, parents in the natural state do have a duty to preserve their children, but it is a duty from which the right of self-preservation can exempt them. With the establishment of a political sovereign, the constant danger everyone poses to everyone else in the state of nature vanishes. The sovereign does not abolish the right of self-preservation; he only eliminates the conditions that necessitate having recourse to this right. Laws governing marriage and parenthood are instituted, and parents no longer have the right of complete and exclusive domination over their children.

One important aspect of Hobbes's theory of parenthood is the view that in a state of nature parental duties are only conditionally valid: duties to children are conditional upon the security of parents. (As we shall see, when conjoined to his theory of human nature, this view leads to conclusions very different from those of Locke.) Another is that the right of parental dominion is grounded, not on the fact that parents brought their child into existence, but on the child's consent. Hobbes's point is not that consent functions as a moral constraint on paternalistic interferences in the lives of children; the child's consent imposes no constraints on the use of parental authority. It is rather that parental authority as such is derived "from the Childs Consent, either expresse, or by other sufficient arguments declared."[4] The giving of consent, whether express or tacit, is essentially the granting of permission, and it is through the granting of permission by children that their parents acquire rights over them. When the con-

---

4. *Leviathan*, ed. C. B. Macpherson (Baltimore: Penguin, 1968), part 2, ch. 20.

sent given by children is tacit, it is their acquiescence in the
power and actions of their parents that constitutes the granting of permission. But the failure to resist the will of parents
cannot legitimately be regarded as acquiescence, nor acquiescence as the granting of a permission, unless in not resisting
their parents, children could know that they are creating and
intend to create in their parents the right of domination over
them; and as Hobbes says in the *Leviathan,* children "had
never power to make any covenant, or to understand the consequences thereof; and consequently never took upon them to
authorize the actions of any Sovereign" (part 2, ch. 26). How
then can parental domination be derived from genuine tacit
consent? Both of the answers discussed in part I—one relying
on the notion of projected consent, the other on the distinction between mature and immature children—are problematic. It is not enough to say that tacit consent is the consent
children will give when they become adults, for a child is not
in fact an adult, and it is not obvious why authority exercised
over a person at one stage of life should be entirely contingent
on decisions that can only be made at a later, and qualitatively
different, stage. If it is then argued that the stages are connected, in that it is only through the exercise of parental authority over young children that consent can later be given,
the suggestion is that parents have an obligation to see to it
that their children reach the age at which they can give genuine consent. Further, by applying the notion of tacit consent
to the mature child alone, we leave ourselves without any
justification for parental authority over immature children,
and this too is troublesome.

Despite these problems in Hobbes's account of the parental
right to command children, his appeal to children's consent
clearly shows that he does not consider children to be the private property of their parents. Since it is only the child's consent that gives legitimacy to parental authority, children are
not merely playthings, whose value consists solely in the grati-

fication they provide their parents. Locke agrees with this implication of Hobbes's theory, but only because he believes that children belong to a higher authority than their parents. Children—all people—are "the Workmanship of one Omnipotent, and infinitely wise Maker"; and "they are his Property, whose Workmanship they are."[5] Those who beget and bear children "are but the occasions of their being" (Treatise 1, sec. 54), for the source of life is God. Further, the authority to discipline children is held and exercised only through divine dispensation. Beginning with Adam and Eve, all parents are placed

> by the Law of Nature, under an obligation to preserve, nourish, and educate the Children, they had begotten, not as their own Workmanship, but the Workmanship of their own Maker, the Almighty, to whom they were to be accountable for them. (Treatise 2, sec. 56)

The law of nature is a declaration of God's will and a standard of right and wrong, and it is God's will that parents shall take care of His property, preserve, nourish, and educate their children on His behalf. Parents' duties and responsibilities are owed in the first place to God. The law of nature also commands us to preserve life, and while in Locke's view the individual is bound to preserve others only "when his own preservation comes not in competition" (Treatise 2, sec. 6), the Lockean state of nature, unlike the Hobbesian, is not characterized by habitual conflict between self-preservation and preservation of others. The duty to preserve one's children, in particular, is usually not rendered void by the right of self-preservation, because next to self-preservation, the strongest desire men have is the one God planted in them "of propagating their Kind, and continuing themselves in their Posterity" (Treatise 1, sec. 88). The duty to preserve one's

5. *Two Treatises of Government,* ed. P. Laslett (New York: New American Library, 1965), Treatise 2, sec. 6.

children is not deduced directly from the existence of this desire, but from the intention of the Creator, which intention is deduced from the existence of the desire. Thus men are "by a like Obligation bound to preserve what they have begotten, as to preserve themselves" (ibid.).

In saying that parents are accountable to God for the job they do rearing their children, Locke does not mean to suggest that if parents do not preserve, nourish, or educate their children, they only fail to do what they are bound to God, not to their children, to do. For in Locke's view, children have a natural right to freedom, and this right entails an obligation on the part of parents to care for their children, and presumably on the part of others not to interfere with the parents' direction of their children. The child's natural right to freedom, like the adult's, is the right to freedom from the arbitrary wills of others, but subjection to the will of parents is not as such arbitrary, because parents are required by the law of nature to govern their child, "and be a Will to him, till he hath attained to a state of Freedom, and his Understanding be fit to take the Government of his Will" (Treatise 2, sec. 59). Though "every Mans Children . . . [are] by Nature as free as himself" (Treatise 2, sec. 73), they are unable to exercise or enjoy this freedom because they lack reason to guide it. Their parents, who already possess reason, must will for them and must induce "a compliance and suppleness of their wills,"[6] so that in time the awe and respect children have for their parents will be transformed into reverence for rationality itself.

From parents' observable desires and children's observable needs, Locke infers a purpose or will of God, and then deduces parents' obligations and children's rights from that purpose or will. Parents are not free to bring up their children according to their own ideas of what is fitting; not free choice,

6. *John Locke on Education*, ed. P. Gay (New York: Teachers College, 1971), sec. 44.

but the antecedent dictate of God, determines the manner and end of childrearing. Further, the Lockean conception of parent-child relationships is not one in which children serve parents in return for their not destroying them when they had the right to do so. For in the first place, Locke's natural right to freedom is limited by the law of nature, which teaches that "no one ought to harm another in his Life, Health, Liberty, or Possessions" (Treatise 2, sec. 6); in the second, the loss of freedom involved in obedience to parents is the price children have to pay in order to attain their own rational freedom. But Locke not only holds that parental authority is *constrained* by parents' obligations to care for their children during their minority. He also argues that parental authority *arises from* these obligations:

> the Power . . . that Parents have over their Children, arises from that Duty which is incumbent on them, to take care of their Offspring, during the imperfect state of Childhood. (Treatise 2, sec. 58)

The family exists to serve the child, not vice versa, and parents have authority over their children only because they need it to carry out their duties to their children. Parental authority is not legitimized by the child's tacit consent, actual or prospective, but by the requirements of an evolving rationality and self-discipline in the growing child. Children, in turn, "are commanded Obedience" to parental power, so "that the pains and care of their Parents may not be increased, or ill rewarded" (Treatise 2, sec. 67).

Locke's contention that "the Nourishment and Education of their Children, is a Charge so incumbent on Parents for their Childrens good, that nothing can absolve them from taking care of it," and that "the power of commanding and chastising them go along with it" (ibid.), is not logically dependent on his theological grounding of parental duty and authority. Other theories of the foundation of parental duty and authority can also make this claim, and in fact there are strong reasons for rejecting Locke's. One problem it raises is epistemological: how can we justify a claim to know what God commands? Another is that Locke attempts to derive an ethical statement concerning our duty to do certain actions from the metaphysical and theological statement that God commands us to do certain things, thereby violating Hume's rule that *ought* cannot be derived from *is*.[7] There is also some merit in the criticism that Locke's method of training the young treats "the child as someone to be molded according to adult preconceptions" and does not consider "seriously the perspective of children themselves in determining their own best interests."[8] Locke's basic insight, however, that parenthood is primarily a matter of duty rather than right, is sound. Children do not have the ability to make rational and autonomous decisions, but they have the capacity to do so, and it is only out of natural necessity that they must be subject to the control of their parents. If children were born, as Adam was, full grown, parental authority would be unjustified.

Following the Lockean conception of parenthood, though not the theory of natural law underlying it or the suggestions of authoritarianism in his method of educating the young, I offer what I shall call the thesis of the priority of parental duties to parental rights. This thesis consists of seven claims:

1. That since parents have duties to do certain things for their children, they *ipso facto* have rights to do those things as well. It is only when parents are at liberty to care for their children, that is, have no duty not to care for them, that parents can have a duty to do so.

2. That within the constraints imposed by the requirements

7. Another difficulty for Locke is this: if we cannot own our children because God made them, how do we come to have property rights in the products of nature? See the discussion in Robert Nozick, *Anarchy, State, and Utopia* (New York: Basic Books, 1974), pp. 287–291.

8. Victor L. Worsfold, "A Philosophical Justification for Children's Rights," *Harvard Educational Review*, 44 (1974), p. 146.

of parenting, parents have the right to a certain latitude in defining and managing child care. This limited right to parental autonomy involves the right to freedom from coercive intervention and too close supervision by the state, and it exists whether childrearing is the primary responsibility of private citizens (e.g., natural, adoptive, or foster parents) or of individuals employed by the state. It is justified on the grounds that such autonomy is critical to the child's healthy psychological development.

3. That parents have a right to the cooperation of their children in the tasks of childrearing, that is, a right to their obedience.

4. That parents have a right to do more than what is obligatory for their children, though how much more is a problem of social justice rather than something for a theory of parenthood alone to decide. Restrictions on what one may inherit from parents, for example, might be justified in order to reduce inequality of opportunity among children (an argument found in Mill, not in Locke).

5. That parents have a right to honor from their children, in consequence of the care and kindness shown, and costs incurred, in bringing them up. Honor can be expressed through actual service in time of need (e.g., caring for aged parents) and in general, through love and devotion.

6. That parents have a right to satisfy their own individual interests, parental and nonparental, as long as this is consistent with the satisfactory performance of their parental duties. These interests include the need for a certain degree of privacy within the family, the desire to engage in activities unrelated to childrearing, and the desire to care for a child. Indeed, in a society that emphasizes the value of individual choice, the quality of child care is to a large extent dependent on parents having the freedom to define and pursue their own interests.

7. That parents have no other rights than these.

The right of paternalistic agency, which authorizes interference with others' freedom of action in order to prevent
them from harming themselves or to promote their good,
does not *always* or only derive from special moral relationships with others and from the duties of care that stem from
these relationships. The right to act paternalistically may rest
on explicit or implicit commitments to particular others (as
in the case of parental paternalism), but even in the absence
of such commitments, it can be grounded in part on the general moral duty to help others further their important and
legitimate interests when we can do so without great sacrifice
or danger to ourselves.

The claim that parental duties take priority over parental
rights has the following consequences. First, parents' rights
are never to be balanced against parents' duties, for the latter
have absolute weight with respect to the former. Parents, for
example, are entitled to take their own interests into account
in discharging their duties; they may not pursue their own
interests *instead* of discharging their duties, for in doing so,
they relinquish the right to control their children's lives.
Second, the failure to discharge a specific parental duty, or
to discharge it fully, is justified only if, on balance and over
the long run, the welfare of the child is advanced thereby. In
certain situations, the performance of one duty may be less
important or less urgent than the performance of another and
therefore may be subordinated to it (e.g., the child's need for
medical care might justify the temporary interruption of normal parental tasks; respect for the child's autonomous choices
might require some adjustments in the parents' other duties).

The Nature of Parental Duties

The theory of parenting expressed by the priority thesis takes
duty as fundamental. It stresses the conformity of parental action to certain standards of behavior rather than parental in-

dependence and freedom of choice, and it justifies parental rights by calling attention to parental duties rather than the other way around. A theory of parenthood that takes rights as fundamental (e.g., Hobbes's) is, as I have tried to show, a theory of a very different character from one that takes duties as fundamental (e.g., Locke's). But theories of parenthood do not only differ from one another in the way each connects the rights and duties of parents. They may also disagree in the particular rights and duties each sets out, as well as in their general conceptions of the kind of duties parents have. In order to distinguish my own theory, therefore, it is necessary to discuss the content and classification of parental duties. I begin with the latter.

One way to describe the duties of parents is to say that they are duties of parenthood, that is, a particular case of *duties of status*. Duties of status are those that persons have in virtue of occupying relatively fixed positions or roles within a hierarchical social order. They are duties that belong in the first instance to roles and only derivatively to those who occupy them. Parental duties, as duties of status, attach to the role of parenthood as defined by the institution of the family. In addition, since parental duties of status are not directly correlated with rights in children but are originally imposed by institutional rules, such duties must be justified in terms of the entire institution in which both parents and children occupy positions.

But parental duties are not merely institutional duties. I say this not because it is possible for children to be raised in public institutions rather than in the family, as this term is normally understood. For those who raise children in public institutions can also be called "parents," and their duties are still defined by (different) institutional norms. I say this, instead, because children have a legitimate claim to what they need to survive and develop, independent of institutional relationships. "Natural needs," says Joel Feinberg, are real claims if only upon hypothetical future beings not yet in existence. I accept the moral principle that to have an unfulfilled need is to have a kind of claim against the world, even if against no one in particular. A natural need for some good as such, like natural desert, is always a reason in support of a claim to that good. A person in need, then, is always "in a position" to make a claim, even when there is no one in the corresponding position to do anything about it. Such claims, based on need alone, are "permanent possibilities of rights," the natural seed from which rights grow.[9]

The needs of children are natural needs in that they lack certain goods because of natural deficiencies, cognitive and emotional, and these needs are deserving of consideration simply as such. Through the institution of the family (or suitable substitutes), society sees to it that someone is in a position to do something about children's need-based claims. Individuals who assume the role of parent have a moral duty to perform their institutional duties, because they have a duty to satisfy the needs of those who are dependent on them. (Who has a duty to supply a child's needs cannot be decided on the basis of the child's needs alone, for, as Feinberg asserts, needs give rise to claims "against the world." Other morally relevant factors have to be considered also. [See chapter two.]) The duties of parents, in short, are *duties of need-fulfillment,* as well as duties of status.

Duties of need-fulfillment should be distinguished from another class of duties that parents have, namely, *duties of respect.* The former are grounded on a concern for the basic helplessness of children and can be performed only if—sometimes, at least—parents exercise their own authority in lieu of the child's. It is assumed, in connection with duties of need-fulfillment, that parents have a right to control those aspects

9. "The Nature and Value of Rights," *The Journal of Value Inquiry,* 4 (1970), p. 255.

of their children's lives that are relevant to protecting their physical, emotional, and psychological development. Duties of respect, in contrast, are duties to respect a child's own desires and wants in matters that are not critical to protecting the child's basic interests, and where these desires and wants, if acted upon, are not likely to impede the child's development or harm others. Locke perhaps had this in mind when he argued that children

> should be allowed the liberties and freedom suitable to their ages, and not be held under unnecessary restraints, when in their parent's or governor's sight. If it be a prison to them, it is no wonder they should not like it. They must not be hindered from being children, or from playing, or doing as children; but from doing ill. All other liberty is to be allowed them. (*On Education,* sec. 69)

To some extent, duties of need-fulfillment and duties of respect overlap, but the primary rationale for the latter is not that respecting children's desires and wants promotes their emotional, intellectual, or moral development. It is rather that depriving another of freedom is morally wrong unless one has adequate justification for doing so, and it is not by itself an adequate justification to say that children lack the capacity for rational decision-making or that the choices they will make will not be fully autonomous. Even if this is true, children should have as much freedom as is compatible with their present needs, the long-range objectives of parenting, and the safety of others. Like duties of need-fulfillment, duties of respect are correlated with rights in children, only with this difference: the rights correlative to the latter are negative rights to noninterference and forbearance, while the rights correlative to the former include positive rights to protection, supervision, and guidance.

The basic rationale for duties of respect is not that children *need* to have their desires and wants considered if they are to develop as they ought to develop, however this is. It is rather that children, as children, have a right to self-determination, a right to be themselves, quite apart from future beneficial consequences to themselves. At the same time, it is only when children's desires and wants are taken into account by those who rear them that they can start to grasp the idea of there being a reason for acting in one way rather than another and thus can engage in purposive behavior. A person acts purposively when he controls his behavior with a view to attaining ends or goals that constitute his reasons for acting. In addition, it is only one's actual objectives that can provide one with a reason for acting, and one's actual objectives are determined by the objects of one's wants or desires. The agent's aims, therefore, are wants or desires, and in every purposive action the agent acts more or less reflectively in accordance with them. As regards the education of children, it is hard to see how they can learn to act for reasons they regard as reasons, unless their parents, or those who care for them, give them some freedom to do what they want to do, simply because they want to do it.

Children have wants as well as needs, and those who bring them up must attend to both. (Very young children perhaps have no desires or wants because they lack the conceptual capacity for beliefs that is presupposed by the ascription of wants and desires, but they still have needs.) An account of parental duties in terms of wants alone makes childrearing too permissive; on the other hand, an account in terms of needs alone could make childrearing too restrictive. However, we expect a theory of parenthood to provide us with a description and explanation of parental duties as well as with a defense and justification of parental authority, and while the notion of a child's right of self-determination explains well enough why parents ought sometimes to refrain from exercising authoritative measures of control over their children, it cannot explain or justify the use of authority over children by parents or anyone else. We cannot argue that parents have rights over their children because parents have a duty to honor their children's right to liberty, for so far from justifying parental authority, respect for children, in the sense of letting them be themselves, actually entails freedom from parental authority. To give children what they need, however, we must rely on more than advice or persuasion, for children may not be aware of their needs, or may not want what they need, or may have no basis for deciding how their needs are to be met. Duties of need-fulfillment are duties that carry authority with them and for this reason occupy a more central place in a theory of parenthood than duties of respect, though who should exercise this authority, to what extent, and for how long, are matters that require separate treatment.

The sentence "a child needs x" can be read in three ways, depending on where the emphasis is placed. The stress on "child" reminds us that we are not talking about adults, and that the needs of children are in many respects quite different from those of adults. The word "needs" is stressed in contrast to "wants." Perhaps the most obvious criterion of need is that a state of affairs is conceived of as absent. Children lack many things: self-sufficiency, education, social skills, etc. But beyond this, the absence of these things does not create a need unless this absence *ought not* to exist. Needs-statements presuppose norms or standards, and in the case of children, these are norms to which those responsible for their upbringing must conform. Questions of want, in contrast, can be settled empirically. As Benn and Peters put it: "To say that a man *wants* food is simply to describe his state of mind; to say that he *needs* food is to say that he will not measure up to an understood standard unless he gets it."[10] Finally, we have to

10. *The Principles of Political Thought* (New York: The Free Press, 1959), p. 165.

establish standards for childrearing in order to determine exactly what it is that children need.

Children's Needs: Primary Goods

What are the norms or standards that are presupposed by statements about children's needs? Or, since duties of needfulfillment entail rightful authority, we can ask the question this way: Granting that authority over children can only be justified in order to prevent children from harming themselves or failing to advance their own good, what are the criteria of "harm" and "good"? "Good" in this context must refer to the child's long-range welfare, to the set of objectives that constitute the ultimate ends of childrearing. A moral theory of parenthood presupposes some conception of the good life for mature human beings, for it is the purpose of childrearing to enable children to lead at least minimally decent and satisfying lives as adults.

There are three conditions that must hold true of a person's life if it is correctly to be judged a good life. First, it must be a unified, integrated whole in which a person is carrying out a rational plan of life. A rational plan of life defines a person's principal goals in life and establishes a harmonious ordering of goals based on the individual's own assessment of their relative importance. Rational plans of life are not chosen once and for all, but are constantly subject to revision and modification as the situations of life change and the future becomes known. Further, rational plans gradually unfold as a reflection of one's choices and values and are only infrequently made the objects of deliberation and calculation. Second, one must autonomously create one's own rational plan of life. Both the ultimate ends and the ordering of one's plan must be the outcome of one's own autonomous decisions. To the extent that they are, a rational plan of life will be the independent and authentic expression of one's own conception of oneself. (For a fuller discussion of autonomy, see pp. 130–36.) Third, in order to successfully execute a rational plan of life that has been autonomously chosen, one must have the opportunity and ability to realize one's basic and less important ends in accordance with their ordering in one's plan of life. One needs health and certain broadly useful traits like self-confidence and intelligence, which will be helpful whatever one's interests and circumstances. One must also be free of interference by others, and have the opportunity for a full range of expression in one's life. One must, moreover, have the general capacity for rational and autonomous decision-making. It is in terms of these opportunities and abilities that parental duties of need-fulfillment are to be specified.

Basic instrumentalities for realizing one's ends, and without which no particular rational plan of life could succeed, are called by John Rawls *primary goods*. Rawls's account of primary goods appears among the premises of his derivation of principles of justice.[11] A specific principle of justice is correct, he argues, provided that it would be chosen over any alternative that could be proposed to a hypothetical group of rational, self-interested persons, each behind an appropriate "veil of ignorance," gathered together for the special purpose of selecting principles that are to govern their basic social and political institutions. The aim of the veil of ignorance, according to Rawls, is "to rule out those principles that it would be rational to propose for acceptance, however little chance of success, only if one knew certain things that are irrelevant from the standpoint of justice" (p. 18). The parties should be equal and should not be in possession of information that would lead them to seek advantages on morally irrelevant grounds like natural endowments, social position, or the stage of development of their particular society. They should also be deprived of knowledge of their particular conceptions of

11. *A Theory of Justice* (Cambridge: Mass.: Belknap Press, 1971).

the good. Ignorant of their specific interests and circumstances in real life, the parties cannot base their decision to adopt a certain principle of justice on the likelihood that it will maximize the satisfaction of their particular desires and interests. But the parties cannot be deprived of all knowledge of themselves, their circumstances, and their society, for then the rational choice of principles would be impossible. They possess general knowledge about economics, politics, and sociology, and know that their society is not so abundantly supplied with goods that principles for regulating conflicting claims on goods are unnecessary. In addition, they know that they have some plan of life or conception of the good, and that there are certain fundamental, general, or primary goods that are necessary for the successful pursuit of virtually any plan of life. These are goods that "a rational man wants whatever else he wants" (p. 92), and he would prefer more of them rather than less. Two types of primary goods are distinguished by Rawls: the social and the natural. Social primary goods include "rights and liberties, powers and opportunities, income and wealth," and "self-respect" (p. 92). The natural include "health and vigor, intelligence and imagination" (p. 62). This list of primary goods, Rawls argues, "is one of the premises from which the choice of the principles of right is derived" (p. 434). If the ideal contractors were allowed to have a fuller conception of their good, the requisite unanimity in the choice of principles would not result.

The contractors are not assumed to want the primary goods merely because they know that in the actual conditions of life they will want to protect and advance their particular conceptions of the good, whatever these happen to be. They also know that their good consists in having and following a rational plan of life and in being able to revise it as circumstances require. In addition, they know that they are to choose principles for a "well-ordered society," one in which everyone always acts justly, all laws are just, and all citizens comply with them. For these reasons, too, the primary goods are essential. Primary goods are necessary for the development and exercise of the capacity to decide upon and modify, and rationally to pursue, a conception of the good, as well as for the development and exercise of a sense of justice.

In *A Theory of Justice,* Rawls considers "the principles which apply to institutions, or, more exactly, to the basic structure of society" (p. 108). It is clear, however, that he believes the same device of an ideal agreement or contract can be used to analyze the concept of morality and to derive moral principles generally. The ideal contractors will find it in their interest to adopt two sorts of principles: (1) those that apply (a) to institutions, principles of justice and the subordinate principle of efficiency, and (b) to individuals insofar as they have voluntarily accepted the benefits of just institutions, the principle of fairness, and (2) those that apply to individuals in abstraction from their relations under common institutions, principles of natural duty, and supererogation. Rawls's two principles of justice, which require the greatest equal liberty and opportunity compatible with a like liberty and opportunity for all and allow inequalities in benefits and burdens only if they are to the greatest benefit of the least advantaged, govern the family as a basic institution of society. Since these principles take precedence over efficiency, the contractors would not agree to the traditional sexist division of labor within the family or to the institution of primogeniture, however efficient these practices might be.

The principles of natural duty include a *principle of paternalism.* Being behind the veil of ignorance, the ideal contractors are deprived of knowledge of their actual age and so do not know if they are children or adults (age, like sex or race, is for Rawls morally irrelevant to the moral point of view). To safeguard their interests in the event they should turn out to be children, the contractors adopt a principle of paternalism to protect themselves against their own irrationality and immaturity. The primary goods play a central role in the definition of this principle, as Rawls notes in the following passage:

> The principles of paternalism are those that the parties would acknowledge in the original position to protect themselves against the weakness and infirmities of their reason and will in society. Others are authorized and sometimes required to act on our behalf and to do what we would do for ourselves if we were rational, this authorization coming into effect only when we cannot look after our own good. Paternalistic decisions are to be guided by the individual's own settled preferences and interests insofar as they are not irrational, or failing a knowledge of these, by the theory of primary goods. As we know less and less about a person, we act for him as we would act for ourselves from the standpoint of the original position. We try to get for him the things he presumably wants whatever else he wants. (P. 249)

Paternalistic decisions regarding the senile or the older comatose patient are to be guided by what we know of their settled preferences and interests (if not irrational), but in the case of rearing children, such decisions should be guided by the theory of primary goods. Young children's preferences and interests fluctuate dramatically and frequently. Even as children mature and develop more stable aims and preferences, paternalistic decisions on their behalf should not take these alone into account. For unlike the senile or comatose cases, children's preferences and interests are still strongly influenced by the desires and beliefs of those who make such decisions for them. Further, the good that paternalism should protect and promote is defined in terms of both types of primary goods, social and natural. Caretakers must protect children's health, develop the physical, emotional, and intellectual competences necessary to rational action, nourish their self-esteem and self-confidence, ready them to take advantage of and responsibly exercise their rights and liberties as citizens, and, as far as possible, provide them with conditions favorable to grasping the educational, occupational, and other opportunities available to them in society.

The principle of paternalism requires that caretakers interfere with and guide children's actions where this is reasonably believed to be necessary to fulfill their needs as defined in light of the theory of primary goods. The principle does not identify these caretakers, however, and in particular, it does not tell us that they should normally be the child's natural parents. The question of *who* the child's caretakers should be raises issues of justice, efficiency, and fairness. Efficiency might dictate that natural childbearers be universally appointed as childrearers, but this would be unjust. It may be more efficient to appoint natural parents as childrearers than to allow children to choose their own guardians, but (as I shall argue in chapter four) removing children from their natural parents and giving them a common upbringing is in a certain respect more just than the traditional family structure. Further, parents who decide to have a child, aware that they are expected to provide for its needs, may have a special obligation to take care of their biological offspring, because they commit themselves to such care through their actions. Institutional rules regulate the relations of parents to children and distribute various benefits and burdens, and if the rules are just or reasonably so in view of the circumstances, then parents who seek to further their own interests by having a child must also bear the burdens associated with the persistence of the institution. If the practice of childrearing is such that the interests of natural parents are not bound up with control over particular children, as in the communal upbringing of the Platonic republic, then fairness does not require that natural parents bear the burdens of care for specific individuals. Conventions of childrearing define the content of parental obligations, where these arise from the principle of fairness, and also determine whether the duty to care for children can be derived from the principle of fairness at all.

I shall not now say more about *who* has, or ought to have, parental duties, for I want to concentrate on *what* these duties require of those who bring children up. Let us begin with the social primary goods. The first thing to note is that the principle of paternalism is a principle of natural duty and that principles of natural duty are chosen by the ideal contractors to regulate their relations apart from common institutions. In selecting such principles, the contractors do not know whether or not their relations to other persons are structured by just institutions. Nevertheless, paternalistic decisions are still governed by the social primary goods, because in addition to the natural duty of paternalistic intervention and guidance, the contractors accept another principle of natural duty—what I shall call the *duty of preparation for just institutions*. This duty complements the natural duty of justice, which Rawls describes as follows:

> This duty requires us to support and to comply with just institutions that exist and apply to us. It also constrains us to further just arrangements not yet established, at least when this can be done without too much cost to ourselves. (P. 115)

The natural duty of preparation for just institutions is to be thought of as the duty to prepare children to take their place within just institutions that exist and apply to us, and the duty to support just institutions by preparing children to participate in them is its corollary. In an unjust society, the duty of preparation for just institutions will require actions that conflict with the process of socialization. Socialization in an unjust society is a process by which people are prepared to perpetuate injustice, whereas preparation for just institutions is in part a process by which children are sensitized to injustice and motivated to challenge the injustice of the social institutions that govern their lives. In addition, since the process of moral education can only be fully carried out within a framework of just institutions, citizens of an unjust society must also criticize and seek to change the social and political context within which children mature, if this can be done without serious cost to themselves.

If society is just, children must be taught respect for the law that guarantees all citizens the equal right to civil and political liberty. Children should also learn early to respect the rights of others, and care should be taken to see that this respect is realized in their actions, for justice demands that the rights and liberties possessed by one person comport with the equal rights and liberties of others. Children who are taught that their wants are paramount are led to expect a continuation of such deference by others outside the context of child-rearing and are ill prepared for group life; they must learn that they can only attain their own ends by allowing others to attain theirs. Discipline is essential here, but it must gradually shift from its position of outward authority to an inner position of self-control, so that obedience becomes the spontaneous expression of self-discipline. At the same time, children should be led to develop a certain attitude concerning their rightful place in a just community. They should be brought to understand and value their own rights, so that in deferring to others they do not deny or disavow their own equality. This acknowledgement and affirmation of one's own equality is also necessarily connected to respect for others. Those who grow up ignorant of their own rights are not in an adequate position to appreciate the rights of others, and if one underestimates the importance of one's own rights, one is liable to place a comparably low value on the rights of others.

As regards the social primary good of opportunity, in a just society, those with similar abilities and motivations have equal chances for culture and educational and occupational achievement. If resources are distributed unequally among adults, and if society is committed to having children raised in the family, then equal opportunity for children requires some transfer of resources to partially equalize the environments of children. Parents, in turn, have a duty to avail themselves of needed support services so that they can provide their children with an environment that affords them access to a full range of future opportunities. If the notion of equal opportunity requires us to view persons independently from the influences of their family life as well as from the influences of their social position, and if the achievement of equal opportunity is a primary social goal, then children will have to be removed from the custody of their natural parents and given an upbringing controlled and supervised by the state. In any case, children are to receive the kind of training, emotional nurture, and guidance that brings out and strengthens their basic tendencies and that prepares them to take full advantage of the equal opportunities formally available to them. To this end, children must be allowed and required to develop initiative and a sense of responsibility for matters that are important to them as children.

Further, children must be equipped with skills that enable them to earn a minimum level of income within the economic system of jobs. Finally, we must arouse the sympathies of children for those less fortunate than themselves, for in a just society, social and economic inequalities are allowed only if they improve the position of the least advantaged members of society (Rawls's "difference principle"). The formation of character in this direction is necessary for the stability and persistence of the practice.

"Perhaps the most important primary good," Rawls asserts, "is that of self-respect" (p. 440), and this good also occupies a fundamental position within a theory of parenthood. Self-respect, which involves both a sense of one's own worth and self-confidence, is the fundamental primary good, because without it persons feel that their plans of life are of little value and hence not worthy of fulfillment, or else they lack the will to pursue them. Self-respect, in addition, is a function of at least two things: the extent and availability of social opportunities and basic liberties, and the attitude of childrearers toward their children's capacities, aspirations, achievements, and moral worth. When we are deprived of the civil and political liberties others enjoy, or when we are debarred from competing for offices and positions carrying advantages of wealth and power, we do not receive confirmation from society that our plans and goals are worth carrying out or that they are as valuable as the plans and goals of others. Because others have greater opportunities and more extensive liberties, we come to believe that what we value, aspire to, and can demand is perhaps of less importance than what others value, aspire to, and can demand, and our self-respect is undermined. But the obstacles to the achievement of self-respect do not lie only in social conditions, and an enduring basis of self-respect must also be established during the childrearing years. Children who do not feel loved, valued, and wanted by their caretakers, whose ambitions and abilities are systematically belittled, whose achievements are minimized, and whose rights are denied or disparaged, will not have enough self-esteem and self-confidence to make full use of the liberties and opportunities equally available to all. Perhaps the most important parental duty is that of providing children with the kind of affectionate, appreciative, and supportive upbringing that gives them a sense of their own value and a confidence in their ability to fulfill their intentions.

As far as the natural primary goods are concerned, their possession is influenced by society more or less depending on who has primary responsibility for childrearing; but "they are not so directly under its [society's] control" (p. 62) as the social primary goods. With the advancement of medical technology and expertise and the equitable distribution of health care facilities and professionals, all children can (and should) receive a healthful diet, prompt treatment of bacterial infections, early immunization against life-threatening diseases, regular physical examinations, and medical correction of many disabling handicaps. Further, children must be allowed sufficient physical liberty to come to terms with the risks of their physical environment, and their innate curiosity and natural exploratory behavior should be supported and encouraged. With respect to the natural primary good of intelligence, children should be exposed to those psychological conditions that causally facilitate cognitive development. The weight of evidence currently favors the age-stage hypothesis, according to which children go through generally invariant stages of intellectual development, progressing along a sequence from concrete to abstract.

Whether deliberately or otherwise, parents do as a matter of fact weight certain primary goods more than others in the upbringing of their children. Imagination might be emphasized rather than physical vigor, wealth and power rather than intelligence. Parents are not to be faulted for this, however, as long as they do what they can to secure at least some minimum amount of each of these primary goods for their children. The list of primary goods is only meant to provide us with a minimal standard below which a child's status or level of well-being must not fall.

Children's Needs: Autonomy

The notion of primary goods helps us to understand both what parenting should be and what it should not be. Paternalistic decisions on behalf of children are to be guided by a generic conception of good, by the primary goods that are the general necessary preconditions for the development of a rational conception of one's own good and the capacity to bring it to realization. At the same time, parents (construing the term broadly) are not to have an unlimited right to determine for their children what their particular conception of the good shall be, or how they shall pursue it. These are decisions that children must learn how to make, and must eventually want to make, autonomously, free from certain kinds of pressures, whether of private or public life. The principle of paternalism is formulated in terms of the primary goods, and parental authority is restricted accordingly, so that children can develop their capacities for autonomous action. It is not the mere possession of a legally guaranteed liberty that should be important to us, but the autonomous action that this liberty permits. Self-confidence is to be valued not only because it is essential to self-respect, but also because it characterizes the especially autonomous person. Since children need autonomy, and since autonomy must be developed and fostered by particular psychological and educational circumstances from very early on in childhood, parents have a duty to expose their children to such conditions.

Before trying to develop a moral principle of autonomy and incorporating it into a theory of parenthood, we should examine the concept of autonomy. On one interpretation of autonomy, autonomy is precluded by the socially structured nature of the child's existence. Because children, from their earliest years, tend to be rewarded for imitating the behavior of significant persons in their lives, and because those who are the major sources of support and control in their environment tend to be potent models for them, it is to be expected that parents will impart their own particular conceptions of the good to their children and heavily influence those they acquire from elsewhere. Autonomy, in the sense of adopting or choosing beliefs, desires, and values *de novo,* is totally unrealistic. If, however, autonomy is not located on the level of first-order considerations but in the second-order judgments one makes concerning first-order considerations, parents can do much to facilitate the development of autonomy in their children. Children cannot adopt their motivations completely

free from parental and other influence, but they can still
come to judge their motivations after the fact. They can come
to reflect on the influences their parents and others have had
over their motives, desires, values, habits, etc., and can independently choose the type of person they want to be and the
way they are to live their lives. They may choose to affirm
these motives and behaviors, that is, identify with them, or
they may choose to reject them because they do not want to
be the kind of person who is motivated in these ways, or who
has these desires and habits. Parents promote autonomy in
this sense when they encourage the development of those capacities that enable children to formulate and act on an independent attitude toward the factors that influence their
behavior, including the characteristics and actions of their
parents.

Autonomy, so understood, is a self-critical ability. To be
autonomous, grown children do not have to reject their parents' attitudes and standards. Rather, they must have the psychological strengths and reflective and critical abilities that
enable them to reject these attitudes and standards if they so
choose and must also be free to make this choice on their
own. Freedom from parents and agreement with them are
not incompatible. Adolescents, to be sure, normally preceive
them to be so. They have an urge to emancipate themselves
from the domination and protection of their parents and
wish not only to be individuals, but independent and grown-up
ones. Accepting the advice or direction of parents is seen by
children to be an acknowledgement of immaturity, and so
they must prove their independence by flouting their parents'
standards. But the disagreement with parents typical of adolescence is not a manifestation of autonomy; it is instead a
necessary and universal part of the struggle toward autonomy.

Further, autonomy, in the sense fundamental to a theory
of parenthood, is an empirical property of persons. Infants
and young children do not possess autonomy; they must de-

velop it, and its development is contingent on the development of certain psychological capacities. Here we must turn to the field of psychology for generalizations and hypotheses concerning the relation between parental practices and the development of autonomy in the child. Overprotectiveness, lax and inconsistent discipline, and an unwillingness to make demands on children have all been shown to inhibit the development of autonomy. In order for children to achieve autonomy, they must be allowed opportunities to experiment and to make decisions within well-defined limits. Within the confines of a secure parent-child relationship, experience should lead children to a sense of capacity to deal with reality through their own judgment rather than through complete compliance to a parent figure. Adolescence, when the issue of autonomy is particularly prominent, poses special problems. Parents must not only be willing to relinquish control over their children (including emotional control), but must also be supportive and accepting of them when the wish to be independent becomes too frightening for them and they feel the need for a more immature parent-child relationship.[12]

It is one thing to apprehend that another is acting autonomously or has the capacity to act autonomously, and quite another to *respect* the autonomy of others or the exercise of their autonomous capacities. In the Kantian philosophy, respect for autonomy is bound up with viewing persons in a certain way, as having unconditional worth and as being ends in themselves who may not be sacrificed or used for the achieving of other ends without their consent. If an object has value

12. For a discussion of the psychological preconditions for the development of autonomy, see Diana Baumrind, "Socialization and Instrumental Competence in Young Children," *Contemporary Readings in Child Psychology*, ed. E. M. Hetherington and R. Parke (New York: McGraw Hill, 1977), pp. 296–308; Erik Erikson, *Childhood and Society* (New York: W. W. Norton, 1963); Irene M. Josselyn, *Psychosocial Development of Children* (New York: Family Service Association of America, 1969); M. Mahler, F. Pine, and A. Bergman, *The Psychological Birth of the Human Infant* (New York: Basic Books, 1975).

because it is a means to some end we judge to be valuable or because it is itself an end we consider worth seeking, the value of that object depends on our valuing it. Persons in contrast, have a worth that does not wholly depend on someone else's considering them to be valuable, and to treat persons accordingly is to act toward them in such a way as always to respect their capacity for autonomous action.

The Kantian injunction to "treat humanity, whether in your own person or in that of another, always as an end and never as a means only,"[13] does not entail that we may never use another person as a means. We do so, for example, every time we buy some article that we want from a storekeeper. But since storekeepers have presumably chosen to carry out sales, we are not using them merely as a means and therefore we are not violating their autonomy. The situation is different with immoral actions. Take Kant's famous example of false promises, that is, promises made by persons who permit themselves to break them at their convenience. In Kant's view, false promise-making is wrong for several reasons including the following: First, it is self-defeating when universalized. If we all were to break promises at our convenience, the would-be promise breaker couldn't make a promise to break. Second, false promise-making is wrong because it treats the promisees as mere means, it involves them in transactions they could not choose to take part in. They could not, as rational agents, both accept the promise and accept that the promise might be broken at the other's convenience. To do so would be to act inconsistently.

If the Kantian formula of the end-in-itself were interpreted to apply only to those who are actually autonomous, it would tell us nothing about how parents ought to treat their children, for children are not yet autonomous. Indeed, if children were treated as mature and autonomous persons, they could

13. *Foundations of the Metaphysics of Morals,* trans. L. W. Beck (Indianapolis: Bobbs-Merrill, 1976), p. 47.

not survive, let alone prosper. Kant himself, however, seems not to have restricted the principle in this way (see above, pp. 86–87). To respect autonomy is fundamentally to respect the *capacity* of an agent to rationally determine for himself what he shall do and be. Children are not merely potential persons, but persons with the capacity for autonomy, and as such they have the right to an upbringing that allows and encourages them to exercise their capacities for autonomous action. Moreover, since some forms of compulsion help rather than inhibit the development of these capacities, parents should not be accused of using their child as a mere means simply because they interfere with the child's liberty of action.

Autonomy, as we saw in part I, is the central value in the educational philosophy of Rousseau's *Émile*. The natural moral goodness of the child, according to Rousseau, can only develop when children are brought up in isolation from and ignorance of social relations. With the intervention of society and its multiplication of "artificial needs,"[14] children become dependent on others and on their opinions and prejudices. This dependence fosters selfishness, and from selfishness spring all "the hateful and angry passions" (p. 174) that make children and others miserable. The educator, therefore, should "regard with suspicion those wishes which they [children] cannot carry out for themselves, those which others must carry out for them" (p. 50). Educators must teach children to rely on themselves, and they do this by giving the child "not what he wants, but what he needs" (p. 49) for the development of his innate intellectual and emotional capacities according to their natural bent. Needs should be fully and promptly met; wants, since they can only be satisfied by relying on others, should be discouraged. Rousseau's commitment to autonomy rests, however, on a claim about the natural goodness of children for which there is no empirical evidence,

14. *Émile*, trans. B. Foxley (London: J. M. Dent and Sons, Ltd. 1974), p. 50.

and his method of educating for autonomy is objectionable on both practical and moral grounds.

A final cautionary word about autonomy: We should be careful not to conceive of it in such an exalted fashion that autonomy becomes indistinguishable from caprice, and we should not be so eager for our children to attain autonomy that we fail to give it adequate developmental support. Autonomy does not develop magically *ex nihilo*. Children need to learn to be autonomous, and this can happen only if they are not autonomous to begin with. Some principles, and in particular the commitment to autonomy itself, must be implanted in children if they are to grow in the proper direction. Moreover, children must already possess at least a tentative character, at least a tentative motivational structure, if they are to be able to autonomously *choose* a different character and different beliefs, desires, and traits. Autonomy, the ability to critically reflect on oneself and the freedom to shape one's life in accordance with changing desires and aspirations, cannot exist in a vacuum; it presupposes some relatively settled beliefs, desires, etc., in short a self, to reason from and with.

Parenting in Unfavorable Circumstances

Though every child is entitled to an upbringing that fosters self-respect and autonomy and should be exposed to the conditions necessary for the enjoyment of the primary goods, as far as his or her natural attributes permit, in actuality those who rear children are often unable to care for them adequately. Many parents lack the knowledge to rear children adequately, and some may be intellectually unfit to do so. Others lack the requisite energy, temperament, or stability, because of inexperience, immaturity, past psychological history, etc. In addition, while favorable socioeconomic conditions do not necessarily ensure that children's needs are met, it is much more difficult to meet these needs in circumstances of severe socioeconomic strain. As the children of the poor grow into adolescence, they become increasingly aware of how limited their chances are of escaping from the multiple disadvantages of poverty, and their self-esteem suffers. Further, in underdeveloped societies, with inadequate educational and health facilities, food maldistribution and malnutrition, and inefficient methods of production, parents cannot provide the care their children should have. Personal qualities, socioeconomic status and the conditions associated with it, and the general nature of their particular society can all adversely affect parents' ability to meet the needs of their children.

If children are reared not by their biological parents, but in institutions controlled and supervised by the state or community, then it is not necessarily wrong to have children one cannot adequately provide for. But if those who decide to procreate are responsible for the upbringing of their offspring, and if they realize (or ought to realize) that they cannot fulfill the responsibilities of parenthood or at least arrange for their fulfillment by competent and willing others, then they should not procreate under these conditions. At the same time, there are important moral differences between the case where the disabilities of prospective parents are due to personal qualities (e.g., temperament or immaturity) and the case where they are due in large measure to insufficient economic resources. By preventing the poor from having children, or by imposing limits on the number of children they may have without imposing comparable limits on more affluent parents, we increase the stigma and lack of self-respect already associated with being poor, and we deny the poor equality of opportunity for parenthood on the basis of characteristics in themselves irrelevant to psychological fitness for raising children. None of this, however, can justify allowing the poor to have children they cannot adequately provide for.

It only points up the need to adopt other policies, relating to employment, income supports, and family services so that the poor can take adequate care of the children they have. In underdeveloped countries, where most parents cannot secure an adequate quality of life for their children, population policies might help society attain a level of economic growth sufficient to meet the needs of children in the long run.

The theory of parenthood I have outlined in this chapter presents a kind of ideal conception of parenting, and does not deal with these pressing problems of our actual imperfect world. It is one thing to establish standards that define a decent upbringing for children and quite another to decide what should be done in case parents cannot raise their children up to these standards. Yet without these standards, we would have no way, other than by intuition, of distinguishing between adequate and inadequate parents. Moreover, it is only in light of such standards that we can rationally assess the impact on children of existing childrearing and other social arrangements and offer suggestions on how to change them if they are found wanting.

CHAPTER TWO

The Assignment of Childrearing Duties

Parents, Natural and Otherwise

In the previous chapter, I set out a moral theory of parenthood consisting of the following main points: (a) parental duties take priority over parental rights (the Lockean thesis); (b) parental duties can be classified as duties of status, duties of need-fulfillment, and duties of respect, that is, as institutional as well as individual duties; (c) to meet the needs of children, guidance and control by others is required, and so duties of need-fulfillment (unlike duties of respect) can account for parental authority; (d) children's needs are to be analyzed with respect to the primary goods and the preconditions for their enjoyment; (e) the principle of paternalism is formulated in terms of the primary goods to give due weight to autonomy for children, the achievement of which also requires an upbringing that encourages children to develop and exercise their capacities for autonomous action. A serious discussion of children's needs must, however, do more than establish priorities for parents or classify and explicate parental duties. It must also answer, in a general way, the following question: Who should be a child's parents? In other words, it must tell us who has parental duties, that is, who has a duty to supply certain needs of children under certain circumstances, or a duty to see to it that all or some of their needs are adequately met by others. A parent in this sense is any adult who has a continuing obligation to direct some important aspect (or aspects) of a child's development, and a child can have several such parents, including those who actually produced the child, relatives, tutors, day-care workers, and schoolteachers.

In its more familiar usage, the word "parents" is reserved for those adults who are most personally and emotionally involved with the child on a day-to-day basis and who have primary responsibility for his or her care and development. Primary responsibility should be distinguished from exclusive responsibility, for it does not follow from the fact that certain adults have primary responsibility for certain children's welfare that they must or can rear them entirely by themselves. The lives parents are leading, and the lives for which they are preparing their children, may be so demanding and complex that the parents cannot have, and often do not want to have, direct supervision of all aspects of their child's care and development. Under these circumstances, they ought to rely on others for help and support in raising their children (if such support and help is available and accessible), and should delegate some of the authority that accrues to them in virtue of their special parental responsibility. Those whom parents authorize to act on their behalf may be granted little discretion in defining and managing child care, or they may be given a great deal of independence to act as they deem best within their limited area of expertise. In any case, as long as parents retain primary responsibility for childrearing, it is they, not their agents, who are ultimately responsible for what happens to their children.

It is possible to arrange childrearing in such a way that pri-

mary responsibility for a child's care and upbringing typically does not rest in the hands of those who are most personally and emotionally involved with the child on a day-to-day
basis. Selection of caretakers and coordination of their activities may even be done by persons who are completely
removed from sustained, direct contact with the child. An
example of the first type of arrangement is the Israeli kibbutz,
where the physical care and rearing of children is basically
the responsibility of the community, not so much of their
natural parents, but also where the emotional ties between
natural parents and their children are much more intimate
and more intense than their ties with other members of the
community. An example of the second type is the large, bu-
reaucratic institution run by administrators who never see
the children whose lives they control. In both cases, experts
do the actual caretaking and childrearing, and to a greater or
lesser extent, primary responsibility for the child's development is detached from emotional involvement with the child.

Biological parents in our society perform functions very
much like those of parents on the Israeli kibbutz and administrators of childrearing institutions.[1] More and more, biological parents today are called upon to act like "the execu-
tives in a large firm—responsible for the smooth coordination
of the many people and processes that must work together to
produce the final product."[2] At the same time, it is a sociological truism that as traditional family functions are transferred outside the family, the task of fulfilling the emotional
needs of parents and children becomes even more concentrated in families than in the past. As specific duties to children are dispersed among various professionals (some of whom
can be considered parents in the broad sense discussed above),

1. Of course, there are many circumstances in our society in which one or
both biological parents do not rear their children. But parental duties are
not standardly assigned to someone other than the biological parents.

2. Kenneth Keniston et. al., *All Our Children: The American Family Under
Pressure* (New York: Harcourt Brace Jovanovich, 1977), p. 17.

the value to us of parent-child relationships is strengthened rather than diminished, and the importance of the emotional ties between parents and children is enhanced. Indeed, it is in large measure because biological parents are believed to have special natural affections for their offspring that they are regarded as especially well qualified to be parents in the non-biological sense of the term and to have primary responsibility for their child's care and development, however attenuated this responsibility may be. For biological parents, the physical realities of conception and birth are a direct cause of emotional attachment to their child, and though there are cases in which this attachment is not sufficiently strong, it is parenthood based on biology that usually provides the model for other varieties of parenthood. For example, the relation between adoptive parents and the child they have adopted is supposed to be similar to what it would have been if the child had been born to them.

Even if biological parents are normally well qualified to rear their children or to decide how and with whom they will share the task of raising their children, this does not explain why biological parents have the right and duty to do so. Does the biological relationship between child and parents itself ground or create the moral duty, or is biology connected to the duty only in a contingent way? In addition, childrearing practices in which biological parents do not have primary responsibility for the upbringing of their children are not only theoretical possibilities but realities in some societies, and the relative merits of alternative arrangements have to be assessed. It is to these two issues, one relating to the grounds of individual responsibility for children, the other to the justification of social conventions of childrearing, that I now turn.

Are Parents' Duties Procreators' Duties?

Adoptive parents, foster parents, stepparents, relatives, teachers, and officials of social agencies can come to have some or all of the duties of biological parents, but it is the biological parents who are usually thought to have first right to the possession of their child, and so it is with the source of *their* duties that I shall begin. That children exist with certain needs, that they must rely on others to supply these needs, and that their biological parents (perhaps by securing the assistance of others) can do so, is not by itself sufficient to establish the parents' responsibility for their children. For as Joel Feinberg argues, "to have an unfulfilled need is to have a kind of claim against the world,"[3] and as yet no explanation has been given for why biological parents should be singled out to meet these needs.

One explanation is mentioned by Henry Sidgwick in *The Methods of Ethics:*

> No doubt children are naturally objects of compassion, on account of their helplessness, to others besides their parents. But on the latter they have a claim of a different kind, springing from the universally recognized duty of not causing pain or any harm to other human beings, directly or indirectly, except in the way of deserved punishment; for the parent, being the cause of the child's existing in a helpless condition, would be indirectly the cause of the suffering and death that would result to it if neglected.[4]

On this account, the duties of biological parents derive from the generally recognized duty not to injure anyone by failing to perform actions that we can perform and that, if performed, would prevent the injury from occurring. Since biological parents can do x, where x involves caring for their offspring themselves or making provisions for others to do so, and since x would prevent y, where y involves harm to a human being, the failure of biological parents to do x can be said to cause y. (Of course, we are not accountable for some outcome simply

3. "The Nature and Value of Rights," *The Journal of Value Inquiry,* 4 (1970), p. 255.
4. (Chicago: University of Chicago Press, 1962), p. 249.

because we are causally responsible for it; other conditions have to be met before the question of moral responsibility can be raised. We must also stipulate that biological parents know, or ought reasonably to know, that they can do x and that their doing x would prevent y.) As to why biological parents are particularly to blame for the harm that would result to their child if neglected, the reason seems to be that biological parents are somehow in a better position than others to care for their children, and to make a difference between this harm's occurring and its not occurring. Though the injunction not to injure children is certainly not addressed exclusively to their biological parents, it is this feature of the relation between biological parents and their child that makes it particularly appropriate to blame them for the failure to prevent y by doing x.

Biological parents are typically in the best position to harm their children through neglect because, in the normal course of events, they are expected to rear their children and are assigned this responsibility. If the expectations were different and it was out of the question for biological parents to do x, they could not be considered causally or morally responsible for the harm that might befall their offspring through (someone else's) neglect. Further, in a society where biological parents are expected to rear their children, and normally do so, decisions to procreate are, and are known to be, decisions to undertake the task of bringing up children or arranging for others to bring them up. The omissions of biological parents necessarily have the most serious impact on the welfare of their children because biological parents are expected to rear their children, and normally do so; and it is in the context of these expectations that decisions to procreate are to be understood as decisions to rear or arrange for the rearing of offspring. Prospective parents may not have given much thought to what parenthood would be like or what it would demand of them, but they know that in their society biological parents are supposed to rear their children, and in deciding to have a child they normally intend to assume responsibility for the care and development of that child. Decisions to procreate can occur before or after conception. Persons may engage in sexual relations with the intention of having a child, or an unwanted and unintended pregnancy that results from (say) rape or a defective contraceptive device may later be accepted and even welcomed. If, however, persons change their minds about having a child after it has been conceived, because they find themselves unable or unwilling to discharge parental duties, or if they unintentionally conceive and do not want the child, they might seek an abortion, if abortions are obtainable and acceptable to them. (I do not discuss here the morality of abortion. Parents may sometimes have duties to children they did not intend to conceive.) If they are not obtainable or if they are felt to be impermissible, the biological parents might put their child up for adoption, either before or after birth. Finally, if alternative caretakers cannot be found and the biological parents cannot countenance deliberate termination of the pregnancy or abandonment of the child, they have no option but to rear him or her themselves. They may not have wanted to become parents and to be responsible for a child's care, but they decide not to avoid parental duties, and so incur them.

It is not procreation itself that creates the duties of biological parents any more than the natural fact of A's having typhoid by itself creates in B a duty to rid A of it.[5] Rather, it is typically the decision to undertake parental duties that is entailed by the decision to procreate. Further, since biological parents ordinarily have parental duties because they undertake them, biological parents and adoptive parents have parental duties for the same reason. To be sure, adoptive parents frequently have a clearer idea of the care and attention

5. See Locke's refutation of the view that procreation is the basis of parental authority, discussed on pp. 74–78 above.

their child will require than biological parents and are less likely to misjudge their desires and capacities to rear. Even if the adoption order were as final as a birth certificate (now there is usually a waiting period between a child's placement with the adopting family and the final order of adoption), adoptive parents would probably not transfer their parental duties to others as often as biological parents. Nevertheless, though the adoptive parent's decision to rear is frequently more deliberate and enlightened than that of the biological parent, and though decisions to procreate should perhaps resemble decisions to adopt more closely than they do (in order to protect children from potentially harmful disruptions of family life), both types of decisions carry with them a commitment to the child. Wherever biological parents are the normal childrearers, parents have some duty with respect to the biological offspring they have chosen to produce, even if not a duty to sacrifice their own interests to the extent required to care for and bring up a child.

As we have seen, biological parents acquire parental duties only if certain background conditions are satisfied. It is not merely because biological parents are the "cause of the child's existing in a helpless condition" that they are causally responsible "for the suffering and death that would result to it if neglected," but because childrearing is arranged in such a way that those who cause a child to exist are in a special position to do something to prevent this harm from occurring. The connection between causing a child to exist and harming the child through neglect is mediated by social customs of childrearing. (In the absence of common childrearing arrangements, and well-established institutional procedures for the care of children, i.e., in a state of nature, the connection depends on other factors.) Moreover, if the duties of biological parents do not follow from the fact of procreation alone but from this fact together with the moral principle that people are responsible for the foreseeable consequences of their voluntary acts (foreseeable at the time the action is performed), then caring for a child must be a foreseeable consequence of having one. But in a society where biological parents are not normally responsible for the performance of parental duties, or for doing what is necessary to fulfill them, this condition is not met.

Parental responsibility is, then, an example of what H. L. A. Hart calls "role-responsibility."[6] Parents in general, whether biological or another kind, are responsible for the upbringing of their charges because they occupy a distinctive place in a social organization, to which place specific duties are attached to provide for the welfare of young children. This organization, and the other social institutions with which it is reciprocally involved, may be just or unjust, efficient or inefficient, oppressive or unoppressive, and many other things as well. In any case, the problem of justifying a practice is distinct from that of explaining how it is that particular individuals typically come to occupy positions within it. Even if the practice of delegating childrearing duties to biological parents is unjust under certain circumstances, those who decide to procreate under this practice are not absolved of all responsibility for their offspring's care. In the long run, perhaps, biology should be irrelevant to the allocation of responsibility for specific children; but to change the rules in the middle of the game, even when those rules are not altogether fair, is unfair to children.

The Parties Affected by Childrearing Practices

Moral principles regulate the relations of parents to children, and among these, the most basic is that parental duties take priority over parental rights. But parent-child relationships, unlike other types of personal relationship (e.g., friendship

6. *Punishment and Responsibility* (Oxford: Oxford University Press, 1968), pp. 212–214.

and companionship), are also governed by law and conven-
tion, by systems of rules constitutive of childrearing practices,
and these laws and conventions can either respect the priority
principle or make it unreasonably difficult for parents to conform to it. Thus society may place an intolerable burden on
parents by, in effect forcing them to choose between their parental obligations and their own legitimate nonparental interests. Under these circumstances, parents will either not
subordinate their own interests to those of their children, as
the priority principle requires, or they will do so, but only
through excessive self-repression. Clearly no set of childrearing arrangements is optimal, or even desirable, where the institutional relationship between parents and children conflicts
with the right ordering of parental duties and rights.

To be acceptable, a childrearing practice should not force
parents to choose between duty and interest but should accommodate both the needs of children and the legitimate nonparental interests of parents. As in any kind of work, long-
term commitment to the job of parenting depends on the
enthusiasm with which the job is performed and the satisfaction derived from it, and parents whose own interests must
always be sacrified to those of their children are likely to end
up not satisfied but miserable and resentful. It is in the interest of children as well as parents that parents have time off
from parenting and the opportunity to engage in rewarding
nonparental work.

But if parents need a wider range of possibilities for personal fulfillment than children alone can provide, individuals
also have numerous interests in having and rearing children
and receive a variety of benefits from parenthood throughout
life. There are, of course, many reasons for wanting children,
and these vary from culture to culture and historical period
to historical period. Some people have children out of political considerations, to promote the goals of a larger community
than the reproductive unit itself (this is an important moti-

vation for having children in Plato's ideal republic). Some want children for economic reasons. The economic returns from children, though deferred for a few years, eventually accrue to the parents in the form of useful work, economic aid, dowry and "bride-wealth," or support in later life. In some societies, people want children for what might be called familial reasons: to extend the family line or family name, to propitiate ancestors, or to enable the proper functioning of religious rituals involving the family. Then, too, having children gives parents power over them, in many cases the most effective power they will ever have the opportunity to exercise on an individual basis. Men and women may also look upon parenthood as providing them with the opportunity to demonstrate competence in an essential social role. Further, persons have children in order to achieve a kind of personal immortality, or because parenthood is considered a part of life, of personal growth, that cannot be experienced in any other way, and hence as an indispensable element of the full life. Finally, persons want children for the altruistic pleasure of having them, caring for them, helping them grow and develop.

The problem of deciding how a childrearing practice should allocate primary responsibility for children is partly that of deciding who should be able to enjoy the benefits that such responsibility brings to those who exercise it. If the desire to raise children is widespread, and if the parental interests in raising children are legitimate, then, other things being equal, the means of acquiring parental responsibility should be widely available. Access to parenthood would not be as easy as it is at present were the community to assign childrearing tasks to child-care specialists rather than to ordinary (biological, adoptive, etc.) parents. But here it is important to note two things: first, that not all interests in rearing children are equally compelling in all cultures and all periods, and second, that at least some of the rewards of having children can probably be enjoyed even though the primary responsibility for rearing them belongs to someone else. With regard to the first point, consider the economic reasons for wanting children. Among the rural poor in developing societies, and in societies without socialized systems of social security, it is reasonable for parents to look to their children as potential guarantors of an acceptable old age. To raise children under these circumstances is to protect oneself against economic insecurity later in life. But in a society where generational responsibility for the aged is collectivized through a social insurance scheme, this reason for wanting children becomes less significant. Moreover, in such a society, childrearing could be collectivized without fear of depriving elderly citizens of an adequate standard of living. As parents become less economically dependent on their children, collective management of children becomes less objectionable, if not completely acceptable.

Similar points can be made about another parental interest in rearing children, the interest in demonstrating competence in an important social role. Men and women who are closed off from other demonstrations of competence, whether through lack of talent or educational opportunity or social status, still have the opportunity to prove themselves in the key role of parent. Throughout history, parenthood has been particularly appealing to women, for as society has defined their role, there is nothing else for grown females to do with their time and energy. Under these circumstances, a childrearing arrangement in which women are freed *from* major responsibility for housework and child care would indeed be seriously objectionable, for they would not at the same time be freed *to* demonstrate their competence in other ways. But in a society committed to sexual equality, where women and men have equal educational opportunity and women are not debarred from competing for offices and positions carrying advantages of wealth and power, it is not unreasonable to think that fewer women would choose to display their talents and skills through motherhood.

As these examples suggest, it is one thing to design an ideal childrearing practice, for a particular society or in general, and quite another to reform an imperfect practice that serves legitimate parental interests. Persons decide to have children in the context of an existing childrearing practice and plan their lives in expectation of the rewards that this practice enables them to enjoy. Major reform of such a practice is going to be unfair to those who rely on it unless, in conjunction with this change, society provides them with some means of satisfying the legitimate interests that were served by the old practice. Thus, if a new childrearing practice is established in which parents (as defined by the previous practice) can no longer look to their children for economic support in old age, society can see to it that they no longer need to do so; and if women must relinquish their traditional responsibilities to the state or community, society can give them the opportunity to demonstrate personal competence in other roles. At the same time, not every interest in rearing children has an alternative nonparental means of satisfaction (as when the reason for wanting children is to have the unique experience of parenthood), and the costs of a childrearing practice in which individuals are deprived of the opportunity for parenthood altogether and contact with children is limited to a relatively few caretakers must be weighed against its advantages.

It is true that in our society, biological parents feel entitled to attribute some of their children's success to their own efforts because they are entrusted with their care, and that if biological parents were denied this responsibility, they would no longer take pride in their children for the same reason. But this motive for wanting children has its dark side, as with parents who "live through their children," often to the latter's distaste and disadvantage, or parents who experience a sense of failure, disappointment, and frustration when their children do not achieve. Moreover, even if biological parents did not carry the main responsibility for child care and childrearing, the desire for children might still be strong and widespread, and perhaps even more widespread than it is now when they do have such responsibility. Since the burdens of disciplining and educating children would be born by others, persons would not be forced to choose between children and careers. Parents-to-be could look forward to intimate and affectionate relations with their children, without fear of foreclosing other avenues of personal development for themselves or encountering the petty quarrels and persistent disagreements that often vex parent-child relationships in the nuclear family. Children would not approach their parents with the special deference that those who direct and control their upbringing (i.e., biological parents) now receive, but the pleasures of having children, watching them grow, and being with them might more than compensate for the loss of power over them. As for the desire to attain a kind of personal immortality through one's children, this too can be satisfied to some extent, even though many aspects of child-rearing are assigned to someone other than begetters and bearers. Finally, even if, as Francis Schrag asserts, "it is scarcely conceivable that a society should exist in which the natural parents were entirely indifferent to what befell their offspring,"[7] there are a number of different childrearing arrangements that can accommodate this parental concern.

I have argued so far that the legitimate interests of children and parents are two factors to consider in assessing a social practice of childrearing. Whether or not, for example, major responsibility for upbringing should be shifted from the nuclear family to public institutions depends on a number of complex theoretical and practical considerations, including relative effectiveness in serving the needs of children, the degree of independence each arrangement affords parents, and the extent to which each respects people's legitimate reasons for wanting children and enables them to enjoy the benefits

7. "Rights Over Children," *Journal of Value Inquiry*, 7 (1973), p. 101.

of parenthood. If there are any parental interests that are not socially created (i.e., innate or natural), these constitute a standard of comparison for different systems of childrearing. Even if the reasons for wanting children are not independent of already existing social practices that allocate childrearing duties, the reference to parental interests does not in principle bar the adoption of alternative practices. For more than one assignment of childrearing duties is compatible with the satisfaction of at least some parental interests, some of the satisfactions that persons now derive from parenthood can be obtained in other ways, and the interests of children may require a change in the dominant mode of childrearing, even though the new practice does not satisfy parental interests as fully as the old. But the interests of children and parents (or those who want to become parents) are not the only factors to consider, because society itself has legitimate interests with respect to procreation and the raising of children, and these interests are intertwined with those of children and parents. (A complete discussion of social interests in this area would set out guidelines for the evaluation of population control policies and assess the importance of the institution of marriage to procreation of the species, but these are subjects that fall outside the concerns of this chapter.) The community's own interests in or with respect to childrearing are to be distinguished from the interests that the community, acting through its government, espouses on behalf of infants and young children when it modifies or terminates the legal relationship between a child and his or her parents.

Society has an interest in childrearing because it has an interest in the process by which children are socialized, that is, acquire the general beliefs, attitudes, and skills that are a necessary feature of any society as well as the specific dispositions and states of mind that are regarded as desirable by that particular (kind of) society. The values and ideals that define the moral life of a community, and which children must internalize to some extent if the community is to sustain itself, are transmitted more or less effectively depending on how responsibility for socializing children is distributed in that society. In a society where the larger community is not an active participant in socialization and children have little opportunity and incentive for meaningful contact with persons older and younger than themselves, children tend to grow up alienated from their community, its customs, values, and responsibilities (whatever these may be), and may even turn to socially destructive activities.[8] In a society whose members are tied together by joint participation in activity toward a common goal that each ranks as his or her most important goal, where the aims of individuals and associations are subordinate to the promotion of group interests, the dominant social values are those of cooperation, altruism, fraternity, and patriotism. Under these circumstances, it is necessarily problematic for the community to assign primary responsibility for socialization to the family rather than to itself, for family ties are based on exclusive and particularistic loyalties that can easily come into conflict with loyalties to the collective.[9] At the same time, it should be clear that being socialized is not necessarily the same as being civilized; the interest in socialization must have an ultimate justification in terms of interests that can be specified independently of socialization. Also, processes of socialization that tend to promote unreflective identification with debatable cultural values and ideals prevent the full development of children's autonomous capacities and are to be rejected for this reason.

In a complex distributive system of child socialization, many agencies, institutions, and professionals are directly or indirectly involved in the process by which children are pre-

8. See Urie Bronfenbrenner, "The Roots of Alienation," *Raising Children in Modern America*, ed. Nathan Talbot (Boston: Little, Brown and Co., 1976), pp. 157ff.

9. Plato understood this, but then proceeded to advocate the absorption of familial arrangements into the political sphere.

pared to participate in their culture or society (these may include the family, schools, churches, and the media). If these agencies are mismatched, the process will be inefficient and possibly ineffective as well. Further, in any large-scale social system, childrearing arrangements themselves are but part of an intricate network of interdependent and interpenetrating subsystems, and these too need to be fitted together to form a coherent set of social rules. On both levels of interaction, there exists what I shall call the problem of institutional coordination, or more generally, the problem of coordinating social practices. This problem is particularly serious during periods of profound social transformation. Changes in family patterns or in the legal, economic, or cultural subsystems of society may put a strain on the entire system that must be relieved by making adjustments elsewhere in the system, for example in the society's childrearing arrangements. Moreover, until these arrangements are adjusted to changes in other social arrangements and practices, that is, until institutional coordination is restored, individuals will often have great difficulty integrating parenting with participation in other subsystems of the society. Persons may therefore choose to limit their range of social opportunities in order to avoid the conflicts that arise from multiple role-playing, or they may find themselves unable to fulfill the divergent requirements of a number of social roles.

From society's point of view, as well as from that of parents and children, no childrearing arrangement is desirable if it is internally inconsistent, and no collection of social practices is acceptable in which the childrearing arrangement is badly coordinated with other types of practices. Coherence is a necessary, though not sufficient, condition of merit. One and the same childrearing arrangement can be badly coordinated under one set of social conditions, and well coordinated under another, and the goals of society must be specified without reference to coherence before deciding whether or not the society's childrearing arrangement should change to serve these goals. In addition, society's interest in institutional coordination is not independent of the interests of parents and children and should not be promoted at the expense of their legitimate interests. Parenting will often be more burdensome than satisfying, and children will often not receive the benefits of consistent and continuous parental care where childrearing arrangements do not keep pace with legal, economic, and other social changes. The justification of a particular childrearing practice and its assignment of duties to care for, educate, and socialize children depends on how well the practice accommodates the various interlocking interests of children, parents, and society. To satisfactorily solve the problem of institutional coordination, therefore, we have to find a coherent set of social practices conferring corollary rights and duties that satisfy the legitimate interests of *all* parties who have a stake in the rearing and education of the young. In some cases, modification of the prevailing childrearing arrangement may be necessary as well as desirable to restore equilibrium to the social system; in other cases, well-coordinated childrearing arrangements may be inadequate because they severely restrict parents' opportunities for self-expression or because they do not allow for the emergence of individuality and independence in children.

The Selection of Childrearers

Biology alone is not a sufficient explanation of the basis of parental duties, because normally procreation is relevant to parental duty only insofar as social practices and customs make it relevant. Ultimately, therefore, our attention must be directed to the social practices and their justification, not to the fact of causation or to the decision to procreate. The justification of childrearing duties—and there is a wide variety of ways in which childrearing practices can and do assign duties to care for children—is a higher-order account that takes into consideration the three distinct, though closely interwoven, sets of interests discussed in the previous section. While this line of argument does not show that there is only one child-rearing arrangement that is justified (social structures and the interests of parents do vary), it does tell us that an assignment of childrearing duties is to be rejected if it fails to satisfy the legitimate interests of all concerned.

Consider the interests (i.e., needs) of children. It seems that, as a general rule, biological parents are most likely (or at least as likely as anyone else) to promote the best interests of their children. Biological parents, especially mothers, have a profound natural concern and affection for their offspring. Ordinarily, as Aristotle and Hegel point out, they do not have to learn to love their children; they love them from birth because they are the product of an intimate and loving sexual union. Moreover, the child is an extension of their own unique selves, and is, therefore, uniquely precious. A baby is not just another child in the world to its biological parents. Contrary to initial impressions, however, a number of considerations can be advanced that might incline us toward placing children under the care and supervision of some party other than their biological parents. Without denying that children need to feel loved, valued, and wanted by their caretakers if they are to develop a healthy self-esteem, we can question whether the kind of love biological parents feel for their child, or at least the circumstances under which this love is manifested, are really conducive to the child's proper development. The very tightness of the bond between children and their biological parents, the very closeness of their identification with each other, might be an obstacle to the parents' objective assessment of their offspring's needs and might interfere with their obligation to prepare them to lead lives of their own. These problems are perhaps not inevitable wherever biological parents have primary responsibility for the upbringing of

children, but as the institution of the biological family is
presently organized and supported by other institutions in
our particular social setting, the positive characteristics of
biological parents must be set against the possible drawbacks
of this mode of rearing. Further, it may be, as B. F. Skinner
has argued, that good child care is "an intricate science, into
which the average mother could not be initiated without years
of training," and that "even when the mother knows the right
thing to do, she often can't do it in a household which is busy
with other affairs."[10]

Consider next the interests of parents, in particular the interests of men and women that cannot be completely satisfied
by the present social arrangement in which women are mainly
responsible for housework and child care and are expected to
perform these jobs without pay. Under this arrangement,
wives are driven into economic dependence on their husbands, a dependence that can make women powerless to defend their legitimate interests and that poses a grave threat
to their self-respect; and husbands are encouraged to separate
public action from private affection and to channel all of
their creative energies into their work, at great cost to their
emotional and psychological well-being. At least two types of
family policy aimed at promoting sexual equality are possible. The first would shift the locus of primary responsibility
for children from the private household to state or communal
agencies. The woman would be relieved of her domestic burdens by means of various institutions of collective living and
could then take her place as man's equal, economically, socially, politically, and intellectually. The danger here, however, is that freedom from parenting altogether will be seen
as a precondition of self-fulfillment, and that success for men
and women alike will be defined solely and narrowly in terms
of nonparental occupations. An alternative approach would

10. *Walden Two* (New York: Macmillan, 1962), p. 142.

involve equalizing the division of home and child-care responsibilities between mothers and fathers rather than transferring
parental duties to nonfamilial social agencies. Parents would
continue to play the decisive part as agents of childrearing, in
some cases in the traditional manner, but society would at
least encourage them to work out more egalitarian family
roles.

Finally we come to the social interest in institutional coordination. A good example of the lack of coordination between childrearing and other practices is the conflict that
exists in our country between the demands of a job and the
demands of a family. On the one hand, we say that parents
are the world's greatest experts about the needs of their own
children, and so we expect parents to take primary responsibility for their care and development. We also profess to be
concerned about the integrity, vitality, and sanctity of family
life. On the other, our country has done very little to bring
work practices into line with families' and children's needs or
to provide supplementary care for children whose parents
both work. Adjustments in the timing and structure of work,
and greater access to quality day-care facilities, would reduce
the conflict between being a good parent and being a productive worker, but so far we have not seriously pursued these
policies.[11] Another example involves our school system, which,
probably more than any other institution, has kept children
insulated from challenging social tasks at a time when they
are reaching physical and intellectual maturity at earlier and
earlier ages.

There is, of course, no general and informative answer to
the question "What way of allocating responsibility for raising fits in best with other social practices?" The answer depends on what those other social practices are. In the early
days of the Israeli kibbutzim, when the new struggling com-

11. For a discussion of the failures of public policy in this area, and recommendations for change, see Keniston, *op. cit.*

munities had very few capital resources for basic investment, most of their resources of manpower and capital were channeled into production.[12] In this context, centralized communal organization of childrearing was very functional, because it freed biological parents for economic production. Under different social conditions—for example, where isolated peasant or rural households predominate—the best match between childrearing and other social practices might be achieved by assigning most childrearing duties to biological parents. Under still other conditions, like those of modern urban society, institutional coordination may dictate the delegation of important childrearing responsibilities to nonfamilial structures of the society, and the retention of the family as a more specialized institution.

Whether rearing by biological parents is likely to be better for the development of the human personality than some other arrangement, whether adult men and women will lead more satisfying lives if parental care is replaced by group care, whether society is better able to maintain a continuity of values by assigning childrearing tasks to ordinary parents or child-development experts—these are questions that can only be settled through observation and experiment. Where there already exists a consensus on norms, it is only on an empirical level that questions about desirable family and childrearing patterns will arise. *If* rearing by biological parents is not socially dysfunctional, psychologically destructive to parents, or harmful to the child's development, then perhaps children should be raised by their biological parents. But it may also be that under a different set of social conditions, other modes of childrearing are preferable. In any case, it is impossible to justify a childrearing arrangement by assigning weights to,

12. For one of the best studies of the interrelation between communal structure and family organization in the Israeli kibbutz, see Yonina Talmon, "The Family in a Revolutionary Movement: The Case of the Kibbutz in Israel," in *Comparative Family Systems*, ed. M. F. Nimkoff (New York: Houghton Mifflin, 1965), ch. 13.

ranking, or aggregating the interests of parents, children, and the community. The interests are too interdependent for this approach. Mutual adjustment of interests, not their ranking or aggregation, is what is required.

CHAPTER THREE

The Duties of Children

The Rights and Duties of Children

My account of the duties of parents is now complete. In chapter one, I classified and described the *duties* that parents have, whether or not they normally think of themselves as having such duties or need to be reminded of their existence; in chapter two, I set out the factors involved in selecting the *parents* who are to have these duties. Children have certain basic needs that must be met if their growth and survival are to be secured, and in societies like ours, where for better or worse child care has traditionally been the obligation of natural parents, all parents who do not surrender their children for adoption implicitly take upon themselves most of the responsibility for their upbringing. However, a moral theory of parenthood is itself only part of a moral theory of the parent-child relationship, for children, like parents, have duties as well as rights and interests. Childrearing practices designate certain persons to protect and promote the interests of young children (interests that cannot actually be isolated from the interests of parents and society), and children in turn have duties regarding those to whom the conventions of childrearing have assigned child-care responsibilities. The next task is to indicate what these duties are and to explain why children have them.

By shifting the discussion from parents' duties to children's duties, I do not mean to suggest that children have no rights against their parents, or that ascriptions of children's rights serve no purpose that could not equally well be served by talk about parents' duties. A few words about children's rights are therefore in order. Rights in general are of two kinds: claim rights and liberty rights, to use Hohfeld's nomenclature.[1] A liberty right is a right to noninterference by others, while a claim right is a right to some good or service from particular others. Infants and small children are incapable of claiming rights on their own, of course, but there is no logical or conceptual reason why individuals must be able to *make* claims before they can correctly be said to *have* claim rights. What is logically necessary is only that right-bearers have interests of their own to be protected by the right, and that the right be assertable by an agent, whether the right-bearers themselves or their representatives,[2] and both of these criteria are satisfied in the case of infants and very young children. Moreover, most of us believe that infants and small children do in fact have claim rights, because we regard parental care and supervision as something owed to them for their own sakes. The appeal to children's (claim) rights does not alter what was said earlier about the content of parents' duties; it only expresses the further moral judgment that these duties are owed to children as their due.

With respect to the liberty rights of children, these vary inversely with their claim rights. Parental authority is limited by the liberty rights of children and should be gradually re-

1. W. N. Hohfeld, *Fundamental Legal Conceptions as Applied in Judicial Reasoning* (New Haven: Yale University Press, 1964).

2. See Joel Feinberg, "Can Animals Have Rights?" in *Animal Rights and Human Obligations*, ed. Tom Regan and Peter Singer (Englewood Cliffs, N.J.: Prentice-Hall, 1976), pp. 190–196.

laxed as the child's moral and intellectual awareness matures. By the time children reach adulthood, their parents no longer have specifically parental authority over them or parental duties to them, though the children may still have duties to the parents, and these duties would set limits to the children's liberty rights. But the authority from which children are eventually to be freed, the dependence that is inherent in childrearing, could not itself be grounded on their liberty rights: this would be logically incoherent. The authority of parents is grounded on their duties of need-fulfillment, not their duties of respect, and the duties of need-fulfillment correspond to children's claim rights, not to their liberty rights. As an empirical matter, children need more than parental noninterference if they are to develop in such a way as to be capable of intelligent and responsible exercise of adult liberty rights. They will not even take an interest in liberty rights if their parents do not actively cultivate their capacities for self-determination while they are growing up. In addition, the duties of children (turning now to a different but related subject) are duties toward specific persons, their parents, and parents occupy a unique place in the lives of their children in part because the parents have, or at one time had, authority over them.

Children's claim rights correlate with the obligations of their parents, first and foremost, and the content and origin of parental duties have already been discussed. Parents who do not give their children, or at least try to give them, a decent upbringing have little or no moral claim to their obedience while young and to their gratitude when grown. On the other hand, there may be a problem with the social practice that allocates childrearing duties, not so much with parents. Parents may do the best they can for their children under a childrearing arrangement that is itself not justifiable. For example, when the interlocking interests of parents, children, and the community are considered, some other childrearing arrangement might be preferable to the one in which biological parents have primary responsibility for the upbringing of their children. While no *conclusive* justification of filial duties can be given without knowing whether the particular distribution of childrearing duties by a social practice is a justifiable distribution, children still have filial duties under these unfavorable circumstances.

The justification of the general system of rules that constitutes childrearing institutions is a higher-order account that takes into consideration three separate, though interrelated, sets of interests. Filial duties, too, can be grounded on such a higher-level account and can be given an institutional justification. For example, one might show that a certain pattern of filial duties is necessary for the stability and persistence of a just social scheme of distributing childrearing duties. The general practice of childrearing might be unstable in a society where prospective parents could not count on some kind of return for their childrearing efforts. But just as the justification of childrearing conventions must be distinguished from the justification of particular applications of these rules to particular cases, so too the justification of conventions regulating the relations of children to parents must be distinguished from the grounds for attributing filial duties to individual children. There are two very different questions here. One question asks why we should have practices that require certain things of (young and adult) children; the other asks for the criteria upon which individual (young and adult) children are judged to have duties to their parents. Utilitarian arguments are appropriate with regard to questions about the practices; but the moral judgments that most of us make about individual cases rely on other sorts of arguments. It is these that I shall develop and evaluate in the following sections.

There can be no single answer to the question "What is the moral basis of children's duties?" because the moral status of children changes over time. The satisfaction of children's legitimate interests occupies a privileged position in the early phases of the parent-child relationship, and during these years the liberty of children should be restricted in order to provide them with the benefits of protection and guidance, not to impose burdens on them for the sake of their parents. To provide these benefits, parents must have obedient children, but it must be an obedience that grows out of confidence in and respect for parents, for it is only this kind of obedience that can develop into the inner discipline essential to complete self-control. As children grow older and obedience to external authority is gradually transformed into the spontaneous expression of self-discipline, parents will find that they do not need to, and that it is unwise to, *demand* obedience from their children as they did before. Nevertheless, as long as the child remains dependent on the parents for protection and guidance, obedience is a necessary counterpart of parental authority.

The ground of grown children's duties is not so clear. Concepts of filial respect and honor are ancient and are explicitly included in the ethical principles of some religions, but today there is little agreement on the requirements of family life after the childrearing years are over. The duties of adult children can be conceptualized in various ways, as duties to repay debts, as duties of gratitude, or as duties of affection and friendship (see Aquinas's distinction between three bases of reciprocity—justice, gratitude, and friendship). When the duties are described in either of the first two ways, the suggestion is that adult children ought to do things for their parents because they are their parents. Less obscurely put, they ought to do things for their parents because they are owed for services rendered and efforts made during the childrearing years. When the duties are described as resulting from friendship rather than prior parental services, the terminology of "owing" seems inappropriate and misleading. Friendship between parents and their grown children is seen as giving rise to duties on the part of children and corresponding rights in parents to emotional support, favors, and services from them, and while the burdens of support, care, and concern born by parents during the childrearing years might partially explain the fact of friendship, they do not create or ground the duties. Family structure also has a bearing on the issue of adult children's duties. In a society where communal institutions carry the main responsibility for maintenance and socialization of children, and the main function of biological parents is to minister to their children's emotional needs, adult children may not have all the sorts of duties to their biological parents that they have under different family arrangements, or they may have one sort of duty to their rearers and another to their biological parents. They would not have special duties of indebtedness to their biological parents, perhaps, for their biological parents did not make any special sacrifices to rear them, but they might still have duties of friendship to them, for it is with their biological parents that they had the most intimate and intense relationship while growing up. Communal arrangements might generate duties of indebtedness to rearers, or more precisely, to the community, since they are its representatives, but the concern of friendship is for particular individuals, and the relatively impersonal care children receive from their guardians in a communal setting tends to inhibit the development of strong emotional attachments to them. For the sake of simplicity, however, I shall concentrate on filial duties as they arise within noncommunal forms of family life, where one and the same set of persons plays an outstanding role in the child's physical care, social rearing, and psychological development.

The Duties of Young Children: Obedience

Duties that dependent children have toward their parents, and that correspond to the parents' duties toward them, are duties of obedience. Young children are not merely to do something or not to do something, but to do something *be-cause* their parents want them to do it or to refrain from do-ing something *because* their parents want them to refrain from it. "Obedience," to quote Aquinas, "makes a person's will ready to carry out the will of another, i.e., a superior."[3] In contrast, obedience is not the basic duty of adult children. Duties of gratitude or friendship oblige them to do something on their own initiative that will benefit their parents and so are not merely special duties included within the general duty of obedience.

Grown children may, under certain circumstances, have a duty to obey their parents as an expression of gratitude or respect, but young children must obey their parents for other reasons as well. They must obey, or more generally cooperate with their parents' reasonable efforts on their behalf, because obedience and cooperation are necessary conditions of the successful performance of parental duties. Parents cannot carry out their responsibilities *to* their children when they meet with resistance *from* them. Young children must do what their more knowledgeable parents want them and tell them to do, if the failure to conform to these requirements would result in their not receiving the benefits of protection and guidance for which they are entrusted to their parents' care. It may be said, therefore, that what is distinctive about the duties of young children is that children have them "to" themselves, and only "toward" their parents. Young children's duty to facilitate their parents' reasonable efforts to discharge their duties has a very different rationale from (say) a bor-rower's duty to repay a creditor. Creditors claim the repay-ment as their due, but parents cannot in the same sense claim obedience as their due. It is the *child* to whom care, educa-tion, and socialization are due, and the duties of obedience characteristic of early childhood are grounded on the child's

3. *Summa Theologiae,* vol. 41, trans. T. C. O'Brien (New York: Blackfriars, 1972), 2a2ae, question 104, article 2.

legitimate interests and upon the child's need for parental control and supervision if these interests are to be protected and promoted. To be sure, parents may properly command obedience if it is called for but not forthcoming and apply sanctions to the child who does not heed their commands. But they are to do this primarily as temporary trustees of the child's welfare. By the time children are able to take complete responsibility for their own lives, childrearing duties have come to an end and so have the concomitant duties of obedience.

In the law, the rights and duties arising from the relation of parent and child are said to be reciprocal.[4] That is, parents are held to have a general duty to support, educate, and protect their children and a correlative general right to the custody and control of their children, to their services and earnings, and to obedience from them. (The doctrine of reciprocity has little practical significance while the family unit remains intact and is normally invoked only when this unity is destroyed by divorce or separation.) From a theoretical point of view, however, the doctrine is a misleading way of explaining the basis of parental authority, and should therefore be abandoned. It is not that parents are entitled to custody and obedience in return for support, education, and protection, or that they must support, educate, and protect in exchange for having custody and receiving obedience. It is rather that children have a right to parental services for as long as parents have a duty to provide them, and parents have a right to custody and obedience so that they can perform their childrearing duties, which duties are to be determined independently of any formula of reciprocity.

In a sense, duties of obedience are duties that children have to themselves rather than to their parents, but it would be wrong to conclude from this that they are simply pruden-

4. See "Note: Reciprocity of Rights and Duties Between Parent and Child," *Harvard Law Review*, 42 (1928–1929), pp. 112–115.

tial duties. Without obedience to parental authority, an obedience based on trust rather than fear, children will not develop the inner discipline essential to complete self-control, and without self-control children will not develop the self-confidence essential to self-respect. Parents, whose most important duty is to foster self-respect in their children, should not demand unconditional obedience, for the children's own self-esteem is closely linked to the esteem they have for their parents. Further, self-esteem is of value not only because without it the agent's ability to achieve further goals and to take satisfaction in what is accomplished thereby become problematic, but also because the absence of self-esteem makes one less likely to respect other persons and renders one liable to violate one's duties to them. In general, the duty of obedience is a *moral* as well as a prudential duty, because obedience makes it possible for children to develop autonomy and enjoy the primary goods, and these are necessary or highly conducive to the fulfillment of social duties. More immediately, we have a moral duty to obey our parents, because they are responsible for protecting us *and* those with whom we come into contact from our irrational impulses.

Very young children do not have any moral duties at all, toward their parents or anyone else, because they lack even a very limited capacity to see or understand or be aware of moral duties. Infants are not even capable of awareness of themselves as separate selves much less as selves with duties to others. Grown children, in contrast, do not have a general duty to follow parental instructions and expectations, because they have a right to determine for themselves how they shall lead their lives. In between infancy and maturity, however, even fairly young children can have some moral knowledge and can, on occasion, be legitimately held responsible for following their immediate natural inclinations rather than obeying their parents. Young children may not be able to grasp all the intricacies of a causal sequence or all the reasons justifying parental orders and prohibitions, but they may still be able to understand, at least in some rudimentary way, what it is to have a moral duty, and their sensitivity to moral duties will increase as they gain experience in making moral decisions and take advantage of opportunities for moral growth.

The duties of young children that correspond to parents' duties to them are based on a more general moral principle, which consists of the following three propositions: (1) If A has a duty to B to do x for B, then B has a right against A to x; (2) If B has a right against A to x, then B may be able to give it up and thereby release A from his duty to do x; (3) If B does not or cannot give up his right against A to x, then B has a duty to facilitate or at least not prevent A's discharging his duty to do x. Thus, where the right arises out of a contractual relationship or some other voluntary undertakings, the right-holder can always change the ethical situation by releasing the respondent of the right from his duty; inalienable rights, in contrast, cannot be given away or disposed of, and the cor-relative duties cannot be cancelled at will. For young children, the option in (2) is not available. Since they lack cogni-tive and emotional powers required for making fully rational decisions and are therefore likely to harm themselves or to fail to advance their own good, they are incapable of releasing their parents from their duties to them. (Parents' duties to care for their children are owed not just to the children them-selves, but also to society, and regardless of the children's level of maturity, they cannot release their parents from their role as agents of society.) By the time the children are able to re-lease their parents, many or all of the parents' duties to them will have ended.

Sometimes even young children have no general duty to obey particular parents. They surely have no duty to obey parents who have shown gross moral or psychological unfit-ness to raise their children or willful failure to give them a decent upbringing. Here again this is due to the fact that duties of obedience are contingent on parents discharging (or making sincere and reasonable efforts to discharge) their duties, not to the child's having released the parents from their childrearing duties.

What Grown Children
Ought to Do for Their Parents

There are many things that grown children can be expected or required to do for their parents, depending on their respective needs, abilities, and resources. Such duties are commonly thought to include supporting aged parents financially; taking care of sick parents; helping parents avoid the isolation and depression of retirement; proffering advice and criticism, not only when asked for but also when not asked for but needed; spending time with parents; sharing one's disappointments and achievements with them; giving parents the opportunity to be with and enjoy their grandchildren. Some of the things adult children ought to do fall under the heading of helping parents when in need or trouble of some kind; others are more appropriately described simply as showing that one cares about, values, and respects one's parents. If parents and children maintain close relations over a long period of time, duties to parents will often be accepted as natural and will not be felt as duties by grown children. Even basically affectionate relationships, however, usually go through cycles of closeness and distance, and sometimes the actions that grown children are required to perform may go against the grain or even seem oppressive.

Parents value the care and concern of their children not merely because they need support in difficult times or enjoy the affection and companionship of others, but also because they want to remain a vital part of their children's lives even after their children leave home and form new families of their own. Adults can provide for their own old age through insurance programs encouraged and subsidized by the society, or they can receive financial assistance from relatives as well as children, but ordinarily there are certain intimacies shared only among members of a nuclear family, and parents value what their children do for them precisely because it is their children who are doing it. Family ties and family feelings are integral to the lives of most of us, and parents who feel that their family is a tight-knit group and that the relationships within it are enduring and viable get particular satisfaction out of the services of their grown children. The services themselves are often less important to parents than what these services betoken: an awareness on the part of grown children that they are still members of the family from which they have departed, an interest in that family, and a desire to preserve and promote its common life.

The filial duties of grown children are commonly thought to involve more than just doing things for parents. Grown children, it is believed, have *special* duties to their parents, in the sense that they must give their parents preferential treatment. More precisely, it is when agents are considered in their private capacity that they are said to have a right or a duty to treat their parents preferentially. Legislators, judges, government administrators, etc., are expected to treat all people alike and to refrain in their official capacity from setting the interests of some particular individuals over those of others. If it is permissible at all for them to give preferential treatment to parents, it must be to parents as a class, not to their individual parents.

A does not treat B preferentially simply by giving him some good that he doesn't give to C, because the good may not be a good for C, or a good only to a very limited extent. A also does not treat B preferentially when he provides him with some good that is not thereby rendered unavailable for C. It is only when the good that A provides B is a good for both B and C, and when A's providing that good to B precludes his providing it to C, that we can properly speak of A preferring B to C. Thus I may choose to give money to my aged parents rather than to friends or charity, or to spend a lot of time with my parents rather than only some time with them and some with others, or even, as in Aristotle's example, to ransom my father out of the hands of brigands rather than to ransom myself. Whether or not I have to choose depends on a number of factors, including the nature of the service to be provided, my resources and abilities, my prior commitments, and the needs and expectations of the potential beneficiaries.

With the possible exception of cases in which individuals must choose between helping or benefiting their parents and helping or benefiting themselves or their own children, many would say that the claims of parents are prior to the claims of equally needy others. Exactly why this should be so will have to be investigated, but as a general point it is true that morality does not require us to treat everyone alike in all respects, or to adopt a purely impersonal standpoint in assessing the alternatives open to us in a given situation. We are permitted, perhaps even obligated, to treat preferentially people to whom we are related by special ties of affection, such as parents, children, spouses, friends, and lovers. The fact that someone is my parent, for example, is or can be a morally relevant reason for helping him rather than a stranger, when I cannot help both. The harder cases, of course, are when I must choose between my parents and others who stand in special relations to me. On Aquinas's view, I owe my parents not only respect, but also something that I do not owe my children, friends, etc.—reverence. Next to God, parents are the "closest sources of our existence and development" (*Summa*, question 101, article 1), and since our indebtedness to them is particularly great, they have the first claim on our services. This conclusion is more difficult to defend, however, when the duties of grown children are regarded as duties of friendship rather than duties of indebtedness. Preferential treatment of friends in general can be defended within a utilitarian framework by showing that the general welfare is best served by our regarding friends as having special claims on us. Since we have a special understanding of our friends' needs, and since we have limited resources at our disposal for bringing happiness to others, more happiness overall would result if each of us made the welfare of our friends his special concern. To show further that among all our friends we have special duties to our parents, we would have to argue that children know their parents' needs better than they know those of other friends. Yet this is often not the case. Children, in fact, tend to perceive their parents only in relation to themselves and, as George Bernard Shaw attests, tend not to conceive of them "as having had youth, passions, and weaknesses, or as still growing, yearning, suffering, and learning."[5]

The Duties of Grown Children:
The Owing Idiom

Parents bear the burdens of support, care, and concern for their children when they are young, and older children, it might be argued, ought to do things for their parents because they are owed for services rendered and efforts made during this period. On Aquinas's view, children are indebted to their parents for their earlier benefactions, indebted not in the sense of having a debt of repayment, i.e., a legal debt, where "the amount given is the measure of the recompense," but in the sense of having a debt of gratitude, i.e., a moral debt, where "the sentiment of the giver" is regarded "more than what he has given" (*Summa*, question 106, article 5). Alternatively, we might wish to confine the notion of indebtedness to cases where it seems appropriate to speak about some form of

5. "A Treatise on Parents and Children," *The World of the Child*, ed. Toby Talbot (New York: Jason Aronson, 1974), p. 380.

repayment, and to characterize gratitude as something owed to another for some other reason. Joel Feinberg takes this approach in the following passage:

> Many writers speak of duties of gratitude as if they were special instances, or perhaps informal analogues, of duties of indebtedness. But gratitude, I submit, feels nothing at all like indebtedness. . . . My benefactor once freely offered me his services when I needed them. There was, on that occasion, nothing for me to do in return but express my deepest gratitude to him. (How alien to gratitude any sort of *payment* would have been!) But now circumstances have arisen in which he needs help, and I am in a position to help him. Surely, I *owe* him my services now, and he would be entitled to resent my failure to come through.[6]

On this view, it would not be inconsistent to claim that grown children owe their parents many things and yet are not indebted to them.

The expression "duty of gratitude" requires some explanation. It does not mean the duty to feel grateful, for feeling grateful cannot be an immediate result of an act of the will. Otherwise, it would be appropriate to say to an ungrateful person, "Stop that at once! Feel grateful!" At the same time, we regard the disposition to feel gratitude for favors received from another as a virtue of character and the inculcation of this virtue as an aim of moral education. One may not be to blame for having a character defect with respect to any of the choices made at a time at which one already has the defect, but it may be appropriate to hold such a person at least partially responsible for *becoming* that sort of person, for not developing the feelings and attitudes involved in gratitude. Further, gratitude is a duty in that one has a duty to *express* gratitude in words or deeds or both. Even persons who can-

6. "Duties, Rights, and Claims," *American Philosophical Quarterly*, 3 (1966), p. 139.

not be criticized for having a defect of character may need to have pointed out to them what they should do in particular circumstances. Sometimes, perhaps because we have forgotten what our benefactors did for us or how valuable it was to us at the time, or because our benefactors need our help now when it is difficult for us to help them, we may have to be reminded that we owe them our gratitude and enlightened as to what would be a fitting response to their prior services.

There are a number of differences between the moral debt of gratitude and the legal debt of repayment (to use Aquinas's terminology) or between the duty of gratitude and the duty of indebtedness (to use Feinberg's). The first concerns the motivations of those to whom these duties are owed. Duties of gratitude are owed only to those who have helped or benefited us freely, without thought of personal gain, simply out of a desire to protect or promote our well-being.[7] The givers may hope for some return, but they do not give in expectation of it. Duties of indebtedness, in contrast, can be owed to those who were motivated primarily by self-interest or by the desire to help only insofar as this was believed to involve no risk or loss to themselves. A second difference has to do with how the notion of sacrifice figures in the account of these types of duties. An important factor in determining whether gratitude is owed is the degree of sacrifice or concession or exertion made by the person who helps or benefits us, because the more a person sacrifices for us (provided the sacrifice is voluntary), the more confident we are likely to be that what the person did for us was done out of a genuine desire to help us and not in order to gain favor. The more our benefactor's actions coincide with his or her own self-interest, the less sure we may be about what lies behind the decision

7. See Fred Berger, "Gratitude," *Ethics*, 85 (1975), pp. 298–309; also Balduin V. Schwarz, "Some Reflections on Gratitude," in *The Human Person and the World of Values*, ed. Balduin V. Schwarz (New York: Fordham University Press, 1960), pp. 168–191.

to help us and hence that gratitude is the appropriate response in the situation. In addition, sacrifice is an important factor in determining *what* is required in the way of specific performance. Though duties of gratitude do not necessarily presuppose sacrifice on the part of our benefactors, more is owed to one who has undergone significant personal hardship in aiding us than to one who has suffered little or not at all. In contrast, sacrifice is relevant to duties of indebtedness not because of what it tells us about the sentiments of the giver, but because of its possible relation to what is given. The person who sacrifices more may give us more as a result, so that we may have a duty to repay that person more. If, however, A has to sacrifice more than B to give us the same x (and we have consented to A's giving us x), then we have a duty to repay A for x, and only x, as well perhaps as a duty to do something extra for A as a token of our appreciation for those efforts. (In the case of filial duties of indebtedness, social customs may help define what constitutes adequate recompense.)

Another difference between duties of gratitude and indebtedness is brought out by asking the question "Do we have such duties with respect to benefits that are owed to us, that is, in situations where those providing them are fulfilling their duties to us?" If A has a duty to provide B with benefits, and this duty does not arise out of a contractual relationship or some other voluntary transaction between A and B, then B has no duty to repay A for those benefits. For example, if A promises C that he will do x for B in exchange for C's doing y for A, and C accepts, it is C, not B, who is indebted to A for x. Similarly for the so-called natural duties, i.e., the duties that obtain between all as equal moral persons, irrespective of their voluntary acts. If I am in need or jeopardy, and you can and do help me at little cost or risk to yourself, I have no duty to repay you for your service. You had a duty to help me under these circumstances, a duty that was not contingent on my performing some service in return. In contrast, I may

have a duty to show *gratitude,* even though those who pro- ✓
vided me with benefits were fulfilling duties that did not arise
out of any express or tacit agreement between us. This is so
for two reasons. First, gratitude "regards the sentiment of the
giver more than what he has given," and though you, the
giver, may have had a duty to help or benefit me in certain
ways, you may not have helped or benefited me solely or primarily because you regarded this as your duty. On the contrary, you may have done so because you cared for me or loved
me. Second, while you may just have been doing your duty,
the fulfillment of that duty may have been onerous for you,
and the fact that you undertook to perform certain duties
that are in themselves exceedingly demanding, or that you
did your duty in circumstances in which many of us would
not, may entitle you to some expression of appreciation from
the recipient of your benefits. Lifeguards, for example, are
responsible for the performance of those specific duties that
are attached to their office, including the rescuing of drown-
ing swimmers, and they should not demand or even expect
repayment from a rescued swimmer when they were only doing their job in rescuing him. But possibly because the job of
a lifeguard is inherently dangerous, or because this lifeguard
incurred more than the usual risk in this particular instance,
the rescued swimmer normally feels grateful to the lifeguard,
and he ought to show that gratitude in some way as well. (For
simplicity's sake, I assume here that the swimmer wanted to
be rescued.)

One of the factors that affect the issue of what we ought to
do to demonstrate our gratitude to another is the degree of
sacrifice or concession made by the one who confers a benefit
upon us. Another is the value of the benefit to us. Yet sometimes grantors do not know whether we will value their services or how highly, and they may think that they do us a
great service when in fact they do us no service at all (as
judged by us) or their services turn out to be less valuable to

us than they had thought they would. If in the first case the
grantor was proceeding on the basis of reasonable (though
unfortunately erroneous) assumptions about what we value,
and had reason to believe that we would want the services,
then it seems we ought to do something to demonstrate our
appreciation for the grantor's benevolent regard, for what he
or she *attempted* to do for us, though not for what was actually *done* for us. That we did not request those services does
not in itself entail that we have no duty to show gratitude for
them. Indeed, since gratitude is essentially a response to benevolence, it seems that we may have a duty to show gratitude
(at some point) for benefits that we did not voluntarily accept but only received, and for benefits which, at the time
they were provided, were judged to be benefits by the grantor
alone, and not by the recipient. But if we did not want the
grantor's services, and let him or her know it, a question
arises as to the grantor's true motives in helping us and therefore as to the appropriateness of gratitude in this situation. In
general, there is an important difference between the case
where benefits are bestowed *without* the voluntary consent of
the recipient, and the case where benefits are bestowed in
disregard of the recipient's voluntary choice. When my wishes
are known, but you claim that benevolence justifies you in
acting contrary to those wishes, you must overcome the presumption that one is better off when one's wishes are respected; when my wishes are not known, and you perform
services for me without my consent, your professed benevolence is not immediately suspect.

In contrast, merely receiving benefits or help from another
does not give rise to a duty of indebtedness. I cannot create
such a duty for you by going ahead and doing something
without your request or knowledge. Thus, if you come back
from vacation and find, to your surprise, that I have cut your
lawn while you were away, it might be ungrateful of you not
to do something in return. But it would not be unjust of you

to refuse to do so. This difference between gratitude and indebtedness with regard to the necessity of consent is not hard to explain. "Gratitude," according to Kant, "consists in honoring a person because of a kindness he has done for us,"[8] and to be sure, we ought to have some control over what others do for us, even out of kindness. Mature individuals have the right to refuse another's gifts, just as they have the right to turn down another's business propositions. But, I submit, it is only when we mistakenly suppose that the aim of gratitude is to rectify some moral imbalance, to restore something that rightfully belongs to another, that we feel the need to protect ourselves against others' kindnesses to the same extent as we protect ourselves against others' claims to repayment (namely, by stipulating that merely receiving benefits of others never creates a duty of gratitude to them).

With these general distinctions between gratitude and indebtedness in hand, we can proceed to consider the special case of grown children's duties to their parents. The question is this: Is it appropriate to describe the things that adult children ought to do for their parents as things *owed* to them? Blackstone, for one, thought so:

> The duties of children to their parents arise from a principle of natural justice and retribution. For to those who gave us existence we naturally owe subjection and obedience during our minority, and honor and reverence ever after; they who protected the weakness of our infancy are entitled to our protection in the infirmity of their age; they who by sustenance and education have enabled their offspring to prosper ought in return to be supported by that offspring in case they stand in need of assistance.[9]

8. *Doctrine of Virtue: Part II of The Metaphysics of Morals*, trans. Mary J. Gregor (New York: Harper, 1964), p. 123.
9. *Commentaries on The Laws of England*, vol. 1 (Philadelphia: J. B. Lippincott and Co., 1856), bk. 1, ch. 16, section 1.

On this view, the relation between parents and grown children is not unlike the *quid pro quo* exchange of a business transaction, where equity and justice dominate. Alternatively, we might argue that though grown children do owe their parents many things and ought to requite their benefits, the monetary metaphor of repayment is fundamentally at odds with the affectionate nature of family life.

To resolve this question, let us begin by applying one of the distinctions between duties of gratitude and duties of indebtedness discussed above. In order for claims to repayment to have any moral force, it must first be established that what parents claim repayment for is something that they were morally at liberty to give to or withhold from their children. If parents have any right to repayment from their children, it can only be for that which was either above and beyond the call of parental duty, or not required by parental duty at all. Thus grown children are not indebted (in the narrow sense) to their parents for having seen to it that they received an adequate education, adequate relative to the children's capabilities and to society's needs, for this was something that the parents, as parents, had a duty to do. They may actually have had a duty to do more, if parents in general ought to provide for their children in a manner commensurate with the parents' particular means and station in life. Parents might also do things for their children which they have no duty to do, as when they continue to support them past the age of majority and they are not in such a feeble and dependent condition physically and mentally as to be unable to support themselves. The principles that govern the content and duration of parental duties serve as a reference point for assessing the validity of parents' claims to repayment from their grown children, and sometimes parents can be shown to have no right to repayment for their prior services simply by appealing to standards of parental care.

On the other hand, it is not necessary for parents to go

beyond their duty, or to do things for their children that they have no duty to do, before it is appropriate to ask what the children must do to show their gratitude to the parents. For though our parents are under a duty to give us a decent upbringing and to care for us to the best of their ability, love is essential to a really good upbringing and sometimes great sacrifices have to be made to provide it, and it is the motive of the giver that gratitude regards, not the obligatoriness of the actions. Indeed, since the degree of obligation to gratitude is to be judged in part by how beneficial the service was to the obligated subject, and since the duties of parents are duties to protect and promote the child's serious interests, grown children may actually have more of a duty to show gratitude for benefits that were owed them than for those that were not.

It is not only because parents were merely discharging the duties of parenthood that their children have no duty of indebtedness to them. For it is also necessary that the benefits received be voluntarily accepted, and young children and infants are not able to choose not to accept the benefits of being born, fed, clothed, nurtured, and educated. Young children cannot exercise genuine choice with respect to the benefits of early care, and until their capacities of rationality and self-control develop sufficiently, they have a duty to cooperate with their parents in their childrearing efforts. Even when parents do what they have *no* duty to do, perhaps in expectation of some recompense from their children when they grow up, they do not thereby make it obligatory for their children to repay them. For when the children are older and have the real capacity for choice, they may quite rationally decide that they would rather not have received these benefits at all than be indebted to their parents for having bestowed them on them. They may feel that they would rather be somewhat less well off than take the lower place of the dependent in relation to their parents. Older children's refusal to accept this dependency cannot, of course, alter the fact that they did receive those nonobligatory parental benefits while young and did (possibly still do) profit from them. But the freedom to decide when, and to whom, one shall become indebted, cannot be abridged in advance by unilateral parental decisions.

Filial gratitude, in contrast, is not to be thought of as the price of parental benefits, a price that older children may not be willing to pay for benefits they could have gotten along without. It is rather an acknowledgement of the generosity of parents. As Kant puts it,

> the minimum of gratitude requires one not to regard a kindness received as a burden one would gladly be rid of (since the person so favoured stands a step lower than his benefactor, and this wounds his pride), but to accept the occasion for gratitude as a moral kindness—that is, an opportunity given one . . . to combine *sensitivity* to others' benevolence . . . with the *cordiality* of a benevolent attitude of will. (*Doctrine,* p. 124)

If children are sometimes afraid to allow themselves to feel grateful to their parents, it is perhaps because they are trying to break free of their emotional dependency on their parents and see any admission of gratitude as an acknowledgment of their parents' superior status. To show gratitude to your parents may seem to be like asking them for a loan when you are trying to prove to yourself and to them that you can be financially self-supporting. Under these circumstances, it is not surprising to hear an older child say, "I didn't ask for your sacrifices on my behalf while I was growing up, so I owe you no gratitude for them." The denial of consent, and hence of any duty of gratitude, is the child's way of maintaining equality with the parents, as well perhaps of defending himself against their persistent accusations of ingratitude. However, the claim that I have no duty of gratitude to X (merely) because I have not consented to X's benefits or help rests on a confusion. As a general attitude, it betrays a deep-rooted suspicion about the motivations of others, an unwillingness or inability to believe that others can be motivated purely by the desire to help us, without any expectation of return from us.[10]

Assuming that grown children do have a duty of gratitude to their parents for benefits received when young, can they ever completely discharge this duty? Kant's view is that gratitude in general is a perpetual or "holy" duty, from which it follows that the duty of filial gratitude, as a special instance, is also perpetual:

> Gratitude must also be considered, more especially, a *holy* duty. . . . A moral object is holy if the obligation with regard to it cannot be discharged completely by any act in conformity with the obligation (so that no matter what he does, the person who is under obligation always remains under obligation). . . . One cannot, by any requital of a kindness received, rid oneself of the obligation for this kindness, since one can never win away from the benefactor his *priority* of merit: the merit of having been the first in benevolence. (*Doctrine,* p. 123)

Kant might have gone on as follows. You have a number of possible objects for your benevolence, but you select me. I ought to be grateful to you not merely because you *helped* or benefited me without expectation of reward, but because you chose *me* to benefit when there were others you might have benefited instead. Further, I am not now in the same position with respect to my benevolence as you were with respect to yours: I must benefit *you* when the circumstances demand it. No matter what I do to show you my gratitude, even if I do the same thing for you that you did for me, I cannot do enough, because I am always only responding to your benevolence. A duty of indebtedness, in contrast, is an "ordinary duty," because repayment completely cancels the debt.

10. Individuals who lack self-respect do not believe that they are worthy of another's caring, and so cannot feel truly grateful.

For Kant, the more beneficial your favor, and the more un-selfishly you bestow it on me, the more gratitude I owe you. These factors, it seems, ought to affect the form that my gratitude should take as well as the duration of my duty. Although first in benevolence, you may only have done me a small favor at little or no personal cost, and it seems that I can compensate for being second in benevolence by doing you a great favor in return at great personal cost. The case of parents and children is particularly complicated, however, for gratitude is owed to parents when they (a) benevolently do more in their child's interest than they are morally required to do, (b) benevolently do things in their child's interest that they have no duty to do, or (c) discharge their duties at great difficulty to themselves,[11] and the fact of having been first in benevolence seems to carry more moral weight in (a) and (b) than in (c). The argument that we can never do enough to show our gratitude to our parents and are, therefore, forever obligated to them because we can never confer on them benefits like those they conferred on us, is open to the following objections: It may or may not be possible for us to give our parents the same or an equivalent benefit, but a great benefit does not entitle our benefactors to much in the way of gratitude if they had a duty to bestow it on us and did so at little personal cost. In addition, even if some form of reciprocation is required and the degree of obligation to gratitude is not slight, we do not need to give our benefactors the same or an equivalent benefit in order to fully discharge our duty of gratitude to them. To claim otherwise is once again to confuse gratitude with indebtedness.

The Duties of Grown Children: Friendship

The owing approach, as I conceive of it, is oriented toward past actions, in that duties of indebtedness and duties of

11. As in economically and culturally disadvantaged families.

gratitude rest on one's own previous acts and/or the previous acts of other persons. In the case of gratitude, the fact that parents have performed certain acts in the past by itself creates certain obligations for children. Grown children may not have much affection for, or be particularly fond of, their parents; they may not desire their parents' company because they do not feel that they have much in common with their parents. However, since duties of gratitude result from prior services and not from the relationship that presently exists between grown children and their parents, these facts do not in themselves show that grown children have no duties to their parents. Of course, neither is this relationship irrelevant to the duties children owe their parents, for the presence or absence of love and friendship between parents and their grown children may tell us something about the kind of upbringing they received. But there are many factors that can prevent the development of friendship between parents and children or that can undermine a friendship that already exists, and even good and loving parents may become estranged from their children when they grow up.

The duty to show gratitude to parents is not the same as the duty to treat parents as friends or the duty to become their friends. Gratitude is not properly friendliness toward benefactors, but rather respect for them, and the relationship of mutual respect between benefactor and grateful recipient is different from the relationship of mutual affection between one friend and another. The principle of gratitude regulates relations between individuals whether or not there is any intimate personal relationship between them. Moreover, while gratitude (unlike indebtedness) may sometimes lead to friendship, the element of choice necessarily enters into the latter. We choose our friends, and we do not have a duty to act on the feelings and desires that motivate actions done out of friendship unless we are already involved in an ongoing or budding friendship with someone. Even in the absence of a

conscious decision to be someone's friend, friendship is still a
voluntary relationship, for it would not be friendship at all
if the parties involved did not endorse or consent to it.

Though gratitude toward parents can blend with and
strengthen the claims that arise out of affectionate parent-
child relationships themselves, friendship and benevolence
are distinct sources of duty. Parents make sacrifices to give
their children proper care and rearing, and children show
their appreciation for what was done, but the feelings characteristic of friendship involve more than appreciation for services rendered. To be sure, if friends are indebted to one another, they will want to discharge their debts, and if they
have performed kindnesses for one another, they will want to
express their gratitude. But friends view these acts in the context of a broader pattern of friendly interactions, interactions
that involve shared activities and interests as well as reciprocal services, and not simply as discrete, isolated incidents. They
are committed to their relationship as such and seek to preserve and strengthen it as something good in itself. Out of this
mutual commitment spring duties of friendship, duties that
can persist after debts have been repaid and gratitude has
been shown.

Friends have duties to one another because, having ac-
knowledged and consented to their special relationship, each
must do what he or she can to nourish that friendship and to
work out problems and tensions that arise between them during the course of their friendship. To blame our "friends"
for not acting as friends ought to act is to accuse them of a
kind of breach of understanding (those who wrong others by
not discharging a duty of indebtedness to them are also guilty
of a breach of understanding, though of a very different
kind). In Henry Sidgwick's words,

> As all love is understood to include a desire for the
> happiness of its object, the profession of friendship seems

to bind one to seek this happiness to an extent proportionate to such profession. . . . Since the profession of friendship—though the term is used to include affections of various degree—must imply a greater interest in one's friend's happiness than in that of men in general, it must announce a willingness to make more or less considerable sacrifices for him, if occasion offers. If then we decline to make such sacrifices, we do wrong by failing to fulfill natural and legitimate expectations.[12]

Duties of friendship are not essentially duties to do things in return for benefits received or sacrifices made, and hence it is inappropriate to regard them as duties *owed* to friends. Parents who say to their children, "We are friends (or at least I thought we were), and friends have the right to make certain demands of one another," are not trying to justify a claim to repayment or gratitude (indeed, gratitude does not seem to be the kind of thing that can be demanded), but are asking the children to live up to their commitment to their mutual relationship. The children can then either do what the parents want them to do, or reject one of their assumptions: that a relationship of friendship actually exists, that they (the children) at least led them to believe that such a relationship existed, or that even friends can be expected to do what the parents ask them to do.

The profession of friendship implies a willingness to do things for our friends even if our own interests are not promoted thereby or we have to make certain sacrifices for them. But a friendship would never begin, or would come to an end, if the individuals involved did not all regard their relationship as being, on balance, a good thing for them to be in (profitable, pleasurable, or valuable in some other way). Thus there can be no friendship between parents and children when parents continually expect their children to sacrifice

12. *The Methods of Ethics* (Chicago: University of Chicago Press, 1962), p. 258.

their own interests for the sake of their friendship, or when parents act as though their friendship gives them the right to make incessant demands on their children's lifestyles. Further, while the duties of friendship are not prudential duties, they do presuppose a relationship that is on balance beneficial to all concerned. (Gratitude, in contrast, does not *presuppose* an interpersonal relationship: it *establishes* one by some form of reciprocation.) Filial duties of friendship may sometimes be quite disagreeable, but they cannot be so disagreeable so often that they stifle the affection from which those duties arise.

Though parents and adult children sometimes like to think of one another as friends, realizing this objective is often hampered by serious obstacles. There are psychological obstacles. We do not, as it were, meet our parents for the first time when we are adults. Our love for them is mingled with memories of former dependencies, and we may feel that we can never be fully the equal of those who know us so much more intimately than we can ever know them. Or we may never altogether forgive our parents for things they did or failed to do. There are also sociological obstacles. In a mobile, rapidly changing society, the child's exit from the family can lead to a loss of affection for or interest in parents and to a diversion of that affection or interest to others. If the relationship with our parents is perceived to have been an affectionate, supportive, nonmanipulative, and honest one, we may make a special effort to resist our growing estrangement from our parents and to find ways of strengthening our ties to them. But sometimes, despite our best efforts, life changes, and the impact of external events preclude the intimacy that friendship demands.

Whether or not genuine friendship is possible between parents and their grown children depends in large measure on the parents' sensitivity to their children's developing capacity for friendship, and on the parents' willingness to deal with their children less and less as superiors and more and more as equals. If the relationship of the early childrearing years is to lead to friendship, it is necessary that parents not wait until their children reach adulthood before admitting them into their lives in a serious way. They must try to interest them in their affairs, confide in them, and seek their advice while they are still young and in a manner appropriate to their level of experience and understanding. As Locke puts it, as children

> grow up to the use of reason, the rigour of government [should] be . . . gently relaxed, the father's brow more smoothed to them, and the distance by degrees abated. . . . Nothing cements and establishes friendship and good-will so much as confident communication of concernments and affairs.[13]

Further, in a society (like ours) where the family is a tiny closed circle and family feeling is therefore particularly intense, the child's exit from the family, via change of residence, work, or marriage, may actually promote the development of friendship between the child and the parents. The child's departure from the home gives them a chance to put a little emotional distance between themselves and to find new (less authoritative, less submissive) ways of relating to one another.

Assuming that parents and older children can be friends, what does this friendship offer children?[14] Personal relationships are many and various, and they satisfy the following interdependent criteria to varying degrees: (a) the responsiveness criterion—the members of the relationship are responsive to each other's peculiarities, individual requirements, temperaments, etc.; (b) the inclusion-of-self criterion—the relationship calls upon and integrates several important parts of

13. John Locke on Education, ed. Peter Gay (New York: Teachers College, 1971), pp. 30, 74.
14. I am not suggesting that the benefits children reap from friendship with their parents are among the causes of, or a basis for, this friendship.

its members' personalities; (c) the spontaneity criterion—the members of the relationship step outside of their official roles and interact in an uninhibited and unforced way. Friendships in general score high in each of these areas, and depending on the degree of affection, intimacy, sharing, and trust involved, some friendships score higher than others.[15] As regards friendship with parents, this can be among a person's closest and most valuable. Parents and children often have very similar styles of mind or ways of thinking, and this can make for a high degree of empathy. In some cases, friends may not know exactly where they stand with one another or how far they can go with one another before putting too much of a strain on their relationship, but children who are confident of their parents' continued love feel that their relationship is resilient enough to withstand open criticism of parents' actions or beliefs, and this can strengthen the bond between them. Further, family life in the modern nuclear family is extremely introverted and private, and this exclusivity often continues long after parental authority has been relinquished, making possible special intimacies between parents and their grown children. Finally, close friendship with parents (like parenthood itself) is inclusive of self to a high degree. Friendship between parents and children is possible only if parents relinquish control and allow their adult children the independence befitting an adult. It develops as children come to terms with their prior dependency and work to integrate their past immature selves into their present mature ones. Through a deepening relationship with parents, the child's self-knowledge and self-respect are enlarged and enhanced.

15. If Aristotle is right that the happy man needs friends (*Nicomachean Ethics*, 1169b3–1170b19), then parents ought to give their children the kind of upbringing that is conducive to the formation of strong personal attachments later in life. Contrary to what Rousseau appears to believe, friendship is not incompatible with autonomy, and the capacity for friendship should perhaps be included among the objectives of parenting.

One final point about friendship as an explanation of filial duty should be made. In permitting others to intervene in their children's lives, parents delegate some of their parental authority and discretion, thereby bestowing on their agents a right to command obedience from their children. However, the contacts between child and caretaker may be too brief, professional, or routine to form the basis of a lasting friendship. Children develop friendships only with those caretakers who meet their emotional needs for affection, companionship, and stimulating intimacy, and it is only this kind of parent-child relationship that can give rise to duties of friendship and their corresponding rights.

The Interplay Between Gratitude and Friendship

If a casual acquaintance unexpectedly favors me with assistance, then I ought to demonstrate my gratitude by my thanks and by means of some benefit I can give in return. In a family that is as it should be, of course, assistance is not unexpected. There is an understanding between parents and children (an understanding that need not be expressly formulated) that parents will act in the interests of their children and provide them with the things that it is good for them to have, and that children will cooperate with their parents as they attempt to do so. The children trust the parents' judgments of right and wrong and their altruistic intentions on their behalf, and count on their support and guidance as they grow in maturity. Yet the fact that growing children expect and have a right to expect certain kinds of help and assistance from their parents which they do not expect or have a right to expect from comparative strangers, in no way shows that children cannot have duties of gratitude to their parents, even for those actions that are included in the parents' moral duties.

The love and affection that normally unite parents and children in the early childrearing years is not friendship, because friendship is, on the whole, an equal partnership, and during these years parents do most of the giving and children most of the taking. Young children have a limited, though ever-growing, understanding of the contribution their own activities can make to the plans and projects of their parents. But this early relationship can perhaps lead to friendship if parents are intimate with their children as they are growing up and if external conditions are not unfavorable. Older children who do become friends with their parents do not thereby cease to owe them gratitude for benefits received and sacrifices made on their behalf while young. Older children not uncommonly do things for their parents partly out of friendship and partly out of gratitude, though it may not be until their friendship comes to an end or is temporarily on the wane that the children are able to differentiate clearly between these two motivational determinants.

A grown child does not have duties of gratitude to his or her parents *because* there is an ongoing friendship between them. Acts of gratitude and acts of friendship are not obligatory for the same reason. But the presence or absence of an ongoing friendship between older children and their parents is relevant to deciding *what* they should now do to show their gratitude to their parents. The way in which we show we care about, value, and respect our parents depends to a large extent on the kind of relationship we have with them. When our parents are also our friends, we should try to express our gratitude in ways that deepen, or do not damage, this friendship. Moreover, since some parent-child relationships are friendly, some cool and distant, and since parent-child friendships themselves exemplify different patterns of affection and sharing, need and response, there is no one act, or specific type of act, that is invariably an appropriate expression of gratitude to parents. Some parents may not be receptive to certain kinds of help from their children, even if they are friends (e.g., financial assistance, or moving into the child's

home after the death of a spouse), and children who insensi-
tively press their services on their parents may only succeed
in arousing their anger and resentment. At the same time,
parents who are friends with their adult children usually
want to preserve this friendship and do not ask for certain
forms of assistance if they have reason to believe that meeting
these requests would put a severe strain on their relationship.

PART III

Problems of Family Policy

CHAPTER FOUR

Equal Opportunity
and the Family

The Family as a Limit to Equal Opportunity

Parents have two distinct sorts of duties with respect to their children. They have a duty, first, to expose their children to the psychological conditions that facilitate the development of their capacities for self-determination, or autonomy. Second, they have a duty to raise their children in such a way as to promote their self-fulfillment, for which primary goods like self-respect and health are necessary. Self-determination itself may also be a causally necessary condition for the achievement of self-fulfillment, but since the value we place on autonomy in making certain choices is not simply derived from our choices promoting our welfare, happiness, or interests, the parents' duty to promote their children's eventual autonomy cannot be subsumed under their duty to promote their personal well-being.

The interrelated ideals of self-determination and self-fulfillment, both of which play essential roles in the discussion of parents' childrearing duties, are conditioned by the distribution of primary social goods in adult society. In a just society, parents ought to raise their children to pursue their ends within the constraints imposed by the public conception of justice, and as far as they are able, they ought to encourage and prepare their children to take advantage of the rights and opportunities available to them in adult society. But the institution of the family, within which parents ready their children for the opportunities offered them outside the home, is itself a basic institution of society to which principles of social justice and equal opportunity ought to apply. A just society, it seems, must give each person not only an equal opportunity for educational and occupational attainment, but also an equal opportunity to enjoy the benefits of early training and nurture. (How this equal opportunity is to be achieved is a major concern of this chapter.) All children should have an equal opportunity to develop their genetically fixed potential for the acquisition of talents and skills, to pursue their natural preferences, and to actualize their basic tendencies. To the extent that they do not, as a result of inherent features of the family system, justice and the family are incompatible.

One might try to defend the family (if defense it needs) by regarding both the natural distribution of abilities and talents and the variations of early upbringing as parts of the "natural lottery,"[1] and then arguing that a just society should not attack or try to eliminate these fortuitous distinctions. It should rather work to ameliorate or moderate as far as possible the effects of these contingencies on the later distribution of social rewards. In other words, the pursuit of equal opportunity should stop at the threshold of the family. But what reasons can be given for including the peculiarities of familial training and nurture in the natural lottery and for excluding them from the purview of the principle of equal opportunity? One suggestion might be that the family is natural, in the sense of being an institution established by nature rather than society.

1. The term is used in John Rawls, *A Theory of Justice* (Cambridge, Mass.: Belknap Press, 1971).

But though this claim looks at first empirical, it is hard to see how any available evidence could actually settle the question of whether natural man lives in families. Further, it is true that the traits that are influenced by a person's genes are also influenced by the environmental conditions present in that person's family and that better than average home environments tend to go along with genetic advantages, worse than average environments with genetic disadvantages. But difficult though it may be to separate the genetic and environmental components of parental influence, this does not really explain why we ought to treat specifically *family* background as if it were a natural accident of birth. Again, it will not do to argue that opportunities are grasped by individuals and that persons must already have identities, formed through interactions within the family, before the issue of opportunity can come up for society. We might be able to show, however, that the conception of self fostered by the family is *preferable* to the conceptions fostered by nonfamilial childrearing arrangements. (I say more about this on pp. 217–23, where I discuss the development of the capacity for love.)

Advocates of the position I am discussing, viz., that the principle of equal opportunity should govern only extra-familial institutions and not the family itself, might recast their claim in terms of respecting parents' rights.[2] To better understand this form of the argument, let us first distinguish between two senses of the term "family background." Family background may refer either to the socioeconomic status of parents or to characteristics of the family of orientation other than its socioeconomic status. Socioeconomic status includes parents' economic status, occupation, and educational attainment; the other factors include the size of the parental family, the child's position among the siblings and their relations with each other, and the educational climate in the home

2. To evaluate this claim, of course, we need a theory of parents' rights. I provide this in chapter one.

(the latter refers to such things as parental involvement with the child, organization of the child's physical and temporal environment, and the parents' attitudes toward achievement). The indices of family socioeconomic level give us an indirect measure of the environmental quality of the home and account for some of the variation in children's prospects of success later in life. But there is also significant variability in childrearing practices that is due to traits and conditions of families other than socioeconomic status.[3] Even within the same social class, parents expend varying amounts of time and effort on their children's growth and development, are more or less responsive to their children's desires and curiosity, have different attitudes toward learning and success, and provide their children with wider and narrower ranges of life possibilities. These differences in outlook and approach, positively associated with but not completely determined by social class, affect both the development of natural abilities and the motivation to use them.

Among the forces responsible for the transmission of a high degree of social and economic inequality from generation to generation, the advantages or disadvantages conferred by one's family of origin are especially strong. Children inherit the advantages (or disadvantages) of their parents' superior (or inferior) socioeconomic status in the form of material wealth, parental pull or connections, and investments in books, tutors, preparatory schools, and the like to speed development in an enriched environment. Since children start life with the economic status of their parents, we can positively affect the opportunities of children by reducing the extent of economic inequality among their parents. This can be done through the provision of direct income supports to supplement low wages or through the equalization of pay scales for different jobs, coupled with income supports for those who cannot or

3. See Peter Blau and Otis Duncan, *The American Occupational Structure* (New York: John Wiley and Sons, 1967), ch. 9.

should not work. Further, these policies do not interfere with the freedom of parents to make basic decisions about how they shall lead their lives and how they shall bring up their children; in fact, they increase the choices of many families. It is the hardships and head starts created by unequal economic origins rather than such parental influences on the ability and productivity of children as genetic endowments, family size, and upbringing that these policies are designed to attack.

Even if the incomes of parents were substantially equalized, however, this would not nullify the effect of family social background on children's educational and occupational opportunities. The quality of a child's home environment is affected not only by the income but also by the degree of education of the parents and their position within the hierarchy of work relations. Moreover, children raised by their natural parents in different families do not all have an equal chance to compete for social rewards if the conditions that are causally effective for the attainment of these rewards vary among families within the same sector of society. There is, in fact, no way to expose all children to uniform early environmental influences as long as society continues to accord a privileged position to the personal childrearing preferences of parents (preferences that differ in part because parents' conceptions of the good life differ) and allows parents to create whatever environment of influence they wish for their children, subject only to minimal standards of parental fitness and social responsibility. Society can move toward greater equality in the life chances of all children by making available to parents economic, social, and educational support services. But since such policies do not intervene in the family, since they preserve intact the decision-making power of parents, children will actually benefit from these services only to the extent that their parents voluntarily avail themselves of them.

Though the privacy of the family may not shield parents

from state intervention when they are guilty of serious physical abuse or refuse to let their children attend school, equal opportunity for children would seem to require a more extensive and fundamental abridgment of parents' rights over children and parental autonomy in childrearing. The issue raised here is not whether the state is ever justified in substituting its own judgment for the judgment of parents with regard to the care of a particular child. Clearly the state as *parens patriae* may and ought to do so in certain circumstances. It is rather whether, given the fact that children raised in the family system do not have completely equal chances to acquire desirable positions and other benefits later in life, the system itself (and its attendant notions of parental autonomy, family privacy, and family integrity) should be abandoned.

"Family life," Mary Jo Bane argues,

> is incompatible with some aspects of equality among citizens. As long as children are raised even partially by families, their opportunities can never be equal; however much resources are equalized, affection, interest, and care remain idiosyncratically centered in families.[4]

It may be that in our class society there is considerable occupational and social mobility, and one's status is not ascribed completely on the basis of the family into which one was born but rests primarily on one's achievements. Still, achievement depends on competence and motivation to succeed, and these in turn are conditioned by the educational and emotional climate of one's family of origin. How should we react to the idiosyncracies of parental affection, interest, and care that influence the educational attainments and occupational chances of children? The appeal to parents' rights does not have to deny that the inherited benefits of early training and nurture create unfair head starts or handicaps in the

4. *Here to Stay: American Families in the Twentieth Century* (New York: Basic Books, 1976), p. 142.

competition for schooling and jobs. The argument may rather be that some types of inherited advantage are more tolerable than others and that, in particular, the competitive advantages and disadvantages resulting from parental as opposed to nonfamilial upbringing are more tolerable than those due to (say) discrimination against inherited traits like race or religion. Society has no right to nullify the differential effects of differences in family upbringing or to attack this source of inequality directly, because the demands of justice for children must be balanced against and limited by the values of parental autonomy, family privacy, and integrity.

The family is not synonymous with the isolated or privatized family. The latter tends to retard the emancipation of children by segregating them from the adult life of the community, and we can move to counteract this tendency without having to place the upbringing of children in the hands of public agencies. The problem of securing equal opportunity for children, on the other hand, presents a much more serious challenge to the institution of the family and to the traditional values surrounding and protecting family life. Yet the basis of our commitment to these traditional values, unlike that of our commitment to equal opportunity, is something of a mystery. Is there a reasonable basis for our reluctance to abandon the family, despite objections from the standpoint of justice, or is this simply a case where the force of habit and custom prevent us from doing what we ought to do? It is this question to which I shall return later in this chapter, after we have seen how present childrearing arrangements would have to be altered to provide greater equality of opportunity for children.

Equal Opportunity and Access to Favorable Family Environments

The notion of equal opportunity requires, at a minimum, that persons not be debarred from competing for offices and positions on the basis of characteristics that have no rational relationship to the capacity or desire for success in those offices and positions. Jobs and schooling should be formally open to all strictly according to competence qualifications, and factors like class, race, religion, and sex should not in themselves bar access to jobs or to the means (education and training) needed to qualify for them. Yet an equal chance to compete for jobs and schools for which one is qualified is small comfort to individuals who, because of social background, do not have an equal chance to acquire these qualifications and to develop their native potentials. Though no one is stigmatized with the stamp of inferiority merely because he or she belongs to a certain class or race, and success must be earned or merited, the qualifications that are relevant to successful performance may in fact be more easily available to persons from some groups than others. When society does not attempt to compensate for the inequities of social position, some persons will be more equal to the opportunities formally available to them than others. The former will receive education and training that develop their natural abilities, that provide them with inspiring role models, and that encourage them to strive for success and to pursue certain sorts of jobs. The latter will have more modest educational and occupational aspirations, because they cannot hope for anything better, and diminished hopes render them liable to underestimate their own merits.

To make equality of opportunity more effective, therefore, we have to do more than remove negative legal and quasi-legal constraints on equal opportunity. In addition to providing formal guarantees of nondiscrimination at the point where an individual is being considered for a certain job or for admission to a certain school, we have to take positive steps to overcome earlier, socially induced inequalities of opportunity that have a cumulative effect on an individual's present competitive position. Otherwise we merely substitute one form of discrimination for another: the injustice of applying the same criteria of selection to individuals who did not all have an equal chance to satisfy these criteria, for the injustice of awarding jobs and socially desirable positions according to irrelevant characteristics like race and sex.

To confer or withhold desirable positions and offices according to irrelevant inborn characteristics or initial social positions is to separate success from ability and effort. Those who are fortunate cannot therefore properly take pride in their success; those who are unfortunate are denied the opportunity to achieve what they are able to achieve and willing to work for, and hence they feel powerless to shape the course of their own lives. They are deprived of an important source of self-respect and satisfaction, the satisfaction that comes from attaining social prestige and status in recognition of one's skills and hard work. Even with the opportunity to fulfill their natural capacities, of course, those who lose in competition are bound to feel disappointed, especially if they have been taught to fear failure and to place a high value on achieving preeminence. But without the opportunity, the disappointment and frustration of failure are even more difficult to accept.

Children acquire the motivation to achieve in part through identification with adults in positions of respect and authority, their parents, for example, and parents whose own prospects of success are severely restricted by their class position tend to transmit their feelings of inferiority and hopelessness to their children. Specific childrearing practices in different social and economic classes also exert a profound influence on the development of children's achievement-related motivations, quite apart from the degree of occupational and social mobility that exists in society. (Equal opportunity does not imply equal results, for considerable economic and social mobility is compatible with great inequalities in the distribution of education, income, wealth, and prestige.) Whether consciously or not, parents tend to impart to their children lessons derived from the conditions of life of their own class and tend to develop orientations and ambitions in their children that prepare them for adequate job performance in the occupational roles of the parents. In this way, our range of life choices is limited by the values and orientations of our parents so that we may not even think it appropriate for us to compete for positions of high status and prestige. And even if we do want to rise in the social and occupational hierarchy, we may have little confidence in our ability to do so.

It is through the family (and school as well) that social class shapes the fundamental personality structures of children; and though the family is not itself a competitive society, there is a kind of preselection process at work here whereby individuals acquire the personality traits and desires upon which later competitive success depends. The contingencies of social class can be regulated only imperfectly, therefore, as long as the institution of the family exists in its present form. (Aside from the fact that the class attitudes of parents affect children's prospects of success, the idiosyncracies of family upbringing lead to unequal chances between individuals.) At least two further steps suggest themselves: the first would alter our present childrearing arrangements to the extent of eliminating the traditional link between childbearing and childrearing; the second would involve the complete elimination of family upbringing and its replacement by some form of common upbringing.

In the first arrangement, children would continue to be reared in families, but at birth they would be randomly assigned to different families in a given population, or perhaps selectively assigned to different families in different social and economic classes, depending on the characteristics of their natural parents. The children of parents with lower than average intelligence, for example, would be matched with adoptive parents who could provide them with better than average home environments for the development of intelligence, and the children of parents with above average intelligence would be matched with parents who could not provide them with such environments. Neither method—random selection, selective assignment—would equalize the distribution of genetic traits or prevent parents from passing on their class attitudes to their children. At the same time, however, neither would simply reshuffle children, leaving things essentially unchanged. For both methods would weaken the correlation of genetic and environmental (dis)advantages and, as a result, lessen the differential impact of family background on children's chances of success. (This proposal rests on the assumption that certain traits with a significant genetic component are positively associated with opportunities for educational and occupational attainment.)

A proposal that bears some resemblance to that of redistributing children at birth is offered by some children's rights advocates. John Holt, for example, argues that the law should give children of all ages the opportunity to seek out and choose "secondary guardians." Secondary guardians are persons, other than natural or adoptive parents, who enter into a voluntary and provisional relationship with children for the purpose of supervising their upbringing. The relationship of secondary guardian is "entered into by the mutual agreement of the child and secondary guardians, either of whom would have the right to end the agreement and the relationship."[5] In contrast, primary guardians, i.e., natural or adoptive parents, have nonreciprocal obligations to their minor children, and must always be available to them if they decide to live at home under their care. This scheme may stimulate the development of independence and self-direction in children and, through the legally protected freedom to select their own childrearing environments, may also lead to an improvement

5. *Escape from Childhood* (New York: Ballantine, 1974), p. 157.

in the opportunities of some children. But from the point of view of equal opportunity for all children, it matters greatly whether the control that is taken *away* from parents is given *to* children or *to* agencies capable of regulating the overall pattern of early environmental influences on children. Legal recognition of private choices in childrearing, whether of parents or children, is an obstacle to full equality of opportunity. Family background affects the quality of a child's primary home environment and through this, the child's ability and desire to take advantage of alternative, secondary environments.

Though a random pairing of infants and parents gives every individual child an equal chance to enjoy the benefits of above average home environments, as a group, those who are born with genetic disadvantages can compete on equal terms with naturally more fortunate individuals only if the former actually have a *better* than even chance to benefit from above average home environments. To the extent that our commitment to equality of opportunity among children rests on a commitment to equality of results among adults, both randomization and selective assignment are inadequate. Redistributive policies that seek to match genetically disadvantaged children with families that offer superior environmental advantages also face other serious problems. In order to effectively and responsibly implement such a policy, we would need to know what traits are passed on genetically and whether and how they affect home environment, we would need evidence that specific genetic traits play a significant role in the intergenerational transmission of social and economic status, and we would need procedures for evaluating specific home environments in terms of their adequacy in compensating for specific genetic disadvantages. Yet even with respect to the one trait whose genetic basis has been the subject of experimental study, viz., intelligence, the findings are inconclusive, and there is little agreement among social scientists on the extent to which inequality of opportunity can be ascribed to differences in IQ.[6]

Another way to deal with the distinctions attributable to family background and their effects on access to other significant goods distributed by society is to eliminate socially and familially relative early differences altogether by doing away with the family as a childrearing institution. In its place, all children, from birth, would be reared and cared for exclusively in communal institutions, where they would be exposed to a common set of psychological, educational, and cultural influences. Childrearing methods could be flexible enough to accommodate the special talents, latencies, and disabilities of individual children, as manifested in the total environment of the collective (families and schools are now only partial environments, the latter functioning largely as supplements to the former). By removing children from their parents before differences in social origins and styles of childrearing have had a chance to influence the development of natural ability and motivation, and by imposing an initial equality of treatment for all children as the basis for the future distribution of social rewards according to merit, common upbringings free achievement from the impact of the home and the dependence on social class.

Equal Opportunity Through Common Upbringings

The form of collective childrearing envisaged here is a replacement for, not merely an addition to, the family, and so is to be distinguished from the contemporary systems of socialized childrearing found in such countries as Israel, the

6. See, for example, Samuel Bowles and Herbert Gintis, *Schooling in Capitalist America* (New York: Basic Books, 1977), pp. 114–122; Christopher Jencks et al., *Inequality: A Reassessment of the Effect of Family and Schooling in America* (New York: Harper and Row, 1972), pp. 64–76.

Soviet Union, and China.[7] Further, such systems might be
established for a variety of reasons, whereas I am primarily
interested in common upbringing as a way of promoting
equal opportunity for children. The early bolsheviks, for example, considered the traditional parent-child tie unsatisfactory, both because parents were apt to be conservative or re-
actionary toward the new regime, and because the family
epitomized the old moral system, one based on blood ties and
sympathy for relatives. By loosening family ties (as well as
weakening the church and transforming the school), the
revolutionists hoped to pave the way for a new culture. The
founders of the Israeli kibbutz also sought to revolutionize
the structure of human society and its basic social relations
and advocated a system of collective upbringing in order to
emancipate women from the burdens of child care and
housework and to perpetuate the values of community life.

Perhaps the most serious obstacle to thinking of a common
upbringing as an instrument for promoting equal opportunity is that common upbringings are usually linked to collectivist goals and aspirations and to a conception of society that
is felt to be at odds with that of an equal opportunity society.
Through communal living and group experience, collective
childrearing arrangements attempt to instill in children
values of mutual understanding, trust, cooperation, and collective responsibility and thereby to lay the foundation for
an integrated and cooperative society. Values like material
prosperity, status, and prestige, in contrast, are by their nature exclusive, for success by some means failure by others,
and a society that takes the notion of equal opportunity seriously subordinates collective activity and social solidarity to
the competitive pursuit of private satisfactions. In short, the
thoroughgoing emphasis on equal opportunity that leads to

7. See Melford E. Spiro, Children of the Kibbutz (Cambridge, Mass.:
Harvard University Press, 1958); Urie Bronfenbrenner, Two Worlds of Child-
hood (New York: Russell Sage Foundation, 1970); Ruth Sidel, Women and
Child Care in China (Baltimore: Penguin, 1974).

common upbringing collides with the very values and ideals transmitted by this mode of childrearing and with the form of social life for which it prepares children. Common upbringings might still be desirable on other grounds, but the use of common upbringings to *equalize opportunities* for children is incoherent. The family, on the other hand, may make it practically impossible to secure equal chances of success for those similarly endowed, but at least it can socialize children into the basic value system of an equal opportunity society.

The response to this objection is two-fold. First, if communal values must be transmitted by communal institutions and introjected in communal settings, then individuals must be reared communally as children if they are to be trained to live communally as adults. Even in a relatively small and cohesive community like that of the kibbutz, where all the participants share common values of cooperation and collective responsibility and work together to promote the good of the community as their highest goal, collectivist values may not be as effectively transmitted by parents as by the community itself. But common upbringing, in the sense fundamental to the creation of equal opportunities, means only that the community takes upon itself to direct the upbringing of children, and collective assumption of responsibility for childrearing does not in itself entail the propagation of any particular set of moral and social values. Second, it is not equal opportunity itself but the inordinate emphasis on achieving high ability and status that precludes communitarian values. Though opportunity is individualistic in the sense that it enables individuals to pursue their particular plans of life and to achieve desirable positions through effort and work, a society committed to equal opportunity is not necessarily one in which self-centered individuals pursue exclusively individualistic aims. Indeed, one way to help prevent such excesses might be to establish some system of collective childrearing, for at the same time that a common upbringing creates more uniform opportunities for children, it can also regulate the pursuit of status and prestige by teaching children to identify with the collective or at least to value collective activity as a good in itself.

There is nothing incoherent, therefore, in the idea of a society open to success through hard work and talent setting up a system of communal childrearing in order to give all children a fair chance of attaining whatever respect, riches, and rewards the society has to offer. Under such a system, children would be reared by nurses and teachers who met uniform standards of competence, so that there could be no difference among children resulting from the differential abilities, intelligence, skills, and emotional capacities of individual parents. The resources of the entire community would be made available to every child so that the opportunities of children could not depend on the economic or social position of their parents. It might still be objected, however, that in the evaluation of alternative childrearing structures we must consider not only equality of opportunity for children, but their psychological health as well, and that the emphasis on equality and equity in collective childrearing precludes the deeply personal care that healthy psychological development requires. Childrearers in a communal setting are not supposed to single out any particular child for special attention, because they are appointed by the community to represent the community, and the community is equally responsible for the well-being of every child. In contrast, the responsibilities of parents in the family system do favor the establishment of intimate relations between rearers and children, for there is a limit to the number of persons for whom one can care deeply at any one time, and in the family, parents are only responsible for relatively few children (those who "belong" to them). Further, privacy is a precondition of intimacy, for we can only enter into intimate relations with other people when we feel that *we* have control over the character of our interactions with them and can decide what is or is not appropriate to the sort of relationship we have with them. Under a system of communal childrearing, however, the organization and management of child care is closely supervised by the community, and caretakers are only agents of the community who, in comparison with parents, have little discretion with regard to childrearing. Here the community does not have to justify intruding upon the relationship between child and caretakers, for this relationship is already by its very nature public.

Of course, this defense of the family does not entail that parents should have all the responsibilities traditionally ascribed to them. A mixed system, in which children are educated and socialized by official representatives of the community but are also deeply attached to their parents, might be a satisfactory alternative. But the community cannot dictate to parents how they shall interact with their children without at the same time destroying the intimacy and warmth of family life, and thus the community cannot in fact see to it that all children receive the same kind of upbringing if it also wants them to have the opportunity for deeply personal care. A comprehensive system of collective childrearing, to which our pursuit of equal opportunity for children has led us, conflicts with the structural prerequisites of healthy psychological development.

Other psychological reasons are sometimes offered for respecting the family unit, and these must be carefully distinguished from the one discussed above. It is claimed, for example, that young children need to have rearers whom they can regard as omniscient and all-powerful, and that this need can be met only by parents who raise their children free from outside control or coercive intervention by the community. But as a defense of the family, even an attenuated form of the family, this argument is clearly inadequate, for it assumes that the community has already decided to let parents raise their own children. Collective childrearing does not have to shake the children's confidence in the wisdom and power of their rearers, and the threat of coercive intervention by the community would be eliminated if the community, in order (say) to secure more equal opportunities for children, took complete control of children's lives. Another argument might be that the young child's need for intimacy and individualized attention must be satisfied in a particular way, viz., regularly and reliably, and that in a system of communal rearing, where the child does not have one primary caretaker from infancy through young adulthood, there is a greater risk of inconsistent and discontinuous care than in the family system. However, the danger of inconsistent care may actually be less, because today's parents are not in fact solely responsible for what becomes of their children, and the community itself is in a better position than most individual parents to supervise and coordinate the activities of all those who share in the task of raising children. Moreover, in a society that favors diffusion of care among several figures in a communal setting rather than concentration of care in the hands of a single parent or set of parents, the loss of one of those figures may be less traumatic to children than the loss of a parent under the family system.

We return, then, to the earlier argument—that communal care that totally replaces family care disturbs the normal course of development because it does not allow caretakers to form primary attachments to particular children or children to experience exclusive and intimate relations with major parent figures. The best system of communal care may be one that encourages some of the emotional atmosphere of the family to develop, but it is still institutional care, and in the opinion of most child psychologists, institutional care cannot provide as satisfactory an emotional environment for infants and young children as that found in most family settings.[8]

8. See, for example, John Bowlby, *Child Care and the Growth of Love* (Penguin, 1973). For a dissenting view, see Lawrence Casler, *Is Marriage Necessary?* (New York: Human Sciences Press, 1974). Casler maintains that "the caretakers in a child-care institution can do at least as good a job of bringing

Family Rearing, the Capacity for Love, and the Good of Society

Parents might not play an outstanding role in the socialization and education of their children or in providing for their physical needs, but wherever the family exists, parents are of crucial importance in the psychological development of the child. Moreover, as long as the family exists, there is some aspect of the child's development over which the community has no control, some type of influence that parents and parents alone exert over children and upon which their future opportunities depend. The family will have the greatest effect on children's opportunities when it is the decisive agent of childrearing, the locus of primary responsibility for the upbringing of children; but even when parents do not as a rule perform those caretaking and training responsibilities that are usually considered to be *parental* responsibilities, they may still provide a developmental base upon which the child's responsiveness to educational efforts and future occupational possibilities rests.

Jencks and his co-workers have recently argued that "equalizing family background and exposure to schooling will not make earnings more equal."[9] This claim, however, does not confront the problem I have posed for the family. For equal opportunity and equal results are distinguishable moral goals, and the failure to insure equal results should not be regarded as a moral criticism of the pursuit of equal opportunity in general or of equal opportunity through common upbringing in particular. The abolition of the family might not do

---

up a child as can his own parents." He concedes that "most institutions lack the emotional intimacy and warmth found in most family settings," but he adds that "there is no evidence that this particular lack has any negative consequences whatsoever" (pp. 77, 108).

9. *"Inequality* in Retrospect," *Harvard Educational Review*, 43 (1973), p. 161.

much to promote economic equality among adults, but it might do a great deal to enhance the quality of some children's lives. Should we nevertheless retain the family in some form? The total elimination of the family might seem to be too high a price to pay for the equalization of children's opportunities, because collective upbringing deprives children of that particular kind of caring that makes a relationship not just personal but intimate and that is essential for psychological health. This vital ingredient will normally be missing, even if in other respects the child's psychological ties to the caretakers are satisfactory.

Why is intimacy between child and caretaker necessary for healthy psychological functioning? This can be understood as a request for factual information, for a description of the family's effects on personality development, and an explanation of why these effects are causally necessary conditions for the attainment of healthy psychological functioning. Ultimately, however, our defense of the family will rest on the values presupposed by statements ascribing psychological health to persons who have been raised in families. One can imagine cultures, cultures with very different institutions of childrearing and systems of socialization, in which the norms invoked by the concept of psychological health do not attach particular significance to the personality traits acquired through intimacy in childrearing. But whatever the possible diversity of conventional norms, some of the reasons for maintaining the privacy of family relations may rest on something a bit more solid than mere cultural contingency. The next objective of this chapter is to explore the possibility that a right to privacy in family life and to intimacy in family relations is required by a basic feature of the conception of a mature and fulfilled human life.

The Rawlsian notion of primary goods (see above, pp. 120–30) identifies the fundamental elements of a good life, among which are liberty, opportunity, self-respect, and health. Another primary good which I touched on briefly in the discussion of filial duties (see above, pp. 191–92), and which is, I believe, of special relevance to the moral analysis of alternative childrearing structures, is the capacity to establish deep personal relations, of which the capacity to establish love relations is the prototype. The capacity to enter into intimate relationships is a basic good not only because deep personal relations afford us a uniquely significant pleasure, but also because they allow us to communicate with and share elements of ourselves that would otherwise remain hidden and to realize creative and emotional possibilities that enhance the quality and meaning of life. Persons who lack the capacity to love also tend to lack a particular kind of self-respect, a sense of one's worth as a *unique* human being.

The capacity for deep personal relationships depends on early childhood experiences and on the way in which these experiences are organized by social practices of childrearing. The individual who is deficient in this capacity need not have suffered a difficult and tormented childhood; he or she may instead be the "normal" product of a system of childrearing that impedes the development of this capacity in all children. Is collective childrearing such a system? There is a close connection between one's self-conception and the kinds of emotional attitudes one is capable of adopting toward others. The emotional attitudes characteristic of profound personal relations are defined by their peculiar aims, beliefs, and experiences, all of which concern particular individuals; such relations are made possible by the capacity to commit oneself to the good of another, not as one among many to whom this commitment can be transferred, but as an irreplaceable individual. The corresponding attitude toward self similarly involves the belief that one is an irreplaceable individual, the desire to promote one's own good as that of a unique individual, and the effort to give expression to the sense of one's specialness through activities that leave one's peculiar stamp upon the world. Yet it is just these sorts of beliefs and desires that collective childrearing arrangements do not, but familial arrangements do, encourage.[10] Collective childrearing, whether designed to revolutionize the structure of human relations or only to enhance the opportunities of children, does not favor the formation of those exclusive attachments in early life out of which the exclusive loyalties of adult intimate relations develop.

This argument, if sound, shows us the importance of allowing the family to play some (nonmarginal) role in the development of children. Children need the family and the protection that privacy in family relations provides, because the capacities for close attachment and love are among the most valuable elements of a good life, and because the environment of the family is ideally suited to the development of these capacities. This argument also fills a gap in Rawls's theory of justice where the family is assumed to exist, but as Rawls himself is aware, no compelling reasons are given for its retention. Rawls admits that the idea of equal opportunity, "taken by itself and given a certain primacy," inclines in the direction of abolishing the family. But he quickly adds that within the context of his full theory of justice, of which a principle of equal opportunity is only a part, "there is much less urgency to take this course" (*Theory of Justice*, p. 511). He advocates instead a compromise position consisting of three elements: the principle of fair equality of opportunity, applied to the treatment of socially induced initial inequalities; the difference principle, applied to the treatment of natural differences; and the rule that fair equality of opportunity has priority over the difference principle (pp. 73–75, 101–102, 300–301, 511–512). Now it might be thought that Rawls does give us a reason for not abolishing the family and thus for

10. This contrast between the family and collective upbringing recalls Hegel's explanation of the difference between the characteristic attitudes of the family member and the citizen. See above, pp. 91–95.

preferring the compromise position in his discussion of moral education (sections 70–72). The sense of justice is said to evolve out of the ties of friendship and confidence among associates and this in turn out of the child's disposition to follow the precepts of authority figures—normally the child's parents, whose position in the hierarchy of the family is defined by certain rights and duties. But Rawls acknowledges that his account of the morality of authority "could, if necessary, be adjusted to fit" alternative childrearing schemes and that "in a broader inquiry the institution of the family might be questioned, and other arrangements might indeed prove to be preferable" (p. 463). Had Rawls considered the role parents play in the development of what might be called the morality of interpersonal relations, he could have told us why a choice *has* to be made between family and nonfamilial upbringing, between preserving parental authority in some measure and enhancing equality of opportunity for children by annulling this authority.

Though this objection to common upbringing is in some ways the central argument on behalf of retaining the family, family upbringing is also desirable because of its relation to an important social good. I refer here to what Mill calls "plurality of paths":

> What has made the European family of nations an improving, instead of a stationary portion of mankind? Not any superior excellence in them, which, when it exists, exists as the effect not as the cause; but their remarkable diversity of character and culture. Individuals, classes, nations, have been extremely unlike one another: they have struck out a great variety of paths, each leading to something valuable.[11]

A community that values "individuality of character and diversity in opinions and modes of conduct" (p. 239) would

11. *On Liberty* (Cleveland: Meridian, 1970), p. 202.

have trouble justifying a common upbringing, for it is largely through the diversity of upbringings in the family system that diversity in values and ideals is preserved. Parents should not be totally free, of course, to create whatever environment of influence they wish for their child, for parental conduct is constrained by the child's need for primary goods and autonomy. But the community also has a legitimate interest in supporting the conditions that foster individuality and therefore in not abrogating the right of parents to transmit their own values (however unconventional) to their children.[12] Moreover, this account of the importance of family upbringing seems to point to a more extensive involvement of parents in the development of their children than that demanded by the previous psychological argument.

I have argued that the pursuit of equal opportunity through common upbringings collides with an individual as well as a social good and that we are committed to valuing the family to the extent that we value intimacy in human relations and diversity in fundamental convictions and styles of life. It is in relation to these three values of equal opportunity, intimacy, and diversity that alternative sets of childrearing practices are to be assessed. We can enhance equality of opportunity for children and also preserve the psychological conditions that causally facilitate the development of the capacity for intimacy by seeing to it that parents do not as a rule perform those responsibilities that are generally considered to be expressions of love and yet have ample opportunity to demonstrate their love to their children in other ways. There are also many ways of improving the opportunities of groups of children without undermining the social conditions that promote diversity in conceptions of the good (through support services for parents and new kinds of educational institutions

12. As children come into contact with diverse opinions and religious, political, and other values, they may of course choose to reject the particular values adopted by their parents.

for children). Though equal opportunity must be balanced against the values of intimacy and diversity, there is still much that can be done (compatibly with these values) to advance social justice through greater collective assumption of responsibility for children.

APPENDIX: Inheritance, Rights, and Opportunities

Gifts *inter vivos* and inheritances constitute the major channels through which the accumulated wealth of a community is transferred to successive generations of owners, and ordinarily a significant part of a person's property passes at his or her death to the members of the immediate family.[1] In our society, the family is both a childrearing institution and a transmitter of property rights. Further, the institution of inheritance plays a major role in the persistence of economic inequality, especially in the maintenance of the wealth and income of the very rich, and also in the persistence of inequality of opportunity, since those who inherit property also inherit opportunity. Those who inherit great wealth can enjoy economic advantages—and the superior status, power, and privilege that go along with them—without having to compete with others at all, or if they choose to compete, they can extend their advantages even more and by inheritance bequeath them to their children. Whatever we may think of the argument for levelling such inheritances from the standpoint of equality in the distribution of economic goods, from the standpoint of equality of opportunity among children a strong case can be made against the inequalities that are perpetuated from generation to generation by inheritance.

Apart from the fact that society has a legitimate interest in the institution of inheritance, deriving from its legitimate interest in the opportunities of its members, children too may have a legitimate interest in the maintenance of some form of inheritance. In societies where the family has primary responsibility for the upbringing of children, it should be presumed that minor children have a *right* to inherit from their parents as an extension of a child's right to care and services from them while the parents live. Locke seems to make essentially

1. By "inheritance" I mean the entry of living persons into the possession of dead persons' property, whether or not the latter have bequeathed it to them.

224

the same point when he says that "the right a son has to be maintained and provided with the necessaries and conveniences of Life out of his Fathers stock, gives him a Right to succeed to his Fathers Property for his own good."[2] While the parents are alive, the minor child has a direct right to their support and nurturing and an indirect right to the economic resources that make that support and nurturing possible; after the parents die, the minor child has a direct right to a portion of the parents' property so that at least certain minimum needs of the child can continue to be satisfied. Put somewhat differently, the parents' commitment to adequately care for those children they bring into the world is to be understood as a commitment to care for them during their minority, not just during the lifetime of the parents, and so parents have an obligation with respect to their minor child to make provisions for their deaths (this includes appointing an appropriate and willing guardian for their minor child).

The right of minor children to inherit from their parents constrains the parents' freedom of bequest and imposes a duty on society if they die intestate. As a general rule, testators may not by will exclude their minor children from a share of their estates to the extent that they desire, and statutory provisions should limit the freedom of testators to dispose of their property at death as they see fit. The right of private property, of which the right of bequest is an instance, is itself not an unrestricted right of individuals to dispose of what they have produced by their own exertions or received without force or fraud from those who produced it. Property rights must be morally assessed not only from the point of view of the persons who possess these rights, but also from the point of view of others whose rights may be infringed by the application of these rights. In the case at hand, a reasonable assessment of the weights of relative rights clearly indicates that the right of bequest should be appropriately limited.

2. *Two Treatises of Government,* ed. P. Laslett (New York: New American Library, 1965), Treatise 1, sec. 93.

For Jeremy Bentham, the right of making a will is "a branch of penal and remunerative legislation" and is "intrusted to individuals for the encouragement of virtue in their families and the repression of vice."[3] In his view, parents should be allowed to use the threat of disinheritance in order to safeguard their own rights and to ensure that the sacrifices made by them during the childrearing years do not go unrewarded:

> By means of an order not payable till after his death, the indemnity for paternal care is increased, and an additional assurance against ingratitude is secured to the father. (P. 421)

Yet aside from the fact that the threat of disinheritance is likely to undermine rather than promote gratitude for parental sacrifices, this argument does not succeed in showing that minor children have no right to inherit from their parents. For this is one of those rights that derive from the child's dependence on the parents for the basic instrumental goods of life, and it is only obedience (or cooperation more generally) that parents may demand of their child as a condition of their meeting his or her basic needs. The right to disinherit minor children cannot be based on consideration of the parents' interests alone, for the minor child may have a prior moral claim to some portion of the parents' property, should they die before the child reaches majority.

In addition to restricting parents' freedom of bequest, as death, a strong case can be made for restricting children's right to inherit. "No one person," Mill argues, "should be permitted to acquire, by inheritance, more than the amount of a moderate independence."[4] Not only do children have no regards those to whom they may bequeath their property at

---

3. "Utilitarian Basis of Succession," in *Rational Basis of Legal Institutions* ed. J. Wigmore and A. Kocourek (New York: Macmillan, 1923), p. 420.
4. *Principles of Political Economy,* ed. William J. Ashley (London: Longmans, Green & Co., 1923), bk. 5, ch. 9, sec. 1.

right to more, since any more would discourage hard work and self-reliance and parents would be derelict in their duty if they did not teach their children to value these things in their own lives; but both justice and expediency demand that "the principle of graduation (as it is called), that is, of levying a larger percentage on a larger sum," be applied to inheritance duties (bk. 5, ch. 2, sec. 3). A limitation on the amount that could be inherited, especially if accompanied by a limitation on the amount that could be acquired by gift, would further the development of the productive resources of society and would diffuse the advantages of leisure among a larger number. By limiting the amounts that could be inherited and acquired by gift, the state could also moderate the tendency toward inequalities of wealth and diminish inequality of opportunities, without imposing a "penalty on people for having worked harder and saved more than their neighbors" (ibid.). A graduated income tax (as Mill admits) would further mitigate inequality of opportunity, for parents with higher incomes can spend more on their children and can provide them with advantages of a more subtle psychological kind. Whether or not it is just to promote equality of opportunity in this manner involves us in a consideration of the principles that ought to govern reward schedules for different jobs or positions and raises issues that go beyond opportunity. If we subject the incomes of one generation of earners to a progressive tax for the sake of greater equality of opportunity among the next, consistency demands that we also subject the incomes of this generation of earners to a progressive tax for the sake of greater equality of opportunity among their descendants. Yet it might be argued that if we do so, we deny subsequent generations of earners the opportunity to enjoy the differential rewards that they have fairly earned. Thus, though the principle of equal opportunity is defined without reference to any particular reward schedule for jobs, not all ways of implementing the former are compatible with all reward schedules.

CHAPTER FIVE

Marriage
for the Sake of Children

The Link Between Family and Marriage

In my discussion of the ethical issues raised by family life and familial arrangements, I have concentrated on the relationship between children and those who bring them up. I have explored the grounds of parental responsibility and authority, the nature and content of parents' obligations, and differing conceptions of filial duty; argued that the network of social practices relating to the rearing of children is to be evaluated in terms of how it accommodates the legitimate interests of children, parents, and society; and accounted for the tension between the family and social justice. It should be clear from the previous chapter that I do not use the term "family" to refer to *any* group that contains members of two or more generations such that the older members care about the welfare of the younger, for I want to contrast certain forms of communal upbringing and familial upbringing. Now I want to focus attention on a different familial relationship, the relationship between the adults who bring children up in the family. For families are typically brought into existence by contracts between adults—marital contracts, though others are conceivable and possibly preferable—and we need to consider how the relationship between parents affects the parent-child relationship and the performance of parental duties. As a result of this investigation, we might decide to recommend a change in our current family system with respect to the ways in which families can or ought to be founded.

Though the most common type of family in our society is still the nuclear family, consisting of a married man and woman with their offspring, there is overwhelming evidence that the arrangements of family life are changing. An increasing proportion of marriages are now disrupted by divorce, resulting in more single-parent families; many children who live with one of their biological parents after divorce also spend a good deal of time in the home of the other, thus becoming the link that connects two families and extends one family over several households; joint custody awards after divorce are likely to become more common in the future; courts are showing a greater willingness to consider, as candidates for the award of custody, parents who are living in informal, nonmarital relationships or who are involved in homosexual relationships. Further, there is an increasing number of births taking place outside legal marriage, and greater social acceptance of such births. "Dependency, not legitimacy, is becoming the basis of entitlement to benefits derived through a parent,"[1] and marriage is losing one of its traditional and important effects, that of distinguishing the legitimate family from all others. New family patterns are also emerging from the changing roles of men and women within marriage, quite apart from the greater frequency of voluntary marital disruption and the growing interest in having and raising children outside marriage.

Higher divorce rates and more liberal divorce laws do not

1. Mary Glendon, "Marriage and the State: The Withering Away of Marriage," *Virginia Law Review,* 62 (1976), p. 715.

in themselves suggest that we are becoming a society of casual sexual encounters rather than more permanent marital relations. In fact, these developments seem "to be taking place within a context of strong and persistent commitment to marriage relationships" and do not signify "a change to quite different sorts of relationships"[2] so much as a change in our expectations of marriage and a growing acceptance of the view that mutual satisfaction and personal compatibility of spouses is the primary justificatory basis of marriage. But if the institution of marriage as such is not being rejected, its ability to provide a satisfactory foundation for family life is being called into question. Indeed, it is becoming increasingly apparent that the nuclear family is not to be taken as the fundamental unit of social organization but is actually an unstable combination of two simpler elements, the monogamic conjugal relationship, or marital union, between parents of the same child or children, and the relationship between parent and child (more precisely, between mother and child, father and child). The traditional view that procreation and childrearing are the primary purposes of marriage and that the central duties of husband and wife are the nonreciprocal and nonprovisional duties of parenthood is giving way to a conception of marriage as essentially involving a serious commitment between two individuals as individuals. It is still the case, to be sure, that most marriages do not end in divorce and that most children are raised by their natural parents, joined in a stable marital union. But as the criteria for evaluating the success of a marriage increasingly tend to focus on the quality of the relationship between husband and wife and on the opportunities this relationship provides for the pursuit of nonparental as well as parental interests, and as people become more accepting of divorce as a solution to an unsatisfying marriage, we have to consider whether the needs of chil-

2. Mary Jo Bane, *Here to Stay: American Families in the Twentieth Century* (New York: Basic Books, 1976), p. 22.

dren would not be better served if society were to institute and give preferred status to novel ways of founding families.

Another aspect of contemporary changes in marriage norms concerns the extent of public control over marriage. Marriage is becoming more and more a private matter, and the entrance of a third party, whether the church or the state, is increasingly looked on with disfavor. The church, which still demands perpetual monogamy, has lost is jurisdiction in marital affairs, and the state is granting greater freedom from governmental control to this form of intimacy in order to promote the growth of love in marriage and harmony in the individual lives of spouses. But as decisions to marry are more and more based on personal individual inclination rather than economic motives or the motive of producing children, and as the institution of marriage is freed from limitations and regulations imposed by church and state, the public interest in the care and development of children becomes more difficult to reconcile with the traditional practice of linking childrearing to marriage. As public demands on marriage are relaxed and the interests of marriage and family diverge, the public's responsibility for the well-being of children calls for more effective controls over parenthood and greater social involvement in the institutions of childrearing.

The instability of the modern nuclear family is a particular example of the more general phenomenon of poor institutional coordination in childrearing arrangements, and since no set of familial arrangements is desirable if its different elements are not all well coordinated, we have to explore alternatives to our traditional practice of linking the parental and the conjugal relationships in the nuclear family. It will be recalled from chapter two that the problem of institutional coordination requires us to find a set of social practices such that the specific rights and duties attaching to the various roles or offices defined by these practices form a coherent whole. Society has a legitimate interest in harmonizing the diverse role demands placed on individuals by their participation in different social institutions. One example of the lack of coordination between childrearing and other practices was discussed earlier: the failure of our society to balance the competing demands of wage work and parenthood, to reduce the conflicts between the family's need for a parent's wages and the socially recognized need of children for parental warmth, attention, and energy. Similarly, the interests of the family and the married couple do not converge harmoniously as they once did, and there has been no systematic attempt to restructure family life so as to tangibly reduce the inevitable conflicts that arise between the social responsibilities of parents and the personal liberties of spouses. Within the nuclear family, the individual performs two roles simultaneously—one is both parent to one's children and companion to one's spouse; but the norms defining these roles with their respective rights and duties are no longer organized into a coherent scheme.

Free marriage, which is a private relationship based on private agreement, might be opposed on the ground that permanent monogamy ought to be maintained for the sake of children. This argument assumes not only that the legitimate interests of children constitute the primary factor in the evaluation of marriage practices, but also that the interests of children can be discussed in isolation from the interests of spouses in the context of the nuclear family. In fact, however, these different sets of interests are too interdependent for this approach. Unhappy marriages of parents have empirically a very demoralizing effect on the growth of the child's character, and it is in the interests of children that the interests of their parents as individual persons be respected by marriage. Indeed, it could be argued that precisely on account of the children the parents' unhappy marriage should be dissolved rather than forcibly maintained.

In passing judgment on the traditional practice of linking

childrearing and marriage, we also have to think about the ways in which parents as well as children are victimized by it. Married persons who feel that they must stay together for their children's sake may have to sacrifice much of their personal well-being in doing so, and if they decide to dissolve their marriage because it has become intolerable, may have to settle for a much less satisfying relationship with their children in the future. As we consider alternative familial arrangements, therefore, our goal should be to find a coherent set of social practices in which the legitimate interests of children and the legitimate parental and nonparental interests of parents can be more adequately met (the interests of society at large are also a factor, but I do not focus on them here). The interests of parents merit consideration both for their own sake and for the sake of the children, whose welfare is closely bound up with that of their parents.

Parenting and Legitimate Sexual Unions

According to Saint Augustine and the tradition he fostered, a tradition that has had a profound influence on conventional Western attitudes toward sex and the relations between the sexes, the only proper end of sexuality is procreation. Sexual intercourse, whether promiscuous or marital, is a natural object of continuing shame, but at least in marriage, "carnal incontinence . . . is turned to the honorable taks of begetting children," and "the concupiscence of the flesh"[3] is tempered by parental affection. Marriage is a good, however, not only or even primarily because it dignifies sexuality by directing it to the production of children and then, through the connection between marriage and the family, represses sexual desire by turning the attention of husband and wife to the upbringing of their children. The principal good for which the

3. *The Good of Marriage*, trans. C. T. Wilcox, M.M. (New York: Fathers of the Church, Inc., 1955), p. 13.

institution of marriage exists is the procreation and proper
education of children, and marriage—that is, unadulterous,
lifelong monogamy—is the best environment in which to rear
children for adulthood. Polyandry, Aquinas argues, "is contrary to certainty as to offspring,"[4] and makes it impossible
for natural fathers to take the part they ought to take in the
direction of their children; and polygyny, while objectionable
principally because it treats wives like servants, also produces
"discord in domestic society" (ibid.), which presumably affects children adversely. Further, Aquinas maintains that the
union of male and female must be a lasting one, because the
human offspring needs attention for a longer time and to a
greater extent than other animals, and that knowledge of the
indissolubility of marriage strengthens conjugal love and promotes collaboration of husband and wife in the task of educating their children.

According to Christian doctrine as expressed by Aquinas,
it is not merely the case that men and women who have sexual
relations with one another with the intent of having children,
or who intend to raise children together, should be married to
one another. The claim is rather that sexual relations are legitimate only within marriage on the following grounds:
(a) sexual intercourse is moral only when it is aimed at procreation (the procreational model of human sexuality); (b)
those who engage in sexual intercourse should provide the
best upbringing they can for those they bring into the world;
and (c) marriage is the most suitable context in which to
bring up children. Contraception and homosexual intercourse
are excluded by (a); extramarital intercourse is forbidden on
the grounds that sexually associating adults must have procreational intentions and, once they procreate, have certain
parental responsibilities that can be carried out only in marriage. On this view, the family is not so much based on
marriage as marriage on the family.

4. "The Divinity of Marriage," in *Sexual Love and Western Morality*, ed.
D. P. Verene (New York: Harper and Row, 1972), p. 129.

The above three propositions rest on distinct considerations—(a) on a definition of unnatural sex and a corresponding notion of a distinctively human nature, (b) on a view of how parental responsibilities arise, and (c) on beliefs about what children require if their upbringing is not to be impaired—and the denial of one of these propositions does not necessarily entail the denial of another. Of the three, the case for (a) is surely the weakest. The argument that nonprocreational sexuality is immoral because it is contrary to nature assimilates human to animal nature and ignores the distinctively human capacity to use sexuality for diverse purposes, including but not limited to procreation. Even if we grant that the natural end of genital activity is procreation, and that procreation is a great human good, it does not follow that anyone who seeks sexual gratification in intercourse that does not aim at or cannot lead to reproduction necessarily acts "contrary to the good for man" (p. 121). One does not deprive oneself or others of the capacity for procreational sex merely by engaging in nonprocreational sex, and one may at other times engage in acts that can and do result in children.

Since the procreational model of human sexuality cannot be sustained, neither can the view that intramarital sex is legitimate only when restricted to procreation. It might still be argued, however, that sexual intercourse ought to be confined to marriage, not because procreation is the only moral function of sexual intercourse, but because a prohibition on extra- and nonmarital sex is a way to help maintain the morally desirable institution of marriage.[5] Further, it is one thing to say that parenthood is not the only proper purpose of sexual partnership and quite another to claim that there is no reason for linking the activity of rearing a child to sexual partnership. That natural parents should or should not be the normal childrearers or that procreation should or should

5. Richard Wasserstrom considers this argument in "Is Adultery Immoral?" *Today's Moral Problems*, ed. Richard Wasserstrom (New York: Macmillan, 1975), pp. 250–252.

not be linked to parental responsibility is not something that can be decided solely on the basis of our model of human sexuality. As I argued in chapter two, the justification of a particular set of childrearing practices and its assignment of duties to care for, educate, and socialize children depend on how the practices accommodate the various legitimate interests of the child, the parents, and the society at large, and it is wrong to suppose, a priori, that a society that rejects the procreational model and also delegates childrearing duties to natural parents must be acting inconsistently or arbitrarily. Then, too, there may be good reasons, relating to the well-being of children, for restricting childrearing primarily to marriage, even if procreation and parenting are not the primary purposes of marriage.[6] (I discuss such reasons below, pp. 247–52.) But if these are not its primary purposes, it is not clear why heterosexual monogamy should be the only permissible form of marital union (polygyny, if Aquinas is right, would still be morally objectionable, because it fails to respect wives). A variety of permissible marital forms is suggested by the separation of marriage and procreation, and which of these is best for, or least detrimental to, children has to be decided on the basis of their psychological consequences and our conception of optimal or proper development.

Marriage and the State's Obligation to Children

The care and development of children is a social interest and responsibility, and society can show its concern for children in either of two ways: by assigning many or most aspects of childrearing to its official representatives, or by allowing parents substantial but not total freedom to raise their children

6. Compare Robert Baker and Fredcrick Elliston on the implications of rejecting the procreational model, in "Introduction," *Philosophy and Sex,* ed. Baker and Elliston (Buffalo, N.Y.: Prometheus, 1975), pp. 4–5.

as they choose and think best. The former approach would appeal to a society that regards the provision of equal opportunity as its most important obligation to children; the latter to a society that seeks to preserve the conditions that foster development of the capacity for intimate human relations. Clearly a society in which children are raised in the privacy of the home must retain some control over parenting by imposing some standards of humanity, health, and education on the parent-child relationship. For however trustworthy parents may be as a class, remedies must exist for the exceptional cases of child abuse and neglect. Traditionally societies have also tried to control parenting through the institution of marriage, though today the effectiveness of this form of regulation is being called into question by the increasing tendency of marriage to focus on the satisfaction of the private interests of spouses.

The marital status is defined in part by laws concerning marriage dissolution. Divorce statutes prescribe procedures for ending a marriage and also customarily authorize courts to award alimony to one of the spouses, to order transfers of property between the spouses, either in addition to or in lieu of alimony, and to issue child support orders. By linking child-rearing to a legal relationship that cannot be broken easily, without any difficulties, the state increases children's chances of enjoying a stable home environment while they are growing up and in this way exercises some control over the activity of parenting itself.[7] The individual who chooses to declare love for another by entering into such a relationship, and who is willing to undertake the risk of legal involvement in divorce and such legal obligations as may be assigned upon divorce, thereby signifies a strong commitment to an enduring relationship and confidence in its durability. These relationships are likely to be more stable than informal, nonlegal re-

7. The presence of more than one parent in marriage is also insurance for the child against the possibility of one parent dying.

lationships between cohabiting adults, or term marriages, which do not end in divorce but simply in the nonrenewal of the previous arrangement; and marriage intended to be of indefinite duration is therefore more favorable to the healthy growth of the child's personality.[8]

Legal regulation of parenting through marriage, thus understood, concerns one crucial aspect of children's psychological development: the degree of stability or continuity in their relations with their parents. (Continuous parental care may, of course, be deficient in other respects.) In general, wherever children are not the direct and primary responsibility of the society itself, the state has an obligation to see to it that parenting is paired with some institution that protects children from hurtful interruptions in their parents' relationship to one another.[9] In societies where the extended family is common and the nuclear family is not isolated from larger kin groupings, kin may be able to perform the same kind of stabilizing function that is performed by marriage in our society. The ready availability of backup caretakers in the extended family could minimize the harmful effects upon children of the dissolution of their nuclear families, and so even allowing that disruption of home life is more likely outside of marriage than within, this would be, under the circumstances, a less compelling reason for linking childrearing to marriage. In societies where extended family groupings or other social networks cannot be relied on to provide unbroken care for children in the event of such disruption, other stabilizing institutions must be paired with parenting. Children have a

8. On the child's psychological need for long-term stable relationships with parents, see John Bowlby, *Child Care and the Growth of Love* (Baltimore: Penguin, 1973); J. Goldstein, A. Freud, and A. Solnit, *Beyond the Best Interests of the Child* (New York: Free Press, 1973). Russell shares this view in chapter 13 of *Marriage and Morals* (New York: Bantam, 1968), where he regards "the family as a reason for stable marriage."

9. Since children internalize the basic moral values of their society through relationships in the family, stable families also contribute to the stable life of the community.

better chance for secure relations with their parents if their parents are married to one another rather than merely cohabit on an informal basis, or if they make a legal agreement to cohabit for an indefinite rather than a limited period of time. But the fact that more and more marriages are ending in divorce suggests that children might have a still better chance if their parents were bound together in a marriage specifically intended for childrearing or by a legal agreement to take responsibility for their child's growth and development.

The state has also used marriage to help ensure some measure of consistency, as well as continuity, of care for children. In our society, where childbearing primarily occurs in the context of marriage, there is a strong, though rebuttable, presumption that the child born to a married woman is legitimate, i.e., that her husband is the child's natural father. The existence of this presumption renders it unnecessary for the state to determine paternity every time the woman makes a claim for child support upon divorce. On the basis of this presumption, and the belief that a parent's obligation to his children does not end merely because he no longer lives with them and cares for them on a day-to-day basis, the state usually requires husbands who do not have custody of their children to support them regardless of who is to blame for the breakup of the marriage. (The system of awarding custody may itself be based on certain indefensible premises about the superior rights or abilities of natural mothers, but children still have rights to support under an unjust social practice.) Unfortunately, whether by absconding, refusing to pay, or fraudulently pleading poverty or inability to work, noncustody parents are often able to evade their continuing parental responsibilities. In other cases, because of remarriage, the income of noncustody parents may not be sufficient to take adequate care of both of their families. Children obviously need greater state protection than that afforded by child support orders alone, entered upon the termination of a marriage, upon a finding of paternity in cases of illegitimacy, or upon the dissolution of some nonmarital legal arrangement between parents.

Dual Marriage and Contractual Families

In our society, the marital status itself normally entitles the persons so united to have children together and found a family. The legal rules defining how valid marriages are made at once confer upon individuals the power to mold their legal relations with one another and to create legal relations with their offspring, who are not parties to the contracts between their parents. There is no set of legal rules, separate and distinct from the rules giving individuals the power to impose upon themselves the legal rights and duties of marriage, specifying procedures by which and conditions under which married persons may become parents of their own children. Suitability for parenthood, it would seem, is taken for granted as long as the prospective natural parents are married to one another, even though rejection of the traditional assumption that the purpose of marriage is childbearing and childrearing has actually left many spouses poorly prepared for parenthood. In striking contrast, those who wish to adopt a child are subjected by law to intensive interviewing aimed at discovering the healthiness of the relationship between husband and wife, the motivation for parenthood, their ability to cope with the stresses of parenthood, and the physical and material conditions that the adopted child will be enjoying. Given that society ought to maximize the probability that children will be raised by competent and willing parents, it is reasonable to argue that marriage should not shield spouses who desire to have and raise children together from having to be evaluated for this purpose in some way, by society and the open community. The point here is only that the discrepancy between natural and adoptive parenthood should be reduced, not that the state should give the same recognition to natural and adoptive parenthood outside of marriage as within.

The social interest in more effective screening procedures for parenthood can be accommodated within marriage by the institutionalization of distinct marital forms having distinct conditions of eligibility. We can imagine an arrangement in which the private and public concerns now confounded in the single institution of marriage would be addressed by two types of marriage. One would be available to individuals who could not have children or agreed in advance that there would be no offspring of their union, and who wished only to take advantage of a certain legal power in order to express, affirm, and cement their commitment to and affection for one another or perhaps to create something analogous to a business partnership. Marriages of this type would include the renewable trial marriage, in which people would explicitly contract for a childless union which would be evaluated after a designated period of time, at which point a completely new decision, such as separation, could be reached, or the license could be renewed; and the permanent childless marriage, in which, again, people would contract for a childless union, but their relationship would be of indefinite duration. After a prescribed length of time, participants in this type of marriage could apply for a license to establish a parental marriage, that is, a permanent marriage explicitly directed toward the founding of a family, if they felt ready for the responsibilities of bearing and raising children or changed their minds about remaining childless. Individuals who entered the first type of marriage would have to meet general requirements of contractual capacity and freely consent to the agreement; candidates for the second would also reasonably be expected to pass genetic tests for biological parenthood and to demonstrate their economic ability to support a child and their psychological fitness for parenting. (Marriage for children would not be short-term marriage. Divorce would not be disallowed, but to reinforce the seriousness of having children, would be available only upon showing exceptional hardship, and giving the state satisfaction that the well-being of the child was secured.) Further, there are strong reasons for not offering childless and parental marriage as two options between which individuals may choose at any time in their marital careers.[10] If every parental marriage, whether children were born into it or adopted, had to be preceded by a harmonious pattern of interaction between spouses within a childless marriage, by a term marriage that indicated readiness for a marriage of indefinite duration, or by a permanent childless marriage that gave every indication of stability, individuals would have the opportunity to discover potential sources of disagreement between themselves (relating to parenting and other matters) and to deal with problems in mutual adjustment before becoming parents. The normal stresses and strains of raising children are only made worse when parents are uncertain about the strength and scope of their commitment to one another or feel trapped into sharing parenthood with an unsuitable partner, and parents who for these reasons experience childrearing as an intolerable burden may see divorce as their only option. Some may sincerely believe themselves to be ready and equipped for parental marriage even before they have gone through a successful childless marriage, but they may misjudge their inclinations or capacities. Moreover, the imposition of a dual marriage sequence is not per se unduly restrictive; the point is not to deprive spouses who genuinely want and can adequately rear children of the right to procreate or adopt. The policy rather aims at getting persons to delay parenthood, to postpone it to a time in their marital

10. This is an essential part of Margaret Mead's proposal for revising marriage customs in "Marriage in Two Steps," in *The Family in Search of a Future*, ed. Herbert A. Otto (New York: Appleton-Century-Crofts, 1970), pp. 75–84.

careers when they may actually be more willing to undertake and more competent to discharge the responsibilities of parenthood. Even if temporarily having to forego parenthood means that some persons will be denied its benefits who once had (but no longer have) the inclination and capacity for parenthood, this seems a relatively small price to pay for helping ensure that children are raised in a reasonably stable home.

Such a marriage policy would be accompanied by a strong emphasis on contraception before spouses are authorized to procreate (a legal requirement that spouses use contraceptives poses moral as well as Constitutional problems), and it could be implemented in a coercive or a noncoercive manner. Penalties could be imposed on persons for having children outside of parental marriage, an extreme example of which would be the forcible removal of the child from the custody of the natural parents. Alternatively, the policy could operate by providing special tax and other social incentives for delaying parenthood until properly licensed to found a family, or by removing public benefits currently provided all parents regardless of when in their married lives they have children. Since the harm to which children are exposed by our current marriage customs has not yet reached epidemic proportions, a coercive policy would seem to be unwarranted.

What makes parental marriage a form of *marriage* is that the mutual commitment to bring up a child is accompanied by, and grows out of, the kind of affection and commitment to one another that is characteristic of a serious, intentionally lifelong marriage relationship. A link between parenthood and sexual intimacy is preserved at the same time that the sequence of marital stages enables spouses to cement their relationship to one another through sexual intimacy before assuming the multiple responsibilities of childrearing. To say only that parenthood should have its own license and that, contrary to present practice, families should be brought into existence by contracts specifically designed for this purpose is not yet to show, however, why this license and this contract should normally be marital, in any familiar sense of the word. We could instead have an arrangement in which marriage conferred no special privilege of parenthood and in which individuals who met certain conditions of eligibility, whether or not they were married to one another (marriage itself would no longer be one of the conditions), could have and raise children together.[11] Individuals who had no desire to cohabit, or who did not feel strongly enough about each other to promise fidelity and support throughout an indefinite future, but who had a common desire for a child, could form a limited partnership in which they legally signified their intention to take responsibility for a child for as long as it needed a stable parental relationship. The child might be their own or adopted. As in dual marriage, individuals who did not intend to engage in parenting would have the freedom to choose between different kinds of marriage and to enter the kind of marriage that suited their individual requirements as private persons; but unlike dual marriage, those who *did* intend to engage in parenting would continue to have this freedom as well as the freedom to avoid marriage altogether. Further, while procreation is not regarded as the primary purpose of marriage, and sex is not restricted to reproduction in either arrangement, dual marriage secures a closer connection between parenthood and sex than a policy that permits individuals to found families outside marriage.

A parental contract (not a marriage) could conceivably be entered into by a small group of consenting adults of varying ages, binding them together in what Shulamith Firestone calls a "household."[12] A group of individuals, each of whom wants to share the experience and responsibilities of parenthood

11. This is the arrangement advocated by Joseph and Clorinda Margolis in "The Separation of Marriage and Family," *Feminism and Philosophy,* ed. Mary Vetterling-Braggin, Frederick Ellison, and Jane English (Totowa, N.J.: Littlefield, Adams & Co., 1977), pp. 291–301.

12. *The Dialectic of Sex* (New York: Bantam, 1972), pp. 230–232.

with the others, applies for a household license and legally signifies its intention to stay together for a limited period of time in order to raise children (the children may or may not be the offspring of a person or couple in the household, and the household may or may not contain married couples.) A system of parental contracts would probably also increase the frequency of a new kind of extended family, in which children are jointly raised by their natural parents, one or each of whom is married to another and may have other children to care for from this union. There is already a growing tendency in our society toward this new kind of family structure, but since it is created by divorce and remarriage, it is vulnerable to the disagreement that led to and the bitterness that remains after the rupture of the natural parents' marriage and is often beset by jealousies and conflicts of loyalty not found in traditional families.[13] The separation of marriage and parenthood would not by itself solve all the problems that such nontraditional blended families face (the roles of stepparents would still have to be worked out, for example), but it would help reduce some of the pressure on them and thus make them more viable.

Both policies, the relatively conservative one of parenthood as a special form of marriage and the more radical one of parental or family contracts, may be understood as responses to the problem of stabilization discussed in the previous section. Both seek to accommodate substantial freedom for adults to create their own individual lifestyles to the child's need for protection against disruption of the parents' relationship to one another. Moreover, both policies regulate parenting by requiring that those who wish to become parents be licensed for it, in recognition of the fact that parenting is too important and too potentially harmful an activity to leave to hap-

13. See Michael Norman, "The New Extended Family: Divorce Reshapes the American Household," *The New York Times Magazine*, November 23, 1980, pp. 26ff.

penstance talent and good-faith effort alone. If despite these similarities it is asserted that parental marriage is preferable to family contracts, the argument could take one of the following forms. First, it might be claimed that procreation and childrearing ought to take place primarily in the context of parental marriage because this helps maintain a kind of personal relationship between adults that is among the most valuable elements of a good life. Though people want to become parents for a variety of reasons, the desire for children is among the most compelling motivations in human behavior and can be used to induce people to get and stay married. If being married were a prerequisite for parenthood, then the spouses in a marriage would be in a position to satisfy for each other an important need or desire that could not be satisfied elsewhere in society. If parenthood were normally restricted to parental marriage, then persons seeking those benefits that are a feature of parenthood would be furnished with explicit social instructions for their attainment, namely parental *marriage*. Second, it might be argued that though both parental marriage and family contracts with or without marriage can provide children with a stable structure in which to grow up, the former is better for children in other ways; and further that the former is more favorable to an experience of family membership that transcends the temporary and relatively limited encounters between parents and their growing children and hence more favorable to the exercise of capacities and enlargement of self that constitute such a richer experience of family life.

As regards the first argument, the priority thesis (see chapone) dictates that children may be used to help maintain especially valuable interpersonal relationships only if these relationships are in fact compatible with at least minimally decent care for children. That they are seems safe to assume, and would not necessarily be denied even by proponents of a family contract scheme who maintain that other arrangements, very different from the marriage relationship, can satisfy this requirement. But if they are right, we might then ask whether it is not unfair to those who can provide such care to deprive them of the opportunity for parenthood just because they are not willing to make a serious, long-lasting commitment to one another. The second argument will be discussed at greater length in the next section. But it should be noted here that the argument does not allege that parental marriage is preferable to parental contracts because family rearing is preferable to nonfamily rearing. Both policies endorse some type of family rearing, and the considerations offered in the previous chapter, particularly concerning the capacity for intimate adult relationships, can be advanced to defend this position.

The Case for Parenthood
as a (Special) Form of Marriage

In parental marriage, conjugal love is not easily separated from parental love. With the appearance of the first child, a new kind of love usually comes into being between spouses which does not replace, but adds to and strengthens, the companionship already existing; and spouses love their children not only for themselves but also as outward signs of the love they have for one another. In contrast, a family contract scheme does not invest parenting with the same emotional significance, for it does not foster the unification of diverse commitments in a single set of relationships and the reciprocal reinforcing of conjugal and parental love. Moreover, it is precisely because marriage can normally endow parenting with such a richness of feeling that a policy linking marriage and parenthood is better for children than a policy giving equal recognition to a variety of ways of contractually initiating families. Parents have duties toward their children and are expected to fulfill them, whether or not they are married

to one another, but when childrearing is restricted primarily
to familistic marriage, these duties will normally be performed
with greater satisfaction and less attendant fragmentation of
energy than is possible in some of the parenting arrangements
permitted by the alternative policy. And the more satisfying
parenting is, the more integrated parent-child relations are
with other intimate, primary relationships that the parents
are involved in concurrently, the more likely it is that children will receive better care.

Parental marriage is beneficial to children in yet another,
more specific, way having to do with how it shapes their understanding of and attitudes toward sexuality. Sex dissociated
from emotions like love and affection and from emotional and
sexual commitment is not per se bad sex, either in a moral or
a psychological sense, but sex provides its most enduring and
enriching satisfactions when it is expressive of these valued
emotions. In families founded on marriage, children typically
have as models adults who are both lovers and in love, and on
the basis of what children see lived out in front of them day
after day, they form impressions about sexual and love relationships that they carry with them into adult life. Provided
parents do not deny their own sexuality to their children, the
rewards of a sexual life in which sex is connected to love will
be evident to the children in the happiness of their parents;
and at a time when children may have difficulty controlling
their sexual impulses, their upbringing can teach them that
sexuality is amenable to emotional control and show them the
value of expressing sexuality in the context of a long-lasting
personal relationship. By contrast, a family contract scheme is
so permissive about parenting arrangements that children can
have parents who are neither lovers nor in love, or who entered into a family contract rather than a marriage because
they did not want sexual intimacy to be taken as a symbol of
a serious, loving relation. On the whole, then, maintaining
some connection between the two institutions of marriage

and the family does more to aid the child's psychosexual development than separating them entirely.

In addition, while some form of competency testing is justified for those who desire to become parents, there are good reasons, having to do with the role of family in the adult lives of parents and children, for not basing our choice of family policy solely on the factor of parenting itself. Like parental marriage, a contractual family is formed for the express purpose of having (or adopting) and raising children; but unlike a parental marriage policy, a contractual family scheme provides no institutional support for the continuation of meaningful parent-child relations beyond the childrearing years. When the children are old enough to take care of themselves and the term of the family contract expires, the family (such as it was) also comes to an end. Parties to a contractual family would probably take some interest in the progress and well-being of their children even after they had grown up; indeed it would be surprising if they did not. But if the parties go their own separate ways after having fulfilled the terms of their family contract, this interest may wane or come into conflict with new loyalties, and the children may have difficulty maintaining a close relationship with both (or all, if there were more than two) of their parents. Even when parenting is linked to marriage, of course, the child's departure from the home may force spouses to reevaluate their relationship and may initiate marital breakup. No defensible family policy can *guarantee* that the family in which children were raised will continue to be available to them as adults. However, partners in parental marriage will commonly be bound together not only by jointly assumed parental responsibilities, but also by deep ties of companionship and love, ties that are enriched by the many shared experiences of childrearing and endure beyond the child's emancipation from the home. Parental marriage thus helps to keep the family intact, not just as a childrearing institution, but as a focal point of important personal relations involving parents and children at various stages in their lives.

A policy linking the family to marriage is more favorable to enduring family relations than a system of contractual families, but these relations can actually survive and develop only if they are given care and attention and are continuously adjusted to the changing roles, personalities, and needs of parents and children. This readjustment frequently requires the growth of self-knowledge and the strength of will to alter long-standing and deeply ingrained patterns of interacting. Emotional dependencies that keep us children long after physical and economic dependence has come to an end and that operate largely unknown or at least unrecognized by us for what they are must be brought to the level of consciousness and worked through if our relations with our parents are to mature. Moreover, the self-knowledge and self-confidence that we gain through continued contact with our parents are very generally significant and enhance our autonomy in other personal relations as well. This is but one of the ways in which family ties sustained beyond childhood can be valuable to us.

Children whose parents disband upon the termination of their contractual obligations and who are thus no longer part of a functioning family unit may also lack a clear, well-grounded sense of their own past. Continued access to my family of origin enables me to experience my life as evolving over time; confronted with many vivid reminders of my earlier self, my personality can attain a coherence that it might not otherwise have.[14] Further, in a society characterized by durable family relationships, parents and children remain united in an active concern for their family of descendants, and family is connected to family in an unbroken chain ex-

14. The importance of this link to the past is only partly explained by the fact that it helps the child accomplish psychological separation from the parents.

tending far into the past. We can trace our roots back through our diverse family histories and in so doing experience history in a way that makes the abstract specific and personally relevant and gain a deeper understanding of and respect for the cultural traditions that have helped shape our lives. The important thing about family roots is not how enviable they are, but that they afford us the reassurance of stability, permanence, and continuity by linking us to previous generations. Through them our perspective is enlarged beyond the here and now. The discovery of special qualities in our forebears, grandparents, and parents can reinforce our own individuality; their aspirations may reconfirm or redirect our own; their accomplishments may inspire us and their failures and disappointments strengthen our resolve. A contractual family scheme, by contrast, would only serve to heighten the sense of historical (or psychohistorical) dislocation that is already widespread in our society, where individuals do not have a strong sense of belonging together, and extended kinship relations beyond the nuclear family are relatively tenuous.[15]

A contractual family scheme is less restrictive regarding the possibilities of family organization than a policy linking parenting to marriage. Some of these are beneficial to adults and children in several ways: they include people of all ages in the childrearing process, they integrate many age groups in one social unit, and they broaden children's personalities by exposing them to many role models rather than to the idiosyncracies of a few. But it would be a mistake to suppose that the adoption of a marriage-oriented family policy can only reinforce family insularity and the social isolation of children. In addition, a family contract scheme would drive

15. See Kenneth Keniston, *The Uncommitted* (New York: Dell, 1970), pp. 157–166, for a discussion of "the cult of the present" and "the fragmentation of identity" as major themes of alienation in our society; Also Robert Jay Lifton, "Protean Man," in *Family in Transition,* ed. Arlene and Jerome Skolnick (Boston: Little, Brown and Co., 1971), pp. 376–386.

the interests of marriage and family farther apart than a policy that connects parenting to a special form of marriage. But while it is certainly desirable to protect the family from the vagaries and transcience of the marriage relationship (assuming here, as I have throughout this chapter, that children are raised for the most part in families), the complete separation of marriage and family is an extreme response to this need.

Bibliography

The items in the first part of this bibliography contain primary sources referred to in part I, as well as some useful critical commentaries and general histories. No attempt has been made to include all works of importance.

Alexander, W. M. "Sex and Philosophy in Augustine." *Augustinian Studies*, 5 (1974), 197–208.

Annas, Julia. "Plato's *Republic* and Feminism." *Philosophy*, 51 (1976), 307–321.

Aquinas, Saint Thomas. *On Aristotle's Love and Friendship*. Providence: Providence College Press, 1951.

———. *Summa Theologiae*, vol. 23. Trans. W. D. Hughes, O.P. New York: Blackfriars, 1969.

———. *Summa Theologiae*, vol. 34. Trans. R. J. Batten, O.P. New York: Blackfriars, 1975.

———. *Summa Theologiae*, vol. 37. Trans. Thomas Gilby, O.P. New York: Blackfriars, 1975.

———. *Summa Theologiae*, vol. 41. Trans. T. C. O'Brien. New York: Blackfriars, 1972.

Arendt, Hannah. *The Human Condition*. Chicago: University of Chicago Press, 1958.

Ariès, Phillipe. *Centuries of Childhood*. London: Cape, 1962.

Aristotle. *Ethica Nicomachea*. *The Works of Aristotle*, vol. 9. Trans. W. D. Ross. Oxford: Clarendon Press, 1966.

———. *Politics*. Trans. E. Barker. New York: Oxford University Press, 1962.

Augustine, Saint. *The Good of Marriage*. Trans. C. T. Wilcox. New York: Fathers of the Church, Inc., 1955.

Barker, Ernest. *The Political Thought of Plato and Aristotle*. New York: Dover, 1959.

Barry, Brian. "Warrender and His Critics." *Hobbes and Rousseau*. Ed. M. Cranston and R. S. Peters. New York: Anchor, 1972.

Bodin, Jean. *Six Books of the Commonwealth*. Trans. M. J. Tooley. New York: Macmillan, 1955.

Charvet, John. "Individual Identity and Social Consciousness in Rousseau's Philosophy." *Hobbes and Rousseau*. Ed. M. Cranston and R. S. Peters. New York: Anchor, 1972.

Cicero. *On Moral Obligation*. Trans. J. Higginbotham. London: Faber and Faber, 1967.

Clark, Lorenne. "Women and John Locke; or, Who Owns the Apples in the Garden of Eden." *Canadian Journal of Philosophy*, 7 (1977), 699–724.

Clark, Mary, ed. *An Aquinas Reader*. New York: Image Books, 1972.

Cooper, John. "Aristotle on the Forms of Friendship." *Review of Metaphysics*, 30 (1977), 619–648.

Deane, Herbert. *Political and Social Ideas of St. Augustine*. New York: Columbia University Press, 1963.

Engels, Frederick. *The Origin of the Family, Private Property and the State*. New York: International, 1975.

Feinberg, Joel. "A Postscript to the Nature and Value of Rights." *Bioethics and Human Rights*. Ed. E. Bandman and B. Bandman. Boston: Little, Brown, 1978.

Fichte, J. G. *The Science of Rights*. Trans. A. E. Kroeger. London: Routledge and Kegan Paul, 1970. First Appendix.

Godwin, William. *Political Justice*. Ed. H. S. Salt. London: Swan Sonnenschein, 1890.

Goldsmith, M. M. *Hobbes' Science of Politics*. New York: Columbia University Press, 1966.

Gray, J. Glenn. *Hegel's Hellenic Ideal*. New York: King's Crown, 1941.

Hamburger, Max. *Morals and Law: The Growth of Aristotle's Legal Theory*. New York: Biblo and Tannen, 1965.

Hampsher-Monk, Iain W. "Tacit Concept of Consent in Locke's Two Treatises of Government: A Note on Citizens, Travellers, and Patriarchalism." *Journal of the History of Ideas,* 40 (1979), 135–139.

Hegel, G. W. F. *Lectures on the History of Philosophy*. Trans. E. S. Haldane and F. Simson. London: Routledge and Kegan Paul, 1963.

———. *The Phenomenology of Mind*. Trans. J. B. Baillie. New York: Harper, 1967.

———. *The Philosophy of Right*. Trans. T. M. Knox. New York: Oxford University Press, 1967.

———. *Reason in History: A General Introduction to the Philosophy of History*. Indianapolis: Bobbs-Merrill, 1953.

Hobbes, Thomas. *Body, Man, and Citizen,* Ed. R. S. Peters, New York: Collier, 1967.

———. *De Cive,* in *Man and Citizen*. Ed. B. Gert. Garden City, N.Y.: Anchor, 1972.

———. *Leviathan*. Ed. C. B. Macpherson. Baltimore: Penguin, 1968.

Howie, George. *Educational Theory and Practice in St. Augustine*. New York: Teachers College, 1969.

Hume, David. *A Treatise of Human Nature*. Ed. L. A. Selby-Bigge. Oxford: Clarendon Press, 1975.

Kant, Immanuel. *Foundations of the Metaphysics of Morals*. Trans. L. W. Beck. Indianapolis: Bobbs-Merrill Co., 1976.

———. *Lecture-Notes on Pedagogy*. Trans. E. F. Buchner. Philadelphia: J. B. Lippincott, 1904.

———. *Metaphysik der Sitten*. Hamburg: Felix Meiner, 1959.

———. *Kant's Political Writings*. Ed. H. Reiss. Cambridge: University Press, 1970.

Leites, Edmund. "Locke's Liberal Theory of Fatherhood." *Having Children*. Ed. O. O'Neill and W. Ruddick. New York: Oxford University Press, 1979.

Locke, John. *John Locke On Education*. Ed. P. Gay. New York: Teachers College, 1971.

——. *Two Treatises of Government.* Ed. P. Laslett. New York: New American Library, 1965.

Lodge, R. C. *Plato's Theory of Ethics.* New York: Harcourt, Brace, 1928.

Loewenberg, J. *Hegel's Phenomenology: Dialogues on the Life of Mind.* LaSalle: Open Court, 1965.

MacIntyre, Alasdair. *A Short History of Ethics.* New York: Macmillan, 1971.

Marx, Karl. *On Education, Women, and Children.* Trans. S. Padover. New York: McGraw-Hill, 1975.

Masters, Roger. *Political Philosophy of Rousseau.* Princeton: Princeton University Press, 1968.

Mill, John Stuart. *On Liberty.* Cleveland: Meridian, 1970.

——. *The Subjection of Women.* Cambridge: MIT Press, 1976.

Nell, Onora. "Innocence and Permissiveness." *Moral Education,* 1 (1969), 3–11.

Okin, Susan Moller. *Women in Western Political Thought.* Princeton: Princeton University Press, 1979.

Ostheimer, Anthony. *The Family: A Thomistic Study in Social Philosophy.* Washington: Catholic University of America Press, 1939.

Plant, Raymond. *Hegel.* Bloomington: Indiana University Press, 1973.

Plato. *Laws.* Trans. A. E. Taylor. *Plato: The Collected Dialogues.* Ed. E. Hamilton and H. Cairns. New York: Bollingen Foundation, 1961.

——. *The Republic.* Trans. Paul Shorey. *Plato: The Collected Dialogues.* Ed. E. Hamilton and H. Cairns. New York: Bollingen Foundation, 1961.

——. *The Statesman.* Trans. J. B. Skemp. *Plato: The Collected Dialogues.* Ed. E. Hamilton and H. Cairns. New York: Bollingen Foundation, 1961.

Plutarch. "Education of Children." *Moralia.* Trans. F. C. Babbitt. Cambridge: Harvard University Press, 1949. Vol. 1.

Rapaport, Elizabeth. "On the Future of Love: Rousseau and the Radical Feminists." *The Philosophical Forum,* 5 (1973–74), 185–205.

Raphael, D. D. *Hobbes: Morals and Politics*. London: George Allen and Unwin, 1977.

Reyburn, Hugh. *The Ethical Theory of Hegel*. Oxford: Clarendon Press, 1967.

Rousseau, J. J. *Émile*. Trans. B. Foxley. London: J. M. Dent and Sons, Ltd., 1974.

———. *The First and Second Discourses*. Trans. Roger and Judith Masters. New York: St. Martin's, 1964.

———. *The Social Contract*. Trans. M. Cranston. Baltimore: Penguin, 1968.

Russell, Bertrand. *Education and the Social Order*. London: Unwin, 1971.

———. *Marriage and Morals*. New York: Bantam, 1968.

Sabine, George. *History of Political Theory*. 3rd ed. New York: Holt, Rinehart and Winston, 1961.

Schaff, P., ed. *A Select Library of the Nicene and Post-Nicene Fathers*. New York: Christian Literature Co., 1888. Vol. 8.

Schochet, Gordon. *Patriarchalism in Political Thought*. New York: Basic Books, 1975.

Selby-Bigge, L. A., ed. *The British Moralists*. New York: Dover, 1965. Vols. 1 and 2.

Seneca, Lucius Annaeus. *On Benefits*. Trans. T. Lodge. London: J. M. Dent, 1899.

Shklar, Judith. "Rousseau's Images of Authority." *Hobbes and Rousseau*. Ed. M. Cranston and R. S. Peters, New York: Anchor, 1972.

Sidgwick, Henry. *The Methods of Ethics*. Chicago: University of Chicago Press, 1962.

Taylor, Charles. *Hegel and Modern Society*. Cambridge: Cambridge University Press, 1979.

Van der Marck, W. H. M. "Toward a Renewal of the Theology of Marriage." *Thomist*, 30 (1966), 307–342.

Verene, D. P., ed. *Sexual Love and Western Morality*. New York: Harper and Row, 1972.

Vinogradoff, Paul. *Outlines of Historical Jurisprudence*. New York: AMS Press, 1922. Vol. 2.

Watkins, J. W. N. "Liberty." *Hobbes and Rousseau*, Ed. M. Cranston and R. S. Peters. New York: Anchor, 1972.

The following books and articles were consulted in writing parts II and III. Those already included in the bibliography for part I are here omitted.

Adams, Richard. "An Inquiry into the Nature of the Family." *Family in Transition.* Ed. Arlene Skolnick and Jerome Skolnick. Boston: Little, Brown, 1971.

Aquinas, Saint Thomas. "The Divinity of Marriage." *Sexual Love and Western Morality.* Ed. D. P. Verene. New York: Harper and Row, 1972.

Baber, Ray. *Marriage and the Family.* New York: McGraw-Hill, 1953.

Baker, Robert and Frederick Elliston. "Introduction" *Philosophy and Sex.* Ed. R. Baker and F. Elliston. Buffalo, N.Y.: Prometheus, 1975.

Bane, Mary Jo. *Here to Stay: American Families in the 20th Century.* New York: Basic Books, 1976.

Baumrind, Diana. "Socialization and Instrumental Competence in Young Children." *Contemporary Readings in Child Psychology.* Ed. E. M. Hetherington and R. Parke. New York: McGraw-Hill, 1977.

Bayles, Michael. "Marriage, Love and Procreation." *Philosophy and Sex.* Ed. R. Baker and F. Elliston. Buffalo, N.Y.: Prometheus, 1975.

Beit-Hallahmi, B. and A. I. Rabin. "The Kibbutz as a Social Experiment and as a Child-Rearing Laboratory." *American Psychologist,* July 1977, 532–541.

Bell, Norman and Ezra Vogel. "Toward a Framework for a Functional Analysis of Family Behavior." *A Modern Introduction to the Family.* New York: The Free Press, 1966.

Benn, S. I. and R. S. Peters. *Principles of Political Thought.* New York: The Free Press, 1959.

Benn, Stanley. "Privacy, Freedom, and Respect for Persons." *Today's Moral Problems.* Ed. R. Wasserstrom. New York: Macmillan, 1975.

Bentham, Jeremy. "Utilitarian Basis of Succession." *Rational Basis of Legal Institutions.* Ed. J. Wigmore and A. Kocourek. New York: Macmillan, 1923.

Berger, Fred. "Gratitude." *Ethics,* 85 (1975), 298–309.

Bertocci, Peter. "The Human Venture in Sex, Love, and Marriage." *Social Ethics.* Ed. T. Mappes and J. Zembaty. New York: McGraw-Hill, 1972.

Bettelheim, Bruno. *Children of the Dream.* New York: Avon, 1970.

Blackstone, William. *Commentaries on The Laws of England.* Philadelphia: J. B. Lippincott and Co., 1856. Vol. 1.

Blaine, Graham B., Jr. *Are Parents Bad for Children?* New York: Coward, McCann & Geoghegan, 1973.

Blau, Peter and Otis Duncan. *The American Occupational Structure.* New York: John Wiley & Sons, 1967.

Block, N. J. and Gerald Dworkin. "IQ: Heritability and Inequality, Part I." *Philosophy and Public Affairs,* 3 (1974), 331–409.

Bowlby, John. *Child Care and the Growth of Love,* Baltimore: Penguin, 1973.

Bowles, Samuel and Herbert Gintis. *Schooling in Capitalist America.* New York: Basic Books, 1977.

Brittain, John A. *The Inheritance of Economic Status.* Washington, D.C.: Brookings Institution, 1977.

Bronfenbrenner, Urie. *Two Worlds of Childhood.* New York: Russell Sage Foundation, 1970.

———. "The Roots of Alienation." *Raising Children in Modern America.* Ed. Nathan Talbot. Boston: Little, Brown and Co., 1976.

Cahn, Edmond, ed. *The Social Meaning of Legal Concepts: Inheritance of Property and the Power of Testamentary Disposition.* No. 1. New York: New York University School of Law, 1948.

Casler, Lawrence. *Is Marriage Necessary?* New York: Human Sciences Press, 1974.

Clarke-Stewart, Alison. *Child Care in the Family.* New York: Academic Press, 1977.

Cole, G. D. H. "Inheritance." *Encyclopedia of the Social Sciences.* New York: Macmillan, 1932. Vol. 8.

Coleman, James S. "The Concept of Equality of Educational Opportunity." *Harvard Educational Review,* 38 (1968), 7–22.

————. "Equality of Opportunity and Equality of Results." *Harvard Educational Review*, 43 (1973), 129–137.

————. "Equal Schools or Equal Students?" *The Public Interest*, 4 (1966), 70–75.

Davids, Leo. "New Family Norms." *The Future of Sexual Relations*. Ed. Robert Francoeur and Anna Francoeur. Englewood Cliffs, N.J.: Prentice-Hall, 1974.

Davis, W. Allison. "Child Rearing in the Class Structure of American Society." *Family in a Democratic Society*. New York: Columbia University Press, 1949.

Dearden, R. F. "Autonomy and Education." *Education and Reason*. Ed. R. F. Dearden, P. H. Hirst, and R. S. Peters. London: Routledge and Kegan Paul, 1975.

————. " 'Needs' in Education." *A Critique of Current Educational Aims*. Ed. R. F. Dearden, P. H. Hirst, and R. S. Peters. London: Routledge and Kegan Paul, 1975.

Dittman, Laura, ed. *Early Child Care: The New Perspectives*. New York: Atherton, 1968.

Donagan, Alan. *A Theory of Morality*. Chicago: University of Chicago Press, 1977.

Donzelot, Jacques. *The Policing of Families*. New York: Pantheon, 1977.

Dworkin, Gerald. "Autonomy and Behavior Control." *Hastings Center Report*, 6 (1976), 23–28.

Eekelaar, J. M. "What are Parental Rights?" *Law Quarterly Review*, 89 (1973), 210–234.

Elliston, Frederick. "In Defense of Promiscuity." *Philosophy and Sex*. Ed. R. Baker and F. Elliston. Buffalo, N.Y.: Prometheus, 1975.

Erikson, Erik. *Childhood and Society*. New York: W. W. Norton, 1963.

Feinberg, Joel. "Can Animals Have Rights?" *Animal Rights and Human Obligations*. Ed. Tom Regan and Peter Singer. Englewood Cliffs, N.J.: Prentice-Hall, 1976.

————. "The Child's Right to an Open Future." *Whose Child?* Ed. W. Aiken and H. LaFollette. Totowa, N.J.: Rowman and Littlefield, 1980.

————. "Duties, Rights and Claims." *American Philosophical Quarterly*, 3 (1966), 137–144.

————. "The Idea of a Free Man." *Educational Judgments.* Ed. James Doyle. London: Routledge and Kegan Paul, 1973.

————. "The Nature and Value of Rights." *Journal of Value Inquiry,* 4 (1970), 243–257.

Firestone, Shulamith. *The Dialectic of Sex.* New York: Bantam, 1972.

Fried, Charles. *An Anatomy of Values.* Cambridge, Mass.: Harvard University Press, 1970.

Friquegnon, Marie-Louise. "Rights and Responsibilities of Young People." *Thinking,* 2 (1980), 11–13.

Geiger, Kent. "The Soviet Experiment." *Family in Transition.* Ed. Arlene Skolnick and Jerome Skolnick. Boston: Little, Brown, 1971.

Gewirth, Alan. *Reason and Morality.* Chicago: University of Chicago Press, 1978.

Glendon, Mary. "Marriage and the State: The Withering Away of Marriage." *Virginia Law Review,* 62 (1976), 663–720.

Goldman, Alan H. *Justice and Reverse Discrimination.* Princeton: Princeton University Press, 1979.

Goldstein, Joseph, Anna Freud, and Albert Solnit. *Before the Best Interests of the Child.* New York: The Free Press, 1979.

————. *Beyond the Best Interests of the Child.* New York: The Free Press, 1973.

Green, Maureen. *Fathering.* New York: McGraw-Hill, 1976.

Harris, John. "The Marxist Conception of Justice." *Philosophy and Public Affairs,* 3 (1974), 192–220.

Hart, H. L. A. *Punishment and Responsibility.* Oxford: Oxford University Press, 1968.

Henley, Kenneth. "Infant Rights and Consent to Medical Research." *Consent: Concept, Capacity, Conditions, and Constraints.* Ed. Lyman Tower Sargent. Wiesbaden: Franz Steiner, 1979.

Hill, Sharon. "Self-Determination and Autonomy." *Today's Moral Problems.* Ed. R. Wasserstrom. New York: Macmillan, 1975.

Hill, Thomas, Jr. "Servility and Self-Respect." *Today's Moral Problems.* Ed. R. Wasserstrom. New York: Macmillan, 1975.

Hohfeld, W. N. *Fundamental Legal Conceptions as Applied in Judicial Reasoning.* New Haven: Yale University Press, 1964.

Holt, John. *Escape from Childhood*. New York: Ballantine, 1974.

Jencks, Christopher et. al. *Inequality: A Reassessment of the Effect of Family and Schooling in America*. New York: Harper and Row, 1972.

——. "*Inequality* in Retrospect." *Harvard Educational Review*, 43 (1973), 138–164.

Josselyn, Irene M. *Psychosocial Development of Children*. New York: Family Service Association of America, 1969.

Kant, Immanuel. *Doctrine of Virtue: Part II of the Metaphysics of Morals*. Trans. Mary Gregor. New York: Harper & Row, 1964.

Keniston, Kenneth, et al. *All Our Children*. New York: Harcourt Brace Jovanovich, 1977.

——. *The Uncommitted*. New York: Dell, 1970.

LaFollette, Hugh. "Licensing Parents." *Philosophy and Public Affairs*, 9 (1980), 182–197.

Leefeldt, Christine and Ernest Callenbach. *The Art of Friendship*. New York: Pantheon, 1979.

Levine, Donald and Mary Jo Bane. *The "Inequality" Controversy*. New York: Basic Books, 1975.

Lévi-Strauss, Claude. "The Family." *Family in Transition*. Ed. Arlene Skolnick and Jerome Skolnick. Boston: Little, Brown, 1971.

Lifton, Robert Jay. "Protean Man." *Family in Transition*. Ed. Arlene Skolnick and Jerome Skolnick. Boston: Little, Brown, 1971.

Mahler, M., F. Pine, and A. Bergman. *The Psychological Birth of the Human Infant*. New York: Basic Books, 1975.

Margolis, Joseph and Clorinda Margolis. "Separation of Marriage and Family." *Feminism and Philosophy*. Ed. M. Vetterling-Braggin, F. Elliston, and J. English. Totowa, N.J.: Littlefield, Adams, 1977.

May, Rollo. "The Sexual Paradoxes of Contemporary Life." *Sexual Love and Western Morality*. Ed. D. P. Verene. New York: Harper and Row, 1972.

Mead, Margaret. *Culture and Commitment*. Garden City, N.Y.: Natural History Press, 1970.

———. "Marriage in Two Steps." *Family in Search of a Future.* Ed. H. A. Otto. New York: Appleton-Century-Crofts, 1970.

Melden, A. I. *Rights and Persons.* Berkeley: University of California Press, 1977.

Mill, John Stuart. *Principles of Political Economy.* Ed. William J. Ashley. London: Longmans Green and Co., 1923.

Moore, Barrington, Jr. "Thoughts on the Future of the Family." *The Family and Change.* Ed. J. Edwards. New York: Knopf, 1969.

Müller-Lyer, F. *The Evolution of Modern Marriage: A Sociology of Sexual Relations.* Trans. I. Wigglesworth. New York: Knopf, 1930.

Nagel, Thomas. "Equal Treatment and Compensatory Discrimination." *Equality and Preferential Treatment.* Ed. M. Cohen, T. Nagel, and T. Scanlon. Princeton: Princeton University Press, 1977.

———. "Rawls on Justice." *Reading Rawls.* Ed. Norman Daniels. New York: Basic Books, 1975.

Norman, Michael. "The New Extended Family: Divorce Reshapes the American Household." *The New York Times Magazine,* Nov. 23, 1980, pp. 26ff.

"Note: Reciprocity of Rights and Duties Between Parent and Child." *Harvard Law Review,* 42 (1928–1929), 112–115.

Novak, Michael. "The Family out of Favor." *Harper's Magazine,* April, 1976, 37–44.

Nozick, Robert. *Anarchy, State, and Utopia.* New York: Basic Books, 1974.

O'Driscoll, Lyla. "On the Nature and Value of Marriage." *Feminism and Philosophy.* Ed. M. Vetterling-Braggin, F. Elliston, and J. English. Totowa, N.J.: Littlefield, Adams, 1977.

Olafson, Frederick. "Rights and Duties in Education." *Educational Judgment.* Ed. James Doyle. London: Routledge and Kegan Paul, 1973.

O'Neill, Onora. "How Do We Know When Opportunities are Equal?" *Philosophical Forum,* 5 (1975), 334–346.

O'Neill, Onora and William Ruddick, eds. *Having Children.* New York: Oxford University Press, 1979.

Parsons, Talcott. "The Normal American Family." *Family in*

Transition. Ed. Arlene Skolnick and Jerome Skolnick. Boston: Little, Brown, 1971.

Parsons, Talcott and Robert Bales. *Family, Socialization and Interaction Process*. Glencoe: The Free Press, 1964.

Rawls, John. *A Theory of Justice*. Cambridge, Mass.: Belknap Press, 1971.

———. "Two Concepts of Rules." *Philosophical Review*, 6 (1955), 3–13.

Reiman, Jeffrey. "Privacy, Intimacy, and Personhood." *Today's Moral Problems*. 2nd ed. Ed. R. Wasserstrom. New York: Macmillan, 1979.

Richards, David A. J. *The Moral Criticism of Law*. Encino: Dickenson, 1977.

———. *A Theory of Reasons for Action*. Oxford: Oxford University Press, 1971.

Ruddick, Sara. "Better Sex." *Philosophy and Sex*. Ed. R. Baker and F. Elliston. Buffalo, N.Y.: Prometheus, 1975.

Schetky, Diane and David Slader. "Termination of Parental Rights." *Child Psychiatry and the Law*. Ed. D. H. Schetky and E. Benedek. New York: Brunner/Mazel, 1980.

Schouler, James. *A Treatise on the Law of Marriage, Divorce, Separation, and Domestic Relations*. 6th ed. Albany, N.Y.: Matthew Bender, 1921. Vol. 1.

Schrag, Francis. "Children: Their Rights and Needs." *Whose Child?* Eds. W. Aiken and H. LaFollette. Totowa, N.J.: Rowman and Littlefield, 1980.

———. "Justice and the Family." *Inquiry*, 19 (1976), 193–208.

———. "Rights Over Children." *Journal of Value Inquiry*, 7 (1973), 96–105.

Schwarz, Balduin. "Some Reflections on Gratitude." *The Human Person and the World of Values*. Ed. B. Schwarz. New York: Fordham University Press, 1960.

Sennett, Richard. *Authority*. New York: Knopf, 1980.

Shaw, George Bernard. "A Treatise on Parents and Children." *The World of the Child*. Ed. Toby Talbot. New York: Jason Aronson, 1974.

Sidel, Ruth. *Women and Child Care in China*. Baltimore: Penguin, 1974.

Skinner, B. F. *Walden Two*. New York: Macmillan, 1962.

Spiro, Melford, E. *Children of the Kibbutz.* Cambridge, Mass.: Harvard University Press, 1958.

———. "Is the Family Universal?—The Israeli Case." *A Modern Introduction to the Family.* Ed. N. Bell and E. Vogel. New York: The Free Press, 1960.

Stephens, William N. *The Family in Cross-Cultural Perspective.* New York: Holt, Rinehart, and Winston, 1963.

Stocker, Michael. "Moral Duties, Institutions, and Natural Facts." *Monist,* 54 (1970), 602–24.

Talbot, Nathan, ed. *Raising Children in Modern America.* Boston: Little, Brown, 1976.

Talmon, Yonina. "The Family in a Revolutionary Movement: The Case of the Kibbutz in Israel." *Comparative Family Systems.* Ed. M. F. Nimkoff. New York: Houghton Mifflin, 1965.

Taylor, Paul. *Principles of Ethics.* Encino: Dickenson, 1975.

Telfer, Elizabeth. "Friendship." *Proceedings of the Aristotelian Society,* 71 (1970–1971), 223–241.

Wasserstrom, Richard. "Is Adultery Immoral?" *Today's Moral Problems.* Ed. R. Wasserstrom. New York: Macmillan, 1975.

———. "Privacy." *Today's Moral Problems.* 2nd ed. Ed. R. Wasserstrom. New York: Macmillan, 1979.

Weiss, Paul and Jonathan Weiss. *Right and Wrong.* Carbondale, Ill.: Southern Illinois University Press, 1967.

Wellman, Carl. "Consent to Medical Research on Children." *Consent: Concept, Capacity, Conditions, and Constraints.* Ed. Lyman Tower Sargent. Wiesbaden: Franz Steiner, 1979.

White, P. A. "Socialization and Education." *A Critique of Current Educational Aims.* Ed. R. F. Dearden, P. H. Hirst, and R. S. Peters. London: Routledge and Kegan Paul, 1975.

Williams, Bernard. "The Idea of Equality." *Justice and Equality.* Ed. Hugo Bedau. Englewood Cliffs, N.J.: Prentice-Hall, 1971.

Worsfold, Victor. "A Philosophical Justification for Children's Rights." *Harvard Educational Review,* 44 (1974), 142–157.

Young, Robert. "Autonomy and Socialization." *Mind,* 89 (1980), 565–576.

Znaniecki, Florian. *Social Relations and Social Roles.* San Francisco: Chandler, 1965.

Index